Peter Doherty is a musician and singer-songwriter. He is one of the frontmen for the rock band, The Libertines, and previously formed Babyshambles and the Puta Madres. Peter's music is as eclectic as it is introspective and is consistently thought of as one of the leading lights on the British rock scene. Born into a military family, Doherty spent much of his youth moving from place to place across Europe. He immersed himself in books and poetry – something that is evident in his lyric-writing to this day.

Praise for *A Likely Lad*

'Reveals unexpected details . . . Intimate, often salacious' *Sunday Times*

'Doherty wasn't just at the heart of that era, he defined it, in ways both good and bad. Who better to capture the excitement but also the bleakness of that period than him?' *Guardian*

'Lucid, candid and, ultimately, hopeful' *Observer*

'Expertly pieced together . . . An extraordinary hymn to indie's own Rimbaud and degenerate noughties London' *Mojo*

'A defiant and humorous look at one of the most infamous rockers of the 21st century' *Far Out Magazine*

'[A]n easily digestible page-turner . . . plenty of new stories' *i News*

'Overloaded with compelling stories – many funny, some haunting' *New Statesman*

Peter Doherty

A Likely Lad

With Simon Spence

CONSTABLE

CONSTABLE

First published in Great Britain in 2022 by Constable
This paperback edition published in 2023 by Constable

3 5 7 9 10 8 6 4 2

A CIP catalogue record for this book
is available from the British Library.

ISBN: 978-1-40871-545-1

Typeset in Minion by Hewer Text UK Ltd, Edinburgh
Printed and bound in Great Britain by Clays Ltd, Elcograf S.p.A.

Papers used by Constable are from well-managed
forests and other responsible sources.

Constable
An imprint of
Little, Brown Book Group
Carmelite House
50 Victoria Embankment
London EC4Y 0DZ

An Hachette UK Company

www.hachette.co.uk

www.littlebrown.co.uk

To Carl, Jai and Katia

I'm now making myself as scummy as I can. Why? I want to be a poet, and I'm working at turning myself into a seer. You won't understand any of this, and I'm almost incapable of explaining it to you. The idea is to reach the unknown by the derangement of all the senses. It involves enormous suffering, but one must be strong and be a born poet. It's really not my fault.

Arthur Rimbaud, *Letters of the Seer*, 1871 (written aged 16)

Contents

Authors' Note

Simon and I started talking in March 2021, both in various stages of lockdown. It was the longest interview I've ever done by some distance – sixty hours or more during that spring and summer. I'd been clean for over a year, but I was still a little bit fragile, and talking to Simon came to be a welcome routine. I was open with him in a way I'd never been with a journalist before – perhaps too open; I told him everything! Over a year later and I'm still straight, which is a bleeding miracle, but I do wonder if the whole book might be different if we started it now.

There's an earthy, brute honesty to parts of the book, a naivety, sometimes a delight taken in certain nihilistic incidents in these pages, that seem now to belong to my past, to youth and, dare I say, to drugs – and increasingly I feel adult and sober. Maybe that's why I find it deeply unnerving, often impossible, to read these conversations written down. I'm amazed Simon's managed to get everything to work chronologically, but I worry if some careless or unvarnished words might offend people. I have no desire to upset – quite the opposite nowadays. Those closest to me do say, however, they recognise my voice in the telling, and I recognise there is a life to this work that would be impossible now to repeat.

I understand how reading this book was especially difficult for the love of my life, my dear darling wife Katia deVidas Doherty. I said when we first started that it would be great if it was an uplifting and funny book. I do think there's a lot of comedy involved in my life. There's sadness and darkness too, often reflected in the songs. When you throw yourself into music, you sometimes have to hold onto the first thing with any meaning, and that can be anger or sorrow, but it's not like I'm promoting those things. It's almost as if for the rest of the time, everything's tickety-boo. You can't really admit defeat.

Peter Doherty, March 2022

I first approached Jai Stanley, Peter's manager, about the possibility of doing a book with Peter's cooperation in 2017. Back then Jai explained how he was not expecting Peter to write his own autobiography, given he used a manual typewriter and tended to flit between literary ideas, but he did say a proper book about Peter was something he'd like to make happen. It was just going to be very difficult. Peter refused to entertain the notion of employing a ghostwriter who would 'put words in his mouth', and although he had a wealth of stories was reluctant to dwell on his past to any real extent.

Over the next three years I checked in with Jai sporadically, and we discussed ways in which we might collaborate on a book. Peter's stance on employing a ghostwriter did not change but, finally, in late 2020, he was persuaded get involved in this work, an authorised biography. I had suggested a minimum of thirty-five hours' interview time and was prepared for a great deal of fucking around – well, he does have something of a reputation! I was confounded at every turn. He was not only conscientious but patient, gracious and generous, always humble and enthusiastic. 'Don't hold back on any subject,' he said. 'Anything you want to talk about, I'm happy to discuss. The things you feel you might hold back on are probably the things you should really ask.'

AUTHORS' NOTE

He took endless questions on the most painful of subjects without flinching or reverting to self-pity. His honesty when discussing his personal dissolution was brutal and at times upsetting. On his broader development as an artist and his twenty-year musical career, he was endlessly enjoyable, refreshingly devoid of cynicism or self-regard. His recall was often remarkable, countless stories playfully tumbling out full of mischief and humour – an ability to laugh at himself is one of his most endearing traits. Twelve months on, and many more hours of interviews than he'd initially agreed to, I will miss him and our morning chats. I have written this story in his words, but I haven't put any in his mouth, simply moved a few around a bit to make the chronology clearer. It is no whitewash of history.

This isn't the book Peter will surely one day write about his life. I know it's not the book he thought I'd write about his life, but I hope I have produced something that rings true and does justice to his music, his electric spirit, vast talent, charm, attitude and wit.

Simon Spence, March 2022

Timeline

2002

June: 'What a Waster', single, The Libertines (Rough Trade) – UK 37

September: 'Up the Bracket', single, The Libertines (Rough Trade) – UK 29

October: *Up the Bracket*, album, The Libertines (Rough Trade) – UK 35

2003

January: 'Time for Heroes', single, The Libertines (Rough Trade) – UK 20

August: 'Don't Look Back into the Sun', single, The Libertines (Rough Trade) – UK 11

September: *I Get Along*, EP, The Libertines (Rough Trade) – US only

2004

April: 'For Lovers', single, Peter Doherty featuring Wolfman (Rough Trade) – UK 7

April: 'Babyshambles', limited edition single, Peter Doherty (High Society) – UK 32

August: 'Can't Stand Me Now', single, The
Libertines (Rough Trade) – UK 2

August: *The Libertines*, album, The Libertines (Rough Trade) – UK 1

October: 'What Became of the Likely Lads', single,
The Libertines (Rough Trade) – UK 9

November: 'Killamangiro', single, Babyshambles
(Rough Trade) – UK 8

2005

May: *Stalking Pete Doherty*, documentary (Channel 4)

August: 'Fuck Forever', single, Babyshambles (Rough Trade) – UK 4

August: *Who the Fuck Is Pete Doherty?*, documentary (Channel 4)

October: 'Their Way', single, Little'ans featuring
Peter Doherty (Rough Trade) – UK 22

November: *Down in Albion*, album,
Babyshambles (Rough Trade) – UK 10

November: 'Albion', single, Babyshambles (Rough Trade) – UK 8

2006

September: 'Prangin' Out', single, The Streets
featuring Pete Doherty (XL) – UK 25

October: 'Janie Jones', single, Babyshambles
& friends (B-Unique) – UK 17

November: *Arena: Pete Doherty*, documentary (BBC Four)

December: *The Blinding*, EP, Babyshambles (Parlophone) – UK 62

TIMELINE

2007

May: *Bloodworks*, art exhibition, Bankrobber Gallery, London

June: *The Books of Albion: The Collected Writings*, Peter Doherty (Orion)

September: 'Delivery', single, Babyshambles (Parlophone) – UK 6

October: *Shotter's Nation*, album, Babyshambles (Parlophone) – UK 5

October: *Time for Heroes – Best of The Libertines*, album (Rough Trade) – UK 23

December: 'You Talk', single, Babyshambles (Parlophone) – UK 54

2008

April: *Art of the Albion*, art exhibition, Galerie Chappe, Paris

June: *Oh! What a Lovely Tour*, album, Babyshambles (Parlophone)

2009

January: *Pete Doherty: In 24 Hours*, documentary (MTV)

March: 'Last of the English Roses', single, Peter Doherty (Parlophone) – UK 67

March: *Grace/Wastelands*, album, Peter Doherty (Parlophone) – UK 17

August: 'Broken Love Song', single, Peter Doherty (Parlophone)

2011

April: *The Libertines: There Are No Innocent Bystanders*, documentary (Pulse Films, directed by Roger Sargent)

2012

February: *On Blood: A Portrait of the Artist*,
art exhibition, Cob Gallery, London

March: The Kooples, Peter Doherty-designed fashion range

August: *Confession of a Child of the Century*, film, lead actor
(Les Films du Veyrier, Integral Films, Warp Films)

2013

August: 'Nothing Comes to Nothing', single,
Babyshambles (Parlophone)

September: *Sequel to the Prequel*, album,
Babyshambles (Parlophone) – UK 10

October: 'Fall from Grace', single, Babyshambles (Parlophone)

November: *Flags of the Old Regime*, art exhibition,
Espace Djam, Paris (part of an itinerant exhibition that
also visited Geneva, Barcelona and Moscow)

2014

May: *From Albion to Shangri-La: Journals and
Tour Diaries 2008–2013*, book, Peter Doherty
and Nina Antonia (Thin Man Press)

2015

March: 'Flags of the Old Regime', single, Peter
Doherty (Walk Tall Recordings)

August: 'Gunga Din', single, The Libertines (Virgin EMI)

2020

April: *All at Sea*, documentary film (Strap
Originals, directed by Roger Sargent)

May: 'Uncle Brian's Abattoir', single, Trampolene
& Peter Doherty (Strap Originals)

December: *In the Fantasy Life of Poetry and Crime*,
art exhibition, Galerie Chappe, Paris

2021

'The Fantasy Life of Poetry & Crime', single, Peter
Doherty and Frédéric Lo (Strap Originals)

2022

'The Epidemiologist', single, Peter Doherty
and Frédéric Lo (Strap Originals)

The Fantasy Life of Poetry & Crime, album, Peter
Doherty and Frédéric Lo (Strap Originals)

A Likely Lad, book, Peter Doherty with Simon Spence (Little, Brown)

1
Army Brat

1979–1990: growing up on army barracks in Belfast, Cyprus and Germany. Discovering Chas & Dave. The Satanic influence of The Simpsons and Beano according to Mum. Hallucinations in Cyprus. Becoming a Christian. Reading George Orwell. Dad goes to war.

'I adored my dad, absolutely idolised him. We share the same name, I was always 'little Peter' or 'Peter Jnr' growing up. He was born in London, grew up in a tight-knit Irish Catholic community. His dad, Ted Doherty, came over to England from Ireland just after the Second World War, in 1946. Ted would sing rebel songs in the pub, so it was quite controversial when Dad joined the British Army. He was an airborne solider, a paratrooper, but he wasn't in the Paras, the Parachute Regiment. He was in the Royal Corps of Signals who were attached to the Paras, 216 Parachute Signal Squadron.

He was busy as a young soldier in the early '70s around Aldershot, but he always found time for football, playing for a Saturday and a Sunday team. One time he played in goal for Hounslow Town, a semi-professional football club in west London. When I was growing up he was always coaching football teams. He was very athletic, into boxing and cross-country running.

One of my earliest memories is when I was five and he took me and my sister AmyJo to Madame Tussauds in London at Christmas. There was this big queue and he said, Na, sod this, and took us charging across London to the Serpentine in Hyde Park instead. I can still see him, moustache bristling, stripping off his army pumps and blue tracksuit and diving in the Serpentine. It was freezing cold. Some bloke came out in a rowing boat with one of those old-fashioned *Beano*-style megaphones, telling him to get out. It was great – me and AmyJo stood holding hands, really proud of our dad.

His mum, Doris, had abandoned him when he was a kid. She was English, from Kilburn, her maiden name was Ford. She had three kids with Ted then had some sort of breakdown when Dad was nine and his brother was about five, and she left Ted in Shepherd's Bush with these two boys. She only went around the corner at first and then moved to Stonebridge Park, a high-rise estate in Brent, northwest London, so it wasn't really that far away, but she wasn't around for Dad and that set his mood for life – emotionally fucked up, I think.

My mum, Jacqueline, did her best to try and forge something more loving from this broken relationship. I'm glad she did, because I'm still close to Nanny Doll; she's in her nineties now. If there's ever a family get-together, we'll sit there singing old music-hall songs and everyone else will sit there rolling their eyes. We did that ever since I was a young kid. I learned the songs from a Chas & Dave record, *Christmas Jamboree Bag*. It was one of the records my mum and dad owned that I loved, that and *The Beatles/1962–1966* and *The Beatles/1967–1970*, the red and blue albums, plus a Cilla Black record or two. As soon I could work the record player I listened to that Chas & Dave record again and again. My mum and dad didn't really know the lyrics, I don't think they really had time for music, but my Nanny Doll knew them all – songs like 'We're Going to Hang out the Washing on the Siegfried Line'. Her sister Vera was a singer. Nanny Doll was strong stuff. For decades, up until she was seventy-five, she worked for some Jewish ladies in Golders Green. I wrote the song '1939 Returning' on my first solo album *Grace/Wastelands* for her.

Growing up, I was fascinated by Dad's childhood. Ted tried really hard but he couldn't cope. Eventually, he called Doris and Dad went back to his mother when he was about fifteen. He was out of control. He left school to work in a travelling funfair. He felt the family disowned him, he wanted out of London. I said to him once, What would happen if the fifteen-year-old me met the fifteen-year-old you? He said, I'd break your nose and take your watch. The big shift in his life happened when he joined the army. He'd say the happiest days of his life were when he was a young recruit. He spent time in Canada and Africa. He'd tell stories about how he was hard as nails as a soldier – he wanted to join the SAS and did some preliminary training but the Royal Corps of Signals wouldn't let him go.

The army became his family. He took his O levels in his mid-twenties and slowly worked his way up through the ranks to eventually become a major. Discipline was his thing. He didn't want me showing him up in any way when I was little. I never got battered – in fact, I never saw Dad swing a punch at anyone. He only hit me once – it was just bend over the bed and get a spanking. Mum says that incident upset Dad more than it did me. He told her afterwards he would never hit a child again. She says that deep down he's even more sensitive than me, that in many ways we're like peas in a pod. But he would put the fear of God in me as a kid. He didn't need to use his hand, he just used his eyes – and, as kids, we knew how to behave.

We were brought up to understand how lucky we were. Dad would say he only got a tangerine for Christmas when he was young, and how hard both he and Mum had worked to get out of their working-class environments in London and Liverpool, respectively. The whole concept of answering back was completely foreign to me and AmyJo as kids. When we were told to get dressed and we were going to go and do something, whether you wanted to in your heart or not, you did it. We jumped when my dad said. I sometimes wonder what would have happened if I'd stood up to him? Maybe if I'd been a bit broader or just a bit more into fighting, but I wasn't. I liked him. I wanted his love.

There were times when he was in a black mood and just wouldn't talk to anyone in the house. It was really dark, really weird. He was holding it all in. I don't know what it was about. When I was little, I thought it was what was going on in the army, but I'm not sure. He was a sergeant major when we were in Belfast, but we never talked about his army life at all.

Being in Belfast with him when he was stationed there in the early '80s is the first strong memory I have of living anywhere. I'd been born in Hexham, Northumberland, not far from Newcastle. At the time, Dad was posted to a Signals station, a former Royal Air Force station, in Ouston in Northumberland. After Ouston we went to Catterick Garrison, North Yorkshire, and then Krefeld, in what was then West Germany, when I was three.

Belfast was one of the few times during my childhood when we didn't live on a barracks. I suppose living in a Protestant community, in army-provided housing, in Belfast was the equivalent of being on a barracks. The kids at the primary school I went to would say, Hey, we love your daddy, he kills Catholics. We looked under the car every morning for car bombs.

I was in Lambeg County Primary School, and I vividly remember coming home one day singing a song I'd picked up but didn't really understand. It was a corruption of the children's counting rhyme 'Eeny, meeny, miny, moe, catch a nigger by the toe', and my dad got really angry with me. I was upset and scared. My Nanny Doll was visiting, and she said, Oh leave him alone, he's just a kid. And my dad went, No, he's got to understand this, and he sat me down and said, Right, how many people does Wembley Stadium hold? And I knew at the time it was a hundred thousand, and he said, Right, now times that by sixty, quite a complicated sum for a six year old, but I said, Six million. He said, Right, that's how many people died in Nazi Germany because of songs like that. I used to repeat that to people. I was on holiday, years later, and some kid at a swimming pool said something to a Chinese kid and I said, Oi, how many people does Wembley Stadium hold?

Certain cartoons became a big deal around then: *Cockleshell Bay* was a favourite, about the adventures of a little boy and girl, Robin and Rosie, in stripy T-shirts in a north seaside town – that was me and AmyJo. Dad had a whistle he used to do, that when we heard it, we knew we had to come back from wherever we were on our little adventures. AmyJo was my best friend growing up. We both had these wonky fringes because Mum would always cut our hair. It looked as if she'd just put a bowl on our heads, cut around that and then tried to do a side-parting. AmyJo was born with a hole in her heart, and when we were in Belfast, she had an operation to fix it, and it was a success. She was told before she went into the hospital, which was right on the Falls Road, if anyone asks you what your dad does, you tell them he works for the Post Office. It was only a few months after that, in 1986, my mum went to hospital again in Belfast and came back with my little sister Emily.

Sport Billy was another favourite cartoon, where he'd kick a football in the opening credits and it went into space. That was my nickname. My dad would call me Sport Billy, which became Billy Bilo. He just used to go, Billy, Billy, Billy, Billy Bilo. Some people still call me Bilo or Billy Bilo now. Dad had other names for me: he'd call me Big Ears or Dog Breath. There was an aspect to his sense of humour that could be quite cruel. He invented this character called Big Otto who me and AmyJo genuinely believed existed. Whenever he saw a fat bloke in the street, he'd go, Look, there's Big Otto, and he'd make me and AmyJo go up to them and ask a question – we'd be told to piss off or just get an odd, quizzical look, but we fell for it every time. He could be crude too: I was out with him one time and there was a girl jogging past and she had quite big breasts and he said, She's going to have a couple of black eyes in the morning. I didn't get it – must have been eight. I said, Why, because the husband is going to beat her up? And he went, No, and did a gesture with his hands. I was really shocked.

We moved to Cyprus when I was nine and stayed for a couple of years. Dad had been newly promoted to regimental sergeant major and the Royal Signals were providing telecommunications infrastructure. I think it was all about intercepting satellite messages, to and fro, from wherever – the civil war between Greek Cypriots and Turkish Cypriots had long died down. There were people there from GCHQ (Government Communications Headquarters), the army, navy and air force. Cyprus seemed to me very open, but when I think back to the giant golf balls, the signal stations, in the mountains and recall the weird strain on my dad at the time, more black moods, perhaps it wasn't for him. He was never out of uniform. Dad got his MBE for his work in Cyprus. I'm not sure exactly what it was for. We don't talk about it.

We were in Ayios Nikolaos, the smallest of the island bases, a tourist hub now but in the mid- to late '80s it was post-battle ground, just a desert. The school was in a tin shed out the back of our barrack house. There were loads of kids there, aged from four to eleven. Different ages were put in the same class doing the same stuff. There was about fifteen in my class, and we would only do from eight o'clock until one o'clock because it was so hot in the afternoons.

The freedom was amazing – we were always out swimming in the sea or running around the *bondu*, the desert. I'd never been swimming before and then the next minute I'm running round Cyprus in my trunks, swimming like a fish. We'd go out snake hunting and climbing into the old lookout towers and bunkers – it was proper little *Lord of the Flies* vibe. To join the local gang of army kids I had to kiss this lizard they had.

It was in Cyprus I started to get the feeling that I was a bit of a let-down to Dad because I couldn't crack it on the athletics field. There's a photo from that time where I'm coming across a finishing line in vest and shorts, looking really fucked. I look at my face now and think, Yeah, you're not really enjoying that. AmyJo was a better athlete. She started to smash it with her cross-country running. For years to come she used to run cross-country for the county, wherever we lived. This is when me and AmyJo started with this rivalry, where I'd say, Dad likes you better, Mum likes me better. We never used to fight about it. We had this *entente cordiale*, this understanding. That's the way it was.

I still got a lot from sport as a kid, especially playing football – loved it. I wanted to be a professional footballer, really, but Dad said I'd never make it, not least because I didn't even clean my boots. I remember playing football for some Sunday-league team, and one time I scored a hat-trick and was really pleased with myself. Dad arrived towards the end of the game and missed my goals but was in time to see me miss a sitter. I came off and I was like, Ah, Dad you missed it, I scored three goals. He could see I was really happy, but he was absolutely fuming about the miss, and in front of everyone he made me do shuttle runs on the road from kerb to kerb by the side of the pitch.

I was never aggressive as a kid, but you have to form a character quite quickly at a young age when you're bouncing around the world as part of the army community – you've got to have a certain presence, other-wise you go proper off the rails. There was an incredible eclectic mix of kids from all over the UK on the barracks, often pretty rough. AmyJo and I weren't brats, but that's what we were all called, Army Brats. We rarely got to know the officers' kids because when they got to eleven or twelve they usually went to private school in England. Alistair Brown was an exception. He was the coolest kid in our school in Cyprus because his dad was a major. I got my first taste of what life might be like on the other side of the tracks when his older brother came over for the summer with a mate of his from their private school. His mate tried to take me off somewhere and pull my trunks down. I remember thinking, *No, this ain't right, not right at all. Fuck you*, and having to leg it.

Ali and me spent the summer of 1988 listening to the *Bullet from a Gun* album by Derek B, a British hip-hop artist who had these mad, sexual lyrics the like of which I'd never heard in my life. I've still got the songs down. It's weird, I've never been into hip-hop, but I can recite Derek B because the songs seemed like fairy stories. I would probably have a lot of Def Leppard down too, but my mum took one look at the picture on the front of the *Hysteria* cassette and said, No, that's anti-Christian, it's Satanic.

My mum was a Christian and quite strict about it. She'd been an army nurse when she met my dad (they married in 1976) but now looked after us kids. She used to put out her own poetry collections: *Time for a Rhyme with Jackie Doherty*. That was her thing: coffee mornings, bible studies. In Cyprus I remember the army newsletter would always have a poem from my mum. Her poems were more like comic rhymes, religious, funny, everyday and homespun.

She could be more heavy-handed with the discipline than Dad, especially later when he was away a lot. She wouldn't let me go to youth clubs or hang out on the street. Around the time we were in Cyprus, *The Simpsons* came out and I was not allowed to watch it because Mum reckoned it wasn't appropriate. I've since become a major fan of *The Simpsons* – watch it all the time. I have fond memories of reading the *Beano* as a kid, but I was never allowed to join the fan club. I'd say, Look, you just send off 20p and you get a Gnasher badge, and my mum was like, No, it's not educational. She was always sticking up stuff on our toilet wall – religious stuff, psalms, or pictures of a sunset with the epithet 'God Is Love'. The Rudyard Kipling poem 'If' was on the toilet wall too.

We'd go to church every Sunday in Cyprus and throughout my childhood. My mum always had a special place for padres, vicars and fathers, people of goodness and trust. They were deity-like figures to me growing up. In church my dad would whisper in my ear when my mum wasn't listening, God please let my horse come in tomorrow and I'll love you for ever, amen. Even though Dad had an Irish Catholic background, neither his mum or dad were really religious. He only went to church because he thought it would be good for us. Sometimes I'd sit with him while he read the newspaper at the back of the church.

I got confirmed when I was twelve, after we left Cyprus and moved to Krefeld, Germany – just after the Berlin Wall came down. I was not pressured into doing it. My mum said you don't do this unless you really believe, and I really did feel the presence of God. I took the vows, the oath – you ask Jesus and the Holy Spirit into your heart, and I remember really feeling it strongly. Years later, when I wasn't a committed Christian and didn't feel the presence of Jesus in my heart very often, I still remembered a time when I did, and I'd feel genuinely safe in that knowledge. Evangelical is the wrong word, but that's the closest word I can think of to describe feeling the presence of God or presence of the spirit.

I was in the choir for about a year: there's a wicked photo of me in my page-boy outfit. The padre made this appeal for more choir members and I got out of the pew there and then and went down the front. Everybody was bemused. The padre asked me what I wanted, and I said, I've come to join the choir. Everyone started laughing. He said, Come to practice next Thursday. They used to put me right at the back of the choir though, because I was so horribly out of tune. In fact, the first time I saw myself singing live was on a family home video, singing at a wedding as a kid, karaoke, doing a Beatles song, and it was so out of tune, it was awful. Among the family, it was always AmyJo who was recognised as the musical one.

Dalton Middle School in Ratingen, near Dusseldorf, was for ten to fourteen year olds, black and red tie. It was an hour on the bus every morning for us to get there from Krefeld. One of my strongest memories from that school involved myself and another lad. We were both twelve, and we'd get taken to the music room at lunchtime by some girls in our year who had all developed a lot faster than us. They took our trousers down, and we were at the mercy of these five or six girls. The headmaster called us into his office one day, secretly, and said, We're worried about the guys in the higher years doing stuff with the younger girls in your year in the music room, and he expected me to tell them what was going on. I didn't know anything about that. I just knew that the girls used to take me and the other lad in there and put their hands down our trousers and make us put our hands down their trousers.

One summer, I went back to Cyprus on my own to visit a kid called Cedric Grandjean for a holiday. Cedric had been the only kid we'd known in Cyprus whose dad wasn't in the army. He was a French businessman who went to work in Russia. Cedric and I became friends because we had a shared love of *Fawlty Towers*. On the barracks we'd always get TV shows three weeks later, if at all, on the British Forces Broadcasting Services, so my Nanny Doll would VHS stuff from the telly in England and send it to wherever we were. She'd record *Fawlty Towers*, *Only Fools and Horses*, *Rising Damp*, *Steptoe and Son* or *Last of the Summer Wine*, all of which my dad loved. I'd always get up early and watch them repeatedly. They were 360-minute VHS tapes. I'd watch them obsessively.

The holiday with Cedric was a disaster. We were jumping off Roman ruins that had been overwhelmed by the sea and something fell on my head from an old wall, and I remember being under a boat not being able to get out and then just hallucinating. I was flying back the next day, and when I got back to England, my Uncle Liam could see something was wrong. He took me to hospital in Watford for a brain scan because I was continuing to have these hallucinations. I was screaming in the street, shouting about how I was being chased by a ball of string. Uncle Liam had moved out of London to Watford with his wife, my dad's sister Christine, and my cousin Adam, who I started a QPR fanzine with later.

I'd actually had these hallucinations before; I had them for a lot of years. I called them the Christmas hallucinations, because I'd maybe get them once a year. I'd start seeing things that weren't there and trying to escape them, trying to escape these digits that were coming down a wire into my brain, shitloads of digits falling from the sky into my face and mouth – I could taste them. And there was this sense that there was rain coming up from the ground, so you'd feel it coming up through your legs, through your body, with an overwhelming sound of static. The first time I injected ketamine I got exactly the same sensation but more in control.

The bang on the head in Cyprus was more about the ball of string, but the taste in the mouth was the same. I think the Christmas hallucinations was just standard fever stuff, when your mind is fevered. It wouldn't last more than a couple of days. It wasn't permanent, like epilepsy – I've read that also involves a lot of digits, tastes and fevers. Occasionally, I'll still get little flashes of that taste.

One of the few times I saw my dad really happy was when we went down in the car to Bavaria: me, Dad and AmyJo. We were walking through the forest, and he was singing 'Meet Me on the Corner' by Lindisfarne. It's such a beautiful song, a bouncier version of the 'Streets of London' but just as melancholic and poetic. I remember saying, What's that? Years later – after my dad had publicly disowned me because of my drug use – I heard the song at random and it just destroyed me. It was so beautiful, and I had such a strong image of us all being happy with my dad walking through this forest.

If Dad took you anywhere or did anything with us, it was always a big deal. While we were in Krefeld, he was away for about six months in Iraq just after the Gulf War. I watched the early US strikes on the telly and then, bang, my dad was gone. I was old enough to understand the narrative, but I was always being told he wasn't fighting; he was just clearing up the mess. I'd write to him, and I remember feeling closer to him than I ever had. I'd tell him things I'd done at school, goals I'd scored, even amazing goals I'd scored on the playground against some of the bigger boys, and a month later I'd get a letter back and he'd tell me how he was clearing up the mess and how the British soldiers would be off to a beheading on a Friday. Hearing about his life made me feel really connected with him – more than I felt when he was at home.

Every Saturday night while Dad was away, we used to dress up – my mum, little Emily, AmyJo and me – and go out to a restaurant in Krefeld town centre. It gave us something to look forward to. We took it in turns to choose where we wanted to go. Emily always chose McDonald's. I liked the posh pizza parlour – it was like a little luxury to have pizza out. I don't know if 1990 was a particular glamorous time for pizza, but to us it was. It must have been hard for Mum, but we were buzzing really that my dad had got close to war – that's what we thought it was about, really. The family vibe was very much an army gang mentality. After the Gulf War, Dad had a few trips away in Bosnia.

My dad always had lots of war books in the house. We had *The Rise and Fall of the Third Reich* and Lyn MacDonald's *Somme*, a famous book about the First World War. There were also anthologies of George Orwell's fiction. I ploughed through them quite early. When you've got a limited library, you really get stuck into the books you do have. They hold great power. Everyone in the family knew and read A*nimal Farm*.

I think my dad even read it aloud to me when I was a kid. I can also remember him reading *Lord of the Rings* to me and being completely sucked in by that. Bilbo Baggins got me early on too.

There was also war poetry in the house, and those poems struck such a deep chord. Dad would recite them to me sometimes. They were these incredibly realistic descriptions of the absolute misery in the trenches. When I first met Carl Barât, we forged a really strong bond over 'Suicide in the Trenches' by Siegfried Sassoon. I loved that poem from when Dad first introduced me to it, and I couldn't believe he'd actually put it to music. There's a Libertines song called 'Anthem for Doomed Youth', about how 'they wish you luck and hand you a gun'. We took the title from the famous Wilfred Owen war poem that I read as a kid. Dad would talk to me about the First World War quite a lot, saying how a generation of young men were killed for half a mile of mud. He had this epic, tragic, overwhelming sense of the futility of it all but was still somehow attached to this romantic idea that there will always be in some foreign field a little piece of earth called England.

I always thought I'd join the army and go to war somewhere. That's what I thought was in store for me. I'd become a soldier and die in a foreign land. It seemed somehow heroic. It was the flag and the idea of being English that was ever present for all us army brats. I suppose it was just this longing to be English, to be in England, this longing for an identity.'

II

Roots

1991–1993: Taxi driving with Grandad Percy in
Liverpool. Auditioning for the Generation Game. *A*
move to Dorset and a TV breakthrough. Queens Park
Rangers becomes an obsession. Youngest fanzine editor
in the country. Sharing Tony Hancock with Dad.

'In the very early days of The Libertines, I told the *NME* I went to primary school in Liverpool, which isn't technically possible. I was christened at St George's on the Everton hill, just up from Anfield, but I really wanted to validate myself as being from Liverpool, to try and communicate this sense of belonging to the city – wishful thinking. AmyJo says I was a terrible liar as a kid. Telling people I'd lived in Mexico was a big one – I had this 'I love Mexico' key ring. I tried it in Anfield when we were visiting my mum's family one time. There were all these urchins kicking a football about in the street, and I tried to convince them that I lived in Mexico, and they told me to fuck off. I ran inside, really upset, and my dad asked, What's the matter? I went, One of the kids told me to fuck off, and he found it hilarious.

A validation of sorts did come years later when The Libertines first went to Liverpool and all the members of my family turned up. I was like, Y'see, I am from this town – even though my Uncle Phil, one of mum's elder brothers, he's dead now, got asked to leave. He'd had one too many and said something really nasty to Gary Powell. Yeah, you've got a good suntan, mate, something like that. Gary's a peaceful guy, but that's not cool.

My mum grew up in 50 Salisbury Road, the terraced house in Anfield where my nan and grandad lived until they died. It was right next to the Liverpool FC ground. She was the only girl in the family, and Nan and Grandad had put money aside for a wedding, and she turned up wed to this soldier from London. They got married about two months after meeting. She wasn't pregnant, they just met and fell in love. My nan apparently got my dad up against the wall on that first night and said, What's so bloody special about you, then?

My dad would always prat about when we'd visit Liverpool. He would say, You know you're in Liverpool when you put your hand out of the car window to indicate and your watch is missing when you pull it back in. We drove an old Mercedes, really square-shaped with the symbol on the front, and another joke we had was that we could never believe the Mercedes symbol was still there when we'd drive away from Liverpool. Eventually it did get nicked when we were visiting the city!

We'd turn up to visit Nan and Grandad with all these little routines worked out. Dad would say, Right, OK, when we get to the house I'm going to say, Right, where does Percy come from? And in a Liverpool accent we'd have to say, Anfield, lad. And then he'd say, When I say what happened to your other grandad, what you going to say? And we'd say, He snuffed it. You think about it now – that's his dad he's talking about. I never knew Ted.

Mum's dad was such an amazing character. He was Jewish. Dad would always take the piss out of his big nose and call him ugly, but over the years a really strong bond developed between them. He was originally called Paris – he changed it to Percy in the 1930s – Percy

Michels. He drove a black cab and was always getting into trouble. One time a Chinese doctor turned up at Liverpool Airport and had to get to the hospital really quickly, but my grandad was the slowest driver. The doctor said, You go faster, you go faster! And my grandad said, Listen, mate, you cook the rice and I'll drive the taxi, all right, and he ended up in court. In his defence, he just pointed at his nose and said, All my life I've been the victim of racism for my nose. Case dismissed. His dream was to buy and sell American cars for the Liverpool market, but he never quite got there.

His mum Channa was Jewish, escaped the pogroms in Russia in 1905. She made her way to Paris, married a Frenchman, a Jewish engineer, and followed him to Liverpool with his work. Then he left her, ran off with the maid, back to Paris. Channa was stranded in Liverpool with five children and pregnant with Grandad. He told a story about seeing his dad during the war in Paris. Grandad was in the British Army as a member of the Desert Rats stationed in Italy and he went to Paris when it was liberated. He had to drive his commander there, and he asked for a twenty-four-hour pass to find his father. The story was that when Percy found his father, a very clever man who spoke thirteen languages, he marched up and said, I'm the son you never met and told him off in three languages, and marched away again. I'd love to do a genealogical unveiling of the whole Michels clan. There's all kinds of stories about Percy's older brothers: one of them, Antoine Michels, was supposed to have been the only man who was allowed to wear every uniform during the Second World War because he was a translator for General de Gaulle, spoke eleven languages, and another one who ended up in a lunatic asylum . . . a mad violin player.

There'd always be a knees-up in Liverpool when we visited. My Uncle Phil would get plastered and dress in my nan's wig and one of her dresses, and all our tearaway scally cousins would be nicking drinks and fags. When Percy died in 1998, he left me his gold Star of David in his will, but my Uncle Phil claimed it before it could be given to me. It was the only thing Grandad left me in his will. At the funeral, Uncle Phil took it off his neck and gave it to me, but I gave it back and told him to look after it for me. I think he sold it a couple of weeks later. Uncle Phil used to have a lot of cash on him and would drive around Liverpool in old Jags. Officially his job was landscape gardening, but I don't know. He was always in and out of trouble with the law over driving offences – he was a well-known tinker, really.

From early on I had this desire, almost desperation, to get on telly. I almost got on the *Generation Game*. My mum and I got auditioned in Bush House, in the BBC studios in London. We had to pretend to be snakes, wriggling on the floor. It was me and Mum in this room with six or seven other kids with their parents trying to get these two available slots. They called us back, but it was for the week we were going on holiday – I was going to see Cedric, and Mum and Dad were going to France to visit the war graves and do Disneyland – so we couldn't do it. We would have been on the first show when Jim Davidson took over as host.

I loved acting as a kid. AmyJo and I would put on little shows for everyone, little sketches. We had a stock trade in characters – we had these two Liverpool football hooligans we'd do when we visited Anfield. That's what a lot of the performance poetry was about later – it was character-based, different accents. I was always phoning my grandad pretending to be Irish or Scottish and booking long cab rides. One time I pretended to be AmyJo's American cousin and got dressed up in her spare Brownies uniform and went along to Brownies with her – there's a photo somewhere. And AmyJo and me were always taping ourselves trying to do our own radio shows.

When we moved from Germany to Blandford Forum Camp in Dorset, Channel 4 came to the local school to do a documentary on this fly called the Blandford fly, which if it stings you, you swell up quite badly. There'd been a major outbreak in the area, and the council was investigating how to destroy the larvae. I pretended I'd lived there all my life and been stung as a baby, life-or-death incident. They were fascinated. There's a Channel 4 documentary somewhere with me as a ten or eleven year old doing this whole routine. Helen Sharman, the astronaut, was presenting the show.

One of the first things Dad and I did together when we were in Blandford was go to a QPR away game at Southampton. They were my dad's local team when he was growing up in Shepherd's Bush. At the game, he pointed out a fella in the crowd and said, Oh my God, that's Alan Barnes, I grew up with him, he lived in my street. This bloke was proper having it with these Southampton fans, looking completely terrifying, fearless, in what my dad christened his 'lucky sneakers'. He developed this idea Alan Barnes had worn these sneakers since the '60s. We didn't approach him at the time, but Alan Barnes turned out to be Mr QPR – the only game he'd missed since the '60s was when Rangers played in Sheffield on the day of his mum's funeral.

After that first game, I pretty quickly became obsessed with every-thing to do with QPR. It became my life. I wrote obsessively to the players and followed them home and away. If I went with Dad, we'd normally drive to away games. He drove me all over the country. I have fond memories of him taking me to Hillsborough and Blackburn. I'd always go to Liverpool. If Dad wasn't going, I'd set off with my little QPR cagoule and take the train. I wasn't allowed to go to after-school youth clubs but going to the football was a different thing. It was encouraged, really. It was a link to Shepherd's Bush, a place like Liverpool, where the family had roots.

Being in the crowd, being on the terrace at QPR, was amazing; I loved the singing and the camaraderie. That was what a lot of it was about for me, getting a sense of strong cultural identity. After seeing

Alan Barnes, I became absolutely fascinated by the Loft Boys, the QPR hard-core supporters who stood in the Loftus Road End part of the ground. They were a really good home-and-away, tight little firm. At the games, I was always right in the thick of it, but I was not really interested in fighting. I just loved being part of the atmosphere. Whenever we played away at any London game, it was always trouble. I remember a police horse being pushed over at Stamford Bridge and seeing darts flying at goalkeepers' backs. It wasn't a good thing to see the violence, but it was a good thing to see the loyalty and passion. Most of the lads just wanted to have a drink and make a fuckload of noise. That was what it was all about – a show of strength for the team, real passion for QPR. It was a proper tribe thing, and the energy, especially on the terraces, was incredible, everyone bursting into the same song at the same time.

When they were deciding to close down the terraces, I used to phone Danny Baker's show, the *Morning Edition* on BBC Radio 5, all the time before going to school, pretending to be different people. I'd put on different accents and complain about the Taylor Report*, trying to build up a bit of momentum because that was the end of going to football for me when they put in seats, in 1994.

Over time I built up this massive collection of QPR fanzines, and that inspired me to start my own. There was one in particular, *A KICK UP the R's*, done by a guy called Dave Thomas, who's a great old Rangers faithful character, always in denim with a Stan Bowles haircut. Dave was like a folk hero to me. The first issue of my fanzine was a bit corny, but I was only fourteen or fifteen. In the editorial, I put, 'Peter Doherty Jnr, youngest fanzine editor in the country', which was so lame. We did four or five issues, and they got better and better. I used to go down the

* The Hillsborough Stadium Disaster Inquiry report that recommended that all major stadiums convert to being all-seater.

training ground, and that's how I got interviews with manager Gerry Francis and star players Ray Wilkins and Les Ferdinand. I had Alan Barnes write something for one issue. I even interviewed the team vicar – there were quite a few committed Christians in that QPR team, which I identified with at the time. Me and my cousin Adam, who helped with the fanzine, went in the director's box for one game to interview the then director Richard Thompson. Adam and his brother Ben and his dad Liam went to QPR every week. The last time I saw Adam was at his dad's funeral two years ago. His two kids were in full QPR strips, and there was a QPR shirt on Uncle Liam's coffin.

I used to do proper research for the fanzine. I'd go down the Arc in Hammersmith, the big public library, and access old articles about hooliganism in the '80s. In one QPR fanzine I used to read, there was this really strange non-football-related regular column called 'View from Flat 302' about a character who lived in one of these flats on the White City Estate overlooking the ground but hated football. Things like that fascinated me, really drove me. The White City Estate was where I thought I was going to end up, living in a flat in one of these massive red-brick tenements. It was built as social housing but basically became a ghetto. On match days all the fans would swarm through, but all the kids on the balcony, young black kids, never came to the game. There was never a lot of black faces on the terraces when you compared it to the percentage of actual black players in the game – probably the same now. I talked to Les Ferdinand for my fanzine, and he was saying as a kid he was scared. He would never go to football matches – he loved football, loved playing, but as a black kid he would never feel comfortable.

All that area around the ground – General Smuts pub, the Springbock pub, South Africa Road, Bloemfontein Road – it was all connected to the Boer War and colonial, imperial Britain. It's closed down now, but General Smuts was a really rough pub, and I wrote a song called

'General Smuts' for The Libertines. It was a demo when we did the first Rough Trade recordings, ended up as a B-side to 'Time for Heroes', but it's always remained one of mine and Carl's favourite tunes.

The year The Libertines played the Leeds festival, 2015, our big comeback year, the QPR players were staying in the same hotel as us, and they found out and Les Ferdinand pretended to be the concierge. He knocked on my hotel-room door and said, Your luggage ready for collection, Mr Doherty? Yeah, yeah, come in ... and it was Les Ferdinand! You can't imagine. This is a guy I used to chase down the Bloemfontein Road if I saw him before a match. He was a proper God to me.

I actually thought, after leaving school, I'd get a job doing the match-day programme at QPR, be an in-house reporter at Rangers. I wrote a few freelance articles for *FourFourTwo* magazine and *When Saturday Comes* and *The Onion Bag*, the only mainstream national football magazine that was fanzine-like – it was absolutely filthy. They used to give away free cassettes with terrace chants on, and I actually invented a song that got put on one of their cassettes – a variation of the Coventry FC football chant 'In Our Coventry Homes': 'In our Liverpool slums, we wear bright pink shell-suits and have curly hair'.

Tony Hancock was another long-standing bond I had with Dad. He was fascinated with this comedian who ended up killing himself aged forty-four, in 1968. My dad loved his comedy, which flirted with topics such as alienation, cynicism, depression, mania, misanthropy and paranoia, but he was interested in his life too. He took me to a few of the Tony Hancock Appreciation soirées, where they'd have screenings on projectors. You'd sit in a dark room with twelve other people and watch it. We'd get the newsletter, and there'd always be Hancock cassettes in the car. We even had matching Tony Hancock ties. I really grew to love his comedy, and over the years I built up a collection of all

Hancock's videos and all his books. I love all situation comedies, but I love *Hancock's Half Hour* especially, the BBC radio show and the TV series, because although it was scripted, it was based on him as a man. He admitted that all the time – a great part of the character he portrayed was really him and how he felt.

I referenced him in 'Up the Bracket', the title track of The Libertines' debut album. It's really a London expression – my dad would say it, or Nanny Doll would say it, as a joke term for the throat, but 'up the bracket' comes up all the time with Hancock. I couldn't believe no one had used it before. In fact, it amazed me that no one really referenced Tony Hancock in pop culture up to that point. I also wrote an early Libertines song called 'Lady Don't Fall Backwards', which ended up on *Grace/Wastelands*, that is the name of this fictional book in *Hancock's Half Hour* in an episode called 'The Missing Page'. It's also the title of Joan Le Mesurier's autobiography. She was Hancock's best mate's missus, and they had an affair, and in the end that's half the reason he killed himself. His suicide note said, 'Tell my mum I'm sorry but things just seemed to go wrong one too many times.' It was really profound.

There was obviously something about Hancock's worldview that Dad could relate to. Hancock was an alcoholic and a depressive. Dad wasn't clinically depressed, but he would have these periods when he'd just not talk to anyone, silent bouts.* He still gets like that. I suppose he is dealing with his feelings, and he doesn't want anyone to know those feelings. I can relate to that. The times he was happy really stand out: while we were living in Blandford, I have this clear image of sitting at the top of the stairs and seeing him downstairs drunk. He didn't really drink, almost never in front of us kids. He looked so happy – he was shadow-boxing in the red jacket, the Charge of the Light Brigade outfit

---

* Peter Doherty Snr's silent episodes are described in Jacqueline Doherty's book *Pete Doherty: My Prodigal Son* (Headline, 2006).

they'd wear for functions. He was saying, I'm Sugar Ray Leonard. I'm thinking, Wow, what's that? And my mum, maybe she'd had some wine as well, saying, Your dad's had a few drinks, go to bed.

One other funny thing I remember about Dad was when we'd go to see QPR we'd often visit this guy Dave Howard, who lived right by the stadium and whom he'd known when he first left school. Dave used to play guitar for David Bowie when he was Dave Jones & The King Bees, and Dad was really amused that he was still bitter about being left behind. One time when my dad was in the other room listening to Dave slag off David Bowie, I said to Dave's wife Sonia, who also knew my dad when he was a teenager, What was my dad like when he was a kid? She said, Oh yeah, he was a lovely boy. I went, Was he? Everyone I'd previously asked about my dad, his brother or his mum, would say, Oh, he was a handful. She said, No, he was a lovely boy, and then she said something that blew my mind. She said, I remember him standing on the platform at Paddington Station in a duffle coat writing poetry. At the time, I think I was spending quite a bit of time stood on train platforms in a duffle coat writing poetry. I brought it up with him later, but he denied it.'

III
Comprehensive

1994–1997: A rude awakening at a new school, the largest comprehensive in the Midlands. Lost in literature and poetry. A crush on Morrissey and The Smiths. First band and an attempt at stand-up. Sally, fantasy literary saucepot. Another appearance on TV. Meeting 'my guitarist' Carl for the first time.

'We moved to Gamecock barracks in Bramcote, Warwickshire, when I was fourteen. I went to 'Nico' – Nicholas Chamberlaine School – in Bedworth, the largest comprehensive in the Midlands. It was unusual because they had no uniform. It was just me and my dad at first – my mum stayed in Dorset with Emily and AmyJo, who was finishing her exams in a previous school – but my mum had said to him, I don't care if there's no uniform, he's wearing uniform. I had to go in black shoes, grey trousers and a white shirt, and everyone else was in tracksuits. It was too much, and in the end I just used to change on the bus.

The first day they put me with this lad who was supposed to show me round, but he just went straight to the bogs and started skinning up with six or seven of the roughest lads in the school. There I am in my uniform with my little backpack. Then the deputy head, a right hard case, came in bawling, and I was absolutely bewildered, terrified. The first lesson hadn't even started. Later someone came up to me and threw an orange in my face, a really squishy orange . . . very upsetting. At the schools I'd been at you'd always had your tearaways, but people who didn't want to learn had been the odd ones out – now if you did want to learn, well, you were just seen as a freak, really.

I did get in the school football team. I suppose I still harboured this ambition to play professional football, even though I wasn't that quick. But at Nico I came across some proper footballers and realised I wasn't going to make it. Jai Stanley, my current manager, was the best one. He was playing for the county, and his heart wasn't in it for the school team. I was very disappointed. I used to look around our team, and we had all these great players, but they couldn't be arsed. I remember we had one game which if we won we were going to play at Highfield Road, Coventry's home ground at the time. Coventry FC was the closest big team to us, and they were in the Premier League then. But Jai and the rest of the lads gave up. I think we lost 5–4 after being 4–0 up. No one was even bothered – they just wanted to get off the pitch. They didn't have any interest in representing the school. They all played for half-decent teams outside school.

It was difficult to make friends. If I wanted to do something with some kids from school on say a Saturday morning, my dad wouldn't let me. Then he'd come back ten minutes later and say, You haven't got any mates anyway, and call me Billy No Mates. To him it'd be funny, but I was quite sensitive, so it stung. I was kept on a tight leash. Dad had all these stories about fighting as a kid and being a tearaway, but the idea I could ever be a tearaway was just so poisonous to him and Mum. There was nothing you could do. There was no rebellion. When she grew up, Emily was the rebel in the family. She said, No, I'm not having it. AmyJo and I were shocked. Ironically, she's ended up in the army. She lives in York now, but she's been bouncing all over the place – Afghanistan, God knows where. She's a right little trooper.

So, I was stuck on the barracks with my dad who got me a job cleaning out the living quarters of the Gurkhas, and on a Monday night we'd go to an auction in Rugby about ten miles from the barracks, where they'd have these crates of books that nobody would be interested in. You could get maybe three or four banana boxes of books for a tenner or fifteen quid. I bought hordes of them. I had boxes and boxes of books, lots of cheap American hardbacks from the '70s for some reason, strange philosophy and literary criticism, a lot of left-wing stuff. I got a huge volume of *Being and Nothingness* by Jean-Paul Sartre. Had it as a doorstop for years – it was impossible to read.

This was when I started to devour books and developed this yearning to be a writer. I actually won first prize in a district poetry competition for an anti-smoking poem I wrote at school. I wasn't allowed to go out after school, but on a Friday night I was allowed to do a glass-collecting job at a pub in nearby Nuneaton. I'd see kids from my year in school in the bar. One night I swiped some fags off a table and tried to smoke them but couldn't hold it down. Then I wrote this poem about it.

School was occasionally a good resource. We got presented with Graham Greene's *Brighton Rock*, and that was a big influence on me. But I got most of my inspiration from the books I picked up at the auction in Rugby. *Trilby* by George du Maurier was one: the best-known character is Svengali, but I also fell for Trilby herself, this beautiful girl wandering around barefoot in rags. I also loved *Waiting for Godot* by Samuel Beckett. I was fascinated by Beckett, loved that photo of him with the really craggy face. It was the same with James Joyce: it was not just the power of the literature; it was the power of the writer's life, their personality and also the culture around them that attracted me. I was seduced by grand names like Beckett, Joyce and Bertolt Brecht, who also had fascinating life – a passionate communist and anti-Nazi.

Another book I got from Rugby was *Ariel: A Shelley Romance* by French writer André Maurois, a fictionalised biography of English Romantic poet Percy Bysshe Shelley. There's a strong image in that book of Shelley being at school and not mixing with the other kids and just going to sit under a tree with a book that I found quite interesting. I wonder why? I also enjoyed John Keats's poetry. I tried to read Lord Byron, *Childe Harold's Pilgrimage*, but I found him a bit stiff, very hard graft, bit uptight, whereas Keats would talk about 'draining dull opiates to numb my weary spirit' – it was intriguing.

I suppose these are the seeds of my desire to try heroin: this romantic vision of the dream-inducing state of a drug – like Coleridge was said to have written these epic narratives such as *Kubla Khan* as visions when he was smoking opium. I never really got on with Coleridge actually, but I did have a copy of *Confessions of an English Opium-Eater* by Thomas De Quincey, and I read Oscar Wilde. My dad once said it was reading Wilde that first put the idea of taking drugs in my head. Probably true – Wilde and Keats. But it was such an alien concept, drugs, at the time I was reading these books. It was not something I ever really saw or had any knowledge of, but these strange little references in certain books I picked up intrigued me, especially to opium – which was described in a luxurious sense, associated with a sensation of peace and accomplishment and a mystical, magical land.

In reality, it turns out Keats had a really bad stomach, so that's why he took it – because of the abdominal pains that killed him, coughing up blood. And Oscar Wilde wasn't actually that into it, wasn't out of his nut on opium.

This only dawned on me when I had a habit and realised how difficult it was to balance being on a constant mission to score with trying to create.

In the early days of The Libertines, I would often talk about books and authors that influenced me and fans would throw books on stage a lot – *Catcher in the Rye* was popular, which was a bit strange, because it was not a book I mentioned. Arthur Rimbaud also came up a lot too – another mystery. I'd absorbed him a little bit as this powerful mystical figure, but I didn't know much about his writing. He was just one of those names you claim to like without even having read him. It would have been a very exotic thing for me to have a collection of Rimbaud's poetry at that time. It was only over the years once they started getting lobbed on the stage I started reading him. I also got a lot of Russian literature thrown on stage: Pushkin, Tolstoy and Dostoevsky. But like Rimbaud they were writers I only really started to get into after the band started. I still get turned onto some good stuff from it coming flying on stage: that's how I discovered the Brazilian novelist Clarice Lispector and Roberto Bolaño, another South American writer.

I did have Baudelaire's *The Flowers of Evil* while I was at Nico. Baudelaire – who inspired Rimbaud – also encouraged excess in the understanding of emotions or people or women or wine ... or anything. It's almost like you couldn't just sit and enjoy the writing to understand it: you had to get a full sense of life. I also loved Jean Cocteau, *Les Enfants Terribles*, and I loved his artwork as well. Jean Genet was another early influence. I was really proud of the Genet and Cocteau books that I got from the auction in Rugby. I thought Genet was hilarious. He was always knocking about with these dodgy characters in the back streets of Marseille and smuggling things across Europe, in and out of jail. I was fascinated by him.

There are certain books that you can really lose yourself in if you're in the right frame of mind, and you've got the time and space around yourself, which I did as a teenager as it happens. It was the equivalent of a drug, really, at that age, for me – it was expanding my mind in all kinds of directions and making me feel different about the world. Then it was going out to look for what I was reading about and a lot of time finding a connection with other people through books. Literature was a big thing for me.

In terms of those formative years and influences, Orwell was the one who really stuck with me, especially *Down and Out in Paris and London*. I really felt a calling after reading that book. I wanted to see that world. I also discovered people like Charles Bukowski and Hunter S. Thompson, who exploded a whole new idea in my head as a teenager that maybe I could just write about an army barracks or Anfield or Shepherd's Bush or any imagined world, the glory or the dregs, anything – I could write what I wanted.

I formed my first band at Nico in my GCSE year, 1995, with Dan De'Ath, my best mate. Dan, a black lad but with an all-white family, had a pretty hard time at school. His dad was from the West Indies, but he'd never met him, and his mum was the daughter of a leading Rotary Club member and left-wing councillor. He had this self-developed refinement – used to say he was Morrissey or that he was Oscar Wilde. He was also really tall, six feet four inches when we were fifteen. He actually left school without any qualifications and ended up working in an all-night garage, but he recently became the mayor of Cardiff for a couple of years.

Dan and I bonded over the Morrissey album *Vauxhall and I*, released in 1994. I fell for that record, and then we both got really into The Smiths. I'd started to develop this vision of maybe being a writer, and I was lonely and frustrated with the world I saw around me, and The Smiths captured a lot of what I was feeling. There was a Music & Record Exchange in Nuneaton, and I'd buy any Smiths vinyl and obsessively listen to it. I would go down and steal books from the public library and sit in Dan's room with all my stolen books and listen to The Smiths. Morrissey's voice and those lyrics were incredible. I saw him on *Top of the Pops* a few times in that period doing the singles 'Alma Matters' and 'Irish Blood, English Heart'.

Something in Morrissey's lyrics, his little sketches of characters and narratives, reminded me of the Chas & Dave songs about fat old policemen and two old girls from Camden Town – there was a similar music-hall element. Morrissey was also quite melodic, even though his voice was really strange on those early Smiths albums. His voice is almost pathologically sombre, this groaning Manchester voice: 'It's time the tale were told' . . . it's a very literary introduction to a band. I just thought this is a really interesting way to go; it's poetry but it's also describing England. Also, there was this Irish connection with Morrissey – it runs through a lot of things I associate with, from Oscar Wilde right through to Beckett.

Initially the band was called Pete's Briefcase. I had this leather attaché case I'd picked up at the auction in Rugby that I thought was the nuts. Then we changed our name to The Peepsters. It was around the time Oasis were kicking off, and all the lads who got into Oasis, like Jai, started a band doing Oasis covers. AmyJo actually really got into Oasis as well. Dad and I drove up to Sheffield to pick her up from an Oasis gig. It was quite exciting seeing all these Oasis fans, and I was a bit jealous that AmyJo had been to a gig, but Oasis didn't really connect with me. Before leaving for school, I'd always put on *The Big Breakfast* on Channel 4, and they'd have a band on every morning, and I was more connected to The Bluetones, The Lightning Seeds and Sleeper. The Lightning Seeds had lyrics about freezing on picket lines, and I heard they were from Liverpool, and I thought, Right, this is a working-class band with a message – intertwining meaningful lyrics with melody. That was really inspirational.

The Peepsters had a song called 'Oranges Are Not the Only Fruit'. We'd just read the Jeannette Winterson book about the lesbian girl and her tough northern mother. And I really got into magic realism at the time. I read Gabriel García Márquez's *One Hundred Years of Solitude* and *Love in the Time of Cholera*.

I sent the two or three songs we had, musically just rip-offs of Sleeper songs, to *The Face* magazine with a photo, convinced they'd put us straight on the cover. It was a picture of me and Dan in the bathtub with bubble jackets on.

Our first gig was in the morning assembly at school. Every Thursday the school crammed in the main hall, and someone would have to get up and perform. This one girl used to do it all the time, sing the same song every week: 'I light up another cigarette and I pour the wine' (Beverley Craven's 'Promise Me'). I thought, Fuck this – we can do this, Dan. In the end, he backed down, so I went up there this one Thursday morning with a mic plugged into a karaoke amp and a guitar I got off a car-boot sale and performed 'Billy the Hamster', my first ever song, a terrible twelve-bar blues with a straight narrative about a hamster getting electrocuted: 'When I was eight I went on to my dad, on and on and on and on, it was driving him mad, no he said you're not getting a pet, you're not old enough yet. When I was nine, a little bit older, one day he tapped me on my shoulder and it was Billy, Billy the Hamster' . . . and then one day he died – he chewed on a cable. I also did the 'Long Song', the second song I wrote, this cyclical number about going to school. Apparently, all you could hear out the front was this droning feedback, eeeeggghhhhhhhhhh, and then everywhere I went round school afterwards kids would just go, Eeeeggghhhhhhhhhh at me. I was absolutely gutted, devastated.

The one other Peepsters gig was in an old lady's front garden just outside the school gate. Dan kept a safe distance from that too. I roped in a rocker kid from school who was supposed to be the drummer – he had a snare drum, anyway. Dan did perform with me one time. We also had this comedy act called Mr Spaniel and Mr Spaniel, which me and Carl later revamped during the early days of The Libertines. So, Dan and I did this one gig at the Digbeth Irish Centre in Birmingham, where one of us was pretending to be an evangelical preacher, and we got really badly racially abused, Dan did, and we got bottled off. But I got in touch with the *Nuneaton Gazette* afterwards and said we're doing this comedy act, we're a really big hit in Birmingham, and they ran this picture in the paper of me and Dan in proper musical-hall attire with an old car horn as a prop – really silly. That was it, I thought, the start of my career as a celebrity entertainer.

I smashed my GCSEs – I did eleven, and I got six A*s, an A, three Bs and a C. It was a badge of honour for a long time – finally someone in the family smashed it at school. For my A levels I chose English literature, history, general studies, which was compulsory, and economics. The sixth form at Nico was actually a bit of joke – the sixth formers used to get attacked, bombarded with fruit or footballs by the younger years. I was quite happy with my A-level results in the end: I got two As, a B and a D in economics. There was a lot of maths involved in economics, and it just doesn't sink in. It's like over the years, I'm ashamed to say, I've never been able to get my head around all the contractual machinations of the music industry, publishing and lawyers and managerial percentages. It's been my downfall, really, but I just have trouble picturing it in my head, working out what's going on.

Jai was in my economics class at A level, and he turned me on to The Stone Roses. I remember cycling the few kilometres to school from the barracks listening to 'Where Angels Play', thinking it was one of the most beautiful songs I'd ever heard, just the melody and hearing the line 'the warm red sun gives up and sinks into the trees', and the line about the ugly little box: 'no place for me and you'. It blew my mind, so beautiful, English, romantic pastoral psychedelia, pure poetry. This is when I started getting more and more into music. I bought 'The Man Don't Give a Fuck' by Super Furry Animals, and *Moseley Shoals* by Ocean Colour Scene was an album I listened to a lot. I can also remember looking at the back cover of the first Supergrass album, *I Should Coco*, where they were all sweaty in their cool clothes, a post-gig photo, and thinking, Yeah, that's the life. I started getting the *NME* every week. It was a key part in building up a fuller picture of the people I was listening to, their lives, what they were wearing in their dressing rooms, or how they held their cigarettes, or what hilarious things they said, or maybe they were really shit. It's part of the fantasy of starting a band: you think you're going to invent this amazing movement or invent these incredible characters.

Girls were always hard work at Nico because you'd see these quite beautiful English roses but then they'd open their mouth and it was, Hey, have you got a big knob? and stuff like that. So, I put a personal ad in the back of *Select* magazine: 'Dashingly pretty, delicately sculptured 16-year-old seeks swinging feminine saucepot for . . .' I don't know. It's so embarrassing – it really is another world. I got a shitload of responses, though, mostly from hard-core Goth teenagers. For a couple of summers, I was doing the rounds of places like Harrow and Pinner – that's where there seemed to be a lot of these eyelinered teenage girls. We'd sit and I'd recite Shakespeare sonnets that I'd memorised. It was generally doomed to failure. They all sent little photos of themselves from a good angle, so it was all very tantalising, but, in reality, not so much.

The *Select* ad was, however, how I got to know Sally Anchassi, and she became my ultimate fantasy literary saucepot. Sally was an important character in my life, especially when I first moved to London. There is a load of intrigue to do with her that we'll get in to. She even became my manager for a while in the early days of Babyshambles. When Sally and I first started writing to one another, she was fourteen or fifteen, this lonely schoolgirl in Wimbledon. In this climate it'll be a bit weird to say it, but I remember being in London for a QPR game and hiding behind one of the pillars at Debenhams where she was working a Saturday job just to see her in the flesh. The Libertines song 'What Katie Did' was originally 'What Sally Did'.

In the summer, after the first year of A Levels, if I wasn't chasing after Goth girls, I'd take the bus and train into Birmingham city centre and sit in the Crown Court, in the gallery, watching the cases, one after the other. It was fascinating. I'd makes notes. Some fella would be shuffled in, and he'd be up for being within one hundred yards of a primary school, really twisted stuff. I'd just be clocking him and looking at his face. I used to see quite a lot people up for infringements of their parole where they weren't allowed within two hundred yards of a certain person or a place where they'd had a fight or something. There was some bloke who'd sworn to burn down a pub and was found with a blanket over his head and a can of petrol just outside the pub.

Then I'd try and do a bit of busking – my first try at it – but I was sixteen or seventeen and couldn't really play anything. I'd just sit on the steps by the Arcadia Centre with my guitar and watch these two black fellas who had a quasi-mod tailors. I used to watch them through the window and see all these Birmingham mods going in and getting their suits done. I used to love watching the scene.

And I actually got myself on telly again. In the pre-New Labour landslide election of May 1997, Channel 4 advertised for two hundred kids aged between fourteen and eighteen to take part in a residential week in Manchester. The programme was called *Generation Next*. John Prescott was there and different leading scientists, academics, sociologists . . . it was some kind of experiment. It sounds weird now, but it was the first time I'd been to an indie nightclub. I was seventeen years old. I can't remember much about the documentary, but I think I had a couple of seconds on screen where I said something about whether or not you get justice depends on whether or not you've got a well-paid lawyer . . . which I didn't really know anything about but is probably true. Ken Livingstone was there as well, and because he had been MP for Cricklewood, which was my nan's area in London, I knew about his obsession with newts and toads. So, I remember getting something in about capitalism being like a pond and him really appreciating it. It was a really interesting show, with kids from all over the country. I was particularly impressed by this kid from Croydon who got sent home on the first day for giving everyone Ecstasy.

This was around when I met Carl for the first time. AmyJo had moved out of home and gone to Brunel University London in Uxbridge to study Sports Science. When she came back from her first term down there, in December 1996, almost immediately she told me she'd met this guy Carl with a ponytail and six-pack and he could play guitar, and I thought, Right, that's it, he's going to be my guitarist. AmyJo also had some weed with her, and we had a spliff – my first spliff. She said, It's all right, all it does is make you laugh. I threw up. It was all part of her meeting this fella with the ponytail and six-pack.

I already had my sights firmly set on going to university in London – all the universities I applied for were in London. I wanted to study English literature. I went to an interview at UCL, which is where I wanted to be really, right in town, the West End, but I felt very intimidated at the interview – all the other interviewees seemed a lot more sophisticated. I also went down to Brunel to visit AmyJo and meet my guitarist Carl. Seeing as we would go on to form The Libertines together, this meeting is quite well documented. I was wearing this red plastic jacket, real Jarvis Cocker style, and he was supposed to be looking after me while AmyJo went to do something. What's not well known is we went to an audition together. He was studying drama. I think it was an audition for a Harold Pinter play or a Joe Orton play. I did the audition as well for a laugh, and I got the part! I obviously had to turn it down, but he's never forgiven me for that – he was absolutely fuming. There was a lot of tension in the air from day one.

After that, Carl and I would sporadically meet, but we'd literally fight and quarrel mostly. I've seen it written that he's two years older, but Carl's only nine months older than me, born June 1978. Sometimes we'd end up with AmyJo and her gang of close mates somewhere in London, but it was always people getting proper pissed up. We'd go to the Wag on a Thursday night, Cigarettes and Alcohol it was called, a messy, sticky night, really. I kept trying to link up with Carl to rehearse.

He had this song called 'France' and I had one called 'Albion'. I tried to build a band with Carl around those two songs, and we wrote our first song together, called 'The Domestic'. Carl had the music and lyrics but we sat down together and rewrote the lyrics. 'Albion' became not just a hit for Babyshambles later on but a recurrent phrase that me and Carl would reference in relation to The Libertines: we'd always refer to our various flats as the 'Albion Rooms' – that was something Carl came up with after he saw a play where the young Oscar Wilde was talking about his 'rooms' at Oxford. We also had this idea about how we were pirates sailing a mythical ship named *Albion* to an illusory utopia called Arcadia, the poet's paradise – my Arcadian dream. People presumed I got the idea of Albion from William Blake, which added to this sort of decadent literary swamp around the band, but I'd never really studied

Blake or read him that widely. I actually got the idea from a book by Mancunian cultural commentator Michael Bracewell called *England Is Mine: Pop Life in Albion*. The book was subtitled 'From Wilde to Morrissey'.'

IV
University

1997–1998: Grave-digging and French New Wave films.
Appearing on MTV at the Oasis album launch. Linda and the
Foundry. Andrew and Trash. First gig – Morrissey, naturally.
Writing songs with Carl and several sexual misunderstandings.
Quitting Uni. Sally, heartbreaker. Francesca, first love.

'The summer I left Nico, before I started at Queen Mary and Westfield in September 1997, which in the end was just the best university that would take me, I moved to my nan's in Dollis Hill near Cricklewood, northwest London. My Uncle Peter, who was married to my dad's eldest sister at one point, was the janitor, the caretaker, on the estate. I spent a good month working in Willesden Green Cemetery. It was proper hard graft. The machine dug the graves, but we had to fill them in while the family mourned. My nan and my Aunt Lil would bring me sandwiches down for my lunch.

I used to be really proud of going into the Willesden Green Library in my overalls from work – 'libraries gave us power' vibes – and they had this foreign film section the likes of which I'd never seen. I can remember watching *Breathless*, the French New Wave movie directed by Jean-Luc Godard, at my nan's flat. Once you've seen a film like

Breathless you can't not go for a year or so thinking you're living in the film, racing round in a fantasy life of poetry and crime.

I'd see these open mic nights advertised in the classified sections of free papers or *Time Out* and I'd turn up and do 'Albion', which was three or four chords, very easy to play. It was the only song I could play. I remember really struggling to get people to shut up. I actually took Carl to the open mic night at this pub in Brentford in west London, and we did 'Albion' together – first time we ever played together on stage.

It was the summer Princess Diana died. I remember wandering down from Cricklewood towards the West End as the crowds were building up in St James's Park and along the Mall on the day of the funeral, and just being swept up by it. There were wreaths everywhere. In the end, I was there all night among the mourning crowds, and I was actually quite close to Westminster Abbey as the princes came through the crowd with their dad to mourn their mother. I'd gone down out of some sort of morbid curiosity but ended up proper being part of the mourning. Seeing the people with this love for the princess changed my quite cynical, sarcastic view of it. I became part of it, reading every single wreath, every single card. It was quite odd because I'd describe myself as being completely anti-royal.

Staying at my nan's was fraught with tension. Halfway through that job as a gravedigger it was already too much staying there – she even gave me a curfew when I had to come home. It defeated the whole point of being in London, so I got a little room in a terrace house just off Cricklewood Broadway, just the other side of Gladstone Park, which Dollis Hill is built around. It was the first time in my life I'd ever had my own roof over my head, paid for by myself, £75 a week. I quit the grave-yard when I got a job as a full-time toy demonstrator for Hamleys in a pop-up shop at the Trocadero centre in the West End, selling wind-up frogs or juggling balls. That lasted five or six weeks until I started uni

– £125 a week. It was great being around the West End. I'd go into Tower Records on Piccadilly Circus for a mooch, and that's where I saw the advert for the new Oasis record coming out, *Be Here Now*. There was going to be an in-store signing, and there was so much hype about it I thought, This'll be a good way to get on telly! Basically, I was trying to wangle a job as a presenter on MTV. I wasn't particularly anticipating the album or into the album – I just had a nice little quote when MTV picked me out in the queue and asked me about Oasis. But it was only years later I saw that clip.* It wasn't shown at the time; it was a cut-off edit that someone saw after The Libertines took off and decided had value.

At that Oasis album launch, I also nicked a cardboard cutout of Noel and Liam from outside the store and then triumphantly jumped onto the back of the number 16 bus to make my getaway. All the press were photographing me on the back step of this bus. The next day I went through every paper in the corner shop trying to find the photo, and it wasn't in any of them. I was confused and heartbroken. It's quite strange when you think about it, that desperate need for fame: disturbing really in a way. I couldn't fathom that they wouldn't want to use this incredible image. There must be a photograph of it somewhere.

I met this Italian hippy girl called Linda in Gladstone Park, where I'd go and sit under a tree and read Keats. She was playing guitar, smoking a spliff, and I just wandered over and said hello. Linda was really tall and really androgynous-looking, quite striking. Years later she went back to Milan and turned up presenting a show on Italian MTV. We used to have these nights at her little house in Dollis Hill where she'd cook pasta for me and we'd watch these films I rented out. I watched *Jules et Jim*, another classic French New Wave movie, for the first time

---

* Viewed 1.8 million times and counting on YouTube.

at Linda's, all about these two friends who fall in love with the same girl, a great film, directed by François Truffaut. I showed it to Carl, and he was into it as well; in fact, Carl and I went on to try and live that film a few times, as you'll discover.

Billy Liar, the early sixties British comedy-drama starring Tom Courtenay, was another film that resonated with me and Carl. I built my whole world around it, really. It was this surreal, grotesque portrait of small-town life in northern England and this yearning to escape. I definitely identified with the feeling of being trapped and plunging, lunging into fantasy. The way Billy was the general of this fantasy world he created in his head, Ambrosia – not that I was dictator in my fantasy, but it sounds suspiciously like Arcadia, doesn't it? Carl and I would quote lines from *Billy Liar*, developing our own private language. 'Today is a day of big decisions' or 'A man can lose himself in London' – we loved that. I'm sure if you went through the script of *Billy Liar* there'd be a few Libertines lyrics in there. There's a song he writes in the film, 'Twisterella, Hasn't Got a Fella', and it was always one of our plans to cover that song even though it was really lame. There weren't a lot of bands we had that connection with, bands we both really loved, but there are certain films we both really swear by, like *Billy Liar*, and a lot of the Ealing comedies and the Marx brothers.

Linda was always trying to groom me and Carl to be in her band. She used to wear these long flowery dresses, paint her face and go down to the Foundry, a venue on Old Street in Shoreditch, east London, which Bill Drummond of the KLF helped set up, and do this really weird version of 'Hard to Handle' on acoustic guitar. The Foundry would become a really significant place for me and The Libertines. It was amazing, a closed little world, full of loads of very clever, very loose, ex-art students getting battered on absinthe. The Foundry was the first place in London where I remember thinking, Fucking hell, I'm home! Carl loved it as well, and we would go down together and end up back at Linda's place with our guitars, writing songs.

It was through Linda I met this old African poet called Apu who dressed in full tribal robes and ran the poetry night in the basement at the Foundry. As well as trying to put together a band with Carl, I was putting together my performance poetry in those first months in London, and my first proper experience on stage as a poet was doing some poems for Apu. It was all stream-of-consciousness stuff that I'd written down and memorised – probably quite twee. I had not had a lot of experience of life. I just had this raging thirst to find a world that was as interesting as the world I thought existed, from this cultural patchwork I had in my head.

The university halls of residence were in Whitechapel, and it was mostly medics – there were about three of us that were at Queen Mary and the rest were at St Barts or the Royal London. It was the last year of student grants, which were being replaced by loans, and that was incredible, getting a grant worth about £1,700 at that age and then every bank offering you an overdraft as well, a complete fantasy.

Andrew Hollis was one of the first people I met in the halls, studying history, really intelligent lad, looked just like Ian Brown, and he dressed a little bit like him as well. I thought he was the nuts, and he introduced me to Trash on a Monday at Plastic People in Soho. It became a place me and Carl would go to religiously, looking to meet Scandinavian birds. It was only a tiny place, held about ninety people. I'm glad people remember it as an influential club night. The guy who ran it always had a skin-tight, wicked Moog T-shirt, and when he put on a record, he'd chuck himself about. He'd always play the Manic Street Preachers' 'Motorcycle Emptiness' at the end of the night. Whenever mates of Carl's from Basingstoke, squaddie types, came to London we'd cover them in eyeliner and take them down to Trash and have a good dance.

We used to go to this drug den on Tottenham Court Road afterwards to get weed, sit there with all these Euro ravers off their nut.

I was a bit confused by the people on my English literature course. They didn't seem to be that into literature. I was very disheartened by the lack of second-hand-bookshop dwellers – there was just shitloads of upwardly mobile eejits. Queen Mary was opposite the Ocean Estate of Stepney, a massive Bangladeshi housing estate. I used to enjoy the walk to the college more than I did the lectures. I continued to discover writers and poets for myself, like Emily Dickinson. She's a rich source of magpie-ing. I wrote a song with Dot Allison called 'At the Flophouse' that Babyshambles recorded and there's a line, 'I took one draught of life, paid only the market price, and now I'm estranged' – it's not her word for word but mostly. I really loved Emily Dickinson, still do. She was proper out there.

I went to my first gig that Christmas, 1997, with Dan De'Ath, to see Morrissey at Battersea Power Station. The next day I jumped the train to Chester to see Morrissey again. I got swept up with fans invading the stage and had a great time, getting bundled off by security, trying to grab Morrissey's leg. Later with The Libertines, I'd always try and encourage fans to do stage invasions. That was always part of the dream.

Carl and Dan got on well. The three of us shared this sort of music-hall comedy vibe. I was always trying to get Carl to rehearse, but he wasn't having it, really. So, when he turned up at Whitechapel Station with his guitar on his back, I remember it being a big moment – a commitment. We wrote a handful of songs – one of them ended up as 'Anthem for Doomed Youth', and bits and bobs would come out in different songs down the years.

I actually wanted to be the singer and have Carl be the guitarist, like Morrissey and Johnny Marr, but Carl said, No, you're not singing, we're both singing, you're going to have to play the guitar as well, so I really had to get it together. I hardly put the guitar down when I was on my own. I knew I had to buck up on the guitar. I wasn't really a natural musician, but I used to love to go and busk at the market on Brick Lane in Shoreditch on a Sunday – often on my own, singing my own songs. Carl was never really that into it, but sometimes I'd persuade him to busk, and we'd do 'Twist and Shout' on repeat. I'd busk at the Underground sometimes, but it was always difficult because they'd move you along.

Carl introduced me to his elder sister Lucie, a budding actress who was in some play in London, and with her little crowd we used to go to the Black Cap in Camden, a gay hotspot known for its drag cabaret. One time we ended up at this theatre producer's house somewhere in Tottenham, and he got me really drunk and took me upstairs. I think I passed out, and when I woke up, he was trying to undo my jeans. I started fighting him off like mad. He was offering me money and some job in some theatre if I let him. I went downstairs really upset, and Carl was laughing, thought it was really funny.

That sort of thing happened a few times to me in this period. Maybe some people felt I was leading them on. Carl knew I wasn't gay. I was actually really randy for birds. I think because of the way I dressed, and probably the way I spoke, people assumed I was gay. I was quite camp and so obsessed with The Smiths and poetry and literature and theatre – the theatre to probably a greater extent than I've ever really acknowledged.

Sally Anchassi actually rescued me the day after we met for the first time. We'd kept writing to one another after she'd responded to my *Select* ad. I'd just got a job at a bookshop at the weekend, Eastside Books on Brick Lane, very strange place, all new books, a shiny pink facade. They hadn't been open long, and there was this one fella who used to come in, quite dandified, had a cravat, and was always interested in the books about east London. He struck me as an interesting man I could share ideas with. It didn't occur to me for a second he was some predatory bloke. I was supposed to be going round this bloke's for Sunday lunch, and Sally decided she'd come with me, and it's a good job she did, because he pulled out this photo album of himself with loads of kids he used to take on this nudist camp holiday every year. Sally had a big row with him and dragged me out of his flat in Bethnal Green.

Sally was really headstrong. She was staying in this flat that we later found out was a bit of a brothel on Holloway Road, where me and Carl would soon end up living. It was a council flat that this girl Sasha had. It had two or three different rooms, and Sally stayed in one of the rooms. To my mind she wasn't working from the flat, she wasn't a hooker or anything – she was just crashing there. She used to wear fishnets and a fur coat and hang around with bands that were on the cusp of the Camden music scene. I didn't really feel cool enough to be a part of that, but I'd been in love with her for years. I remember saving up all my money and going to Notting Hill Music & Video Exchange and buying her a copy of *This Is Hardcore*, Pulp's new album. Then she broke my heart. We were at Sasha's, and I played her a new song Carl and me had written, 'You're My Waterloo', and she said, Look, it's not just that you can't sing, you can't write songs either, Peter. It fucking killed me. I was destroyed. She also said, Look at your actions, you're stalking me. And as soon as she said that, I thought, That's not right at all, I thought you were going to fall in love with me. I completely cut off all ties with her. That fucked me right up.

I told Carl what had happened, and he thought it was quite funny, especially what she said about 'You're My Waterloo', which ended up being one of The Libertines' big songs. There's a line in that song, 'You're the survivor of more than one life', which is about Carl – his twin brother died when they were just weeks old – but the actual subject matter of the song was Sally. 'You're My Waterloo' was also an important song for the development of Carl and me as songwriters. I had these chords and lyrics and bang, he came out with the bridge straight away. He wrote the musical melodies in answer to the lyrics that were about him, the idea being they entwine in rhapsodic ecstasy. It was a real symbol of what we could do together. It became our party piece, because we'd never really had a structured song that we could play with two guitars, and the power of it would always come over acoustically when we would be playing at open-mic acoustic nights or busking on the street or just playing for a few people in a kitchen in flat somewhere. At some point we went to Coventry and recorded a four-track demo of 'You're My Waterloo' and 'Albion' with someone he knew – our first ever demo.

Carl was always trying to break away from the idea we had to throw everything into the band in those early days. He'd got work selling programmes at the Victoria Theatre or the Old Vic and was dossing at some actress's place. That was his main source of income for years and years, working in the theatre: selling programmes or ice cream, taking tickets off people when they come in. He was obsessed with the theatre; his dream job really was to be an actor. We had a lot of dreams and schemes aside from the band: I was convinced we were going to be models! We would take pictures on my little Kodak and go down to King's Road to the model agencies with these pictures. We'd obviously be booted out and we'd sit outside these agencies watching all the male models come and go and say, Look at him, I'm better-looking than him. We'd have conversations about putting Vaseline on your lips to make you look famous, stuff like that, before going down to Trash.

Different girlfriends Carl had would say, What are you doing, wasting your time with Peter and this band? I'd be putting pressure on him to rehearse and his girlfriend would say, No, I don't want you talking to Peter any more. You need to stop doing this band. I was always like, No, no, no, and I'd go and meet him with my guitar after he finished at the theatre. He'd always be late. I distinctly remember having a blazing row with him one night about it when he was working *The Iceman Cometh* with Kevin Spacey at the Old Vic. He was really late, and they were joking that Kevin Spacey wants to bum everyone who's selling programmes, saying how they might get a part in one of his films if they played it cool. I was waiting for him, walking by the river, along the Embankment, with my little paperback copy of the Tony Hancock biography. A lot of it was about Tony moping around London after the war. I was sort of moping around London waiting for Carl.

It was on one of those nights waiting for Carl that I again got mixed up in a misunderstanding over my sexuality. I was walking along the Embankment by HMS *Belfast* with my guitar, and I thought how cool it'd be to get on the battleship and sit playing. It must have been two or three in the morning, and it was easy to climb aboard, round the railing, up the gangplank, but this security guard grabbed hold of me, What you doing? I went, Oh, I just wanted to have a look round. It was a bit odd, but he offered to give me a guided tour, and he showed me all these bits that were off the tourist path, secret cabins and secret war-meeting rooms. Then he took me to this bit where the tourists watch their audio-visual guides, and he put this hardcore gay porn on the video screen. He went, I'll just leave you with this for a couple of minutes, and if you want to go, you can go. I legged it back down the gangplank.

I fell for this Swedish drama student, Evelina. I got called in for a meeting with the uni tutor about all the lectures I was missing. I'd stopped going in, couldn't be arsed, and I told him, I'm leaving England, I'm going to Stockholm with this Swedish girl to get married. I didn't go to the airport in the end. Years later, Evelina popped up in one of the tabloids with a kiss and tell, saying something like, Oh yeah, Peter was really sweet, but he'd cry after we had sex. That was complete bollocks.

I don't remember that at all – typical tabloid embarrassing twist on the story.

There was also a girl called Farran who was at my college who I fell for completely. I wrote a song for her, 'She Is Far', that eventually ended up on *Hamburg Demonstrations*. That song really paints a picture of that time, where I was at – just walking around London in love, full of these lofty ideals. There's also a line in that song about monuments to blood spilt in foreign lands. I took Farran to Loftus Road, just to sit in the empty stadium. You could hop over the fence and get in. In fact, I got into the changing rooms and stole a pair of socks and a pair of shorts, prized possessions.

Francesca Piazza became my first long-time serious girlfriend. Linda introduced us. She was in London at Christmas, and Linda said, Here you are, this is my friend Peter, I'm not going to be around for Christmas, he'll show you around London. I fell head over heels in love with Francesca – this beautiful foreign girl in London. She was amazing, very dramatic, very Sophia Loren-looking. We were really tight for the next few years on and off. She was at the Central School of Drama in Finchley Road and obsessed with Samuel Beckett. She was all about independent theatre groups, community theatre, and she'd take me to some strange performances, strange shows. She worked part-time at the Italian bookshop in Covent Garden, an Italian cultural hub, and knew a woman called Ornella who had a flat on Finchley Road where we'd crash sometimes. There were loads of amazing films and books in that apartment. It was the first place in London where I felt safe and warm.

I'd hang out at Poetry Café in Covent Garden. There'd be an open mic night in a tiny room downstairs once a week, and the only way in was the deep end, so I'd perform some poetry. In the end, I built up a regular thing there. The place was well maintained and had quite a posh café upstairs. It was like the state-sponsored poetry venue. I tried but failed to get a job in the café, but I became such a regular face in there they let me go behind the counter and pour my own coffee. There was a really good-looking boy who worked there called Fran who everyone said was also a TV presenter for Nickelodeon, so I was obviously interested in that. He was going out with this girl Belinda, a Brummie, and they were this gorgeous couple.

The idea was I was going to make a go of the band with Carl, or I was going to crack it with the poetry. I didn't go back to uni for the second year. I signed on the dole, got a room in a flat, eight floors up in one of the tower blocks not that far from Queen Mary – £80 a week. The flat belonged to this strange East End fella called Phil who used to clean windows in the morning – we'd sometimes go out together. He took me to some strange places. Once I was trying to buy some trainers, and he took me to this flat that was all cages inside and they had everything in there – electric scooters, trainers, shitloads of TVs. The whole flat was full of this stuff. I can also vaguely remember Phil talking to me about crack. He was always smoking spliff, but I remember him saying, Yeah, I get a little bit of crack and heroin at Christmas, just once a year. That was definitely the first time I ever did coke, with Phil, off his ironing board. It was years later before I ever did it again.

Carl would sometimes come over to stay at Phil's flat. He'd also quit university. I took a leaf out of his book and started working at the theatres. The first job I had was at the Vaudeville Theatre collecting ticket stubs for performances of *Loot*. I loved that play, and I found Joe Orton's life story quite interesting, coming to London from Leicester and trying to be an actor and then being in this really strange intense relationship with Kenneth Halliwell who eventually murdered him. Carl and I were never homosexual, but we had this really intense creative relationship – we were trying to write, trying to create something, trying to create a little world. Joe Orton became a big influence.

I worked full-time at the Vaudeville for *Loot* – short bursts of work, like an hour and a half, but every night, twice on Saturday – as well as other productions I did there part-time. Now and again Carl would also phone me saying that they'd need someone at the Old Vic for two nights or the Victoria where *Annie* and other big musicals played. The Victoria was great. I had a proper fiddle going on there. It was shameful really, but all the old biddies who used to come to the matinee would buy ice cream, and if they paid with a tenner, you'd give them the change as if they'd given you a fiver, and they never ever complained. I used to come away jangling.

In the end, I got in a proper dodgy situation with Phil at the flat. It all went wrong. Fran and Belinda had fallen out, and Belinda came to crash at Phil's – took the front room. But I think Phil must have been trying it on with Belinda or something, and it got a bit dark: he kicked Belinda out, and then he tried to get me in a threesome with him and one of his girlfriends. I didn't want to. I said I saw him as more of a father figure than a sexual partner, and he pulled a knife out on me. He said, I'm going to wipe that smile off your face. I barricaded myself in my room, and Carl had to come and rescue me. It was a bit of a moody situation. We had to get all my stuff out. It was like, Well, where are we going to go now? I had a couple of bags of stuff. So, we went and crashed, top and tail, in Belinda's spare room in Delaney Mansions, the original Albion Rooms, a dive – 258-360 Camden Road, a chopped-up old house full of little bedsits. This is when we first moved to Camden, and everything changed with the dynamic of the band.'

V
Camden

1998–1999: A move to Camden. A new singer, Scarborough Steve.
The naming of the band and first gig. John Hassell, bassist. The
changing faces of Johnny Borrell. The truth about the suicide pact.
A rejection by Food Records. Fights with Carl. Living in a brothel.

'We met Scarborough Steve Bedlow on the night bus coming back from Trash. We could hear him laughing at the back of the bus with three girls. I was sat with Carl after an unsuccessful night's hunting. Because he had a French pin badge on his jacket, we decided he was French. Look at him coming over here taking all the girls. Then he got off at our stop with these girls, and I heard him go, C'mon, it's this way, girls, in this broad Yorkshire accent. I was like, Hang on a minute, he's not French at all – and we followed him down the road, and it turns out he lives in Delaney Mansions too.

The next morning, he was in the garden hanging out his Thee Hypnotics T-shirt, the band he'd followed down to London from Yorkshire, on the washing line, and I asked him to be the singer in the band. This is when the idea we might be able to make it suddenly reached fever pitch for me and Carl. Steve became our God: he used to have a skin-tight Moog T-shirt, like the DJ at Trash, and flares and a little black leather jacket. He was just the nuts. I couldn't see him failing as a lead singer. I couldn't see the world not loving him the way that every boggle-eyed indie girl that ever met him in the Camden Good Mixer pub did.

He sort of dressed us – I'd get his hand-me-downs. He used to have a knack of turning up with the most amazing shoes. He had these brown and white leather patch proper '70s platform shoes. I had them for a while. He also gave me this amazing jacket, pigskin with brown artificial fur lining. It's still knocking around.

Carl and I started to bum around Camden, just getting out and about. It was really exciting. There was like an army of kids in bell-bottom Levi's and leather jackets. It was pre-Strokes but after Blur, and there was a void, loads of terrible Scandinavian kids trying to start bands, but it was great too, because you thought, Hey, it maybe could still happen, there maybe could still be another great band to emerge. We'd hang out at pubs like the Good Mixer and the Dublin Castle, a complete shithole in the best possible way. We actually bumped into Liam Gallagher in there. I said, Liam, we've got a band, come back to our place and have a jam. He went, No, mate, I'm the devil's dick, I don't do that kind of thing.

The idea of meeting anyone who was in a band in person was magical, like meeting a knight of the Round Table. It was kind of the be all and end all. Steve actually knew Menswear, who had just broken up but were still Camden faces, and he sorted it so I could go round to see the singer Johnny and play him a few songs. This was a big deal for me – I'd bought their single 'Stardust' when I was at Nico – but I ended up really embarrassing myself. Steve had taught me this song he joked he had written which I thought was really beautiful, and I played it to Johnny. It was actually 'Signed DC', a great Arthur Lee song by Love. I obviously hadn't listened to Love at the time and was going around saying the band have got this great new song. Johnny and his mates all looked at each other, really confused. They went, You wrote that, did you? I said, Yeah, well, me and my mate. I was laughed out. I was heartbroken.

At the time, we were still working nights at the theatre, on and off, and in the mornings Carl and I started working on Camden Market, cash in hand on second-hand-clothes rails. It's my first memory of seeing Mick Whitnall, who'd go on to become the Babyshambles guitarist. He also worked the clothes rails – him being this ridiculously cool-looking Suedehead assisting eager tourists. I also started to go down Camden Market with a little blanket, put my collection of bric-a-brac and books out on it, and try and flog stuff. I only had one thing of value really – my dad's Spirit of Ecstasy that he'd ripped off a Rolls Royce when he was fifteen. It was my family heirloom, but I got offered silly money for it, and, I regret it now, I sold it.

Mum and Dad actually came to see me at Delaney Mansions. Dad had been posted back to Germany – so they'd moved back there with Emily. They brought me a load of duty-free tobacco and a crate of German lager. I'd seen them since quitting uni, back in Bramcote barracks before they left for Germany, and although that news hadn't gone done too well, I'd sort of reassured them everything was OK. I was quite excited to see them. It was the first time they'd been to London to see me living on my own. Dad came in and said, This is a bit of a shithole. It was the first time Carl had met him. I was a bit upset. He also commented on Carl's hair being so long. I think Dad was a mix of amused and bemused. To my parents, it maybe looked as if I was in free fall, living top and tail in this slum, whereas I genuinely felt that as a songwriter I was getting better every day. I was starting to master my craft.

I was getting turned on to so many different types of music at that time, a lot of '60s stuff that Steve loved, like The Stooges and Arthur Lee. When I first heard 'Daydream' by The Lovin' Spoonful, it took me on a whole other songwriting vibe – into those early songs, such as 'Dilly Boys', which actually ended up as a B-side on 'Can't Stand Me Now'. There was a creative explosion when we moved to Camden – songs just started popping up everywhere, really.

The band name came from this Marquis de Sade book I had called *The Lusts of the Libertines*. I bought it from the Music & Video Exchange in Notting Hill, and it was just absolute filth. I'd read it out loud sometimes, and it would just crack us up – 'this libertine will ravage a goat'. Before settling on The Libertines, we'd been The Albion, then The Cricketers and The Strollers. I didn't know proto-punk New York band Television had thought about calling themselves The Libertines, but this band The Libertines from Bury popped up with this song called 'Cola Queen'. It was the early days of the internet, but they had a website and everything, and I was gutted. Then I thought, Fuck this, and I remember getting on their message board posing as different people, saying stuff like 'But isn't there a different Libertines in London who have been around longer?', sowing these seeds of doubt in their mind that they were the first Libertines. You won't find any information about them on the internet now. Good. My work here is done. They were a clear and present danger, an existential threat to our very fabric of being. So, they had to be dealt with!

It's been written into Libertines folklore that Carl and I supposedly made a suicide pact in this period. I still had quite a few books from the auction days, and one I recall knocking about for years is a book about suicide, *The Savage God: A Study of Suicide* by Al Alvarez, like a literary poem to Sylvia Plath in a way. But there was no suicide pact. It was more like me talking him out of it, saying, No, I'll tell you what, if we're still not signed in a year, then we'll do it. It was like, This time next year, Rodders, we'll be millionaires! It was always like that. I'd say, Just hang on, it's going to be fine, we've just got to practise.

He had this thing about throwing himself off a tall building. That was the big one, shooting yourself as you fell down to the street. And if we were ever by water, he'd jump in, and he couldn't swim, so I used to have to save him. He went in the canal in Camden a few times. It was a test to see if I cared about him, if I dared dive in after him. The night we were trying to choose a name for the band, Carl, Steve and I were on the banks of the canal at three or four in the morning, and it was whoever could hit the wine bottle floating in the canal with a stone got to choose the name of the band. I maintain it was my choice of band name, I hit the bottle. I don't know how the other stories go, but I do know Carl dived in at some point.

We got our next place when I offered to help the people in the house next door to Delaney Mansions move. They'd bought this townhouse further down Camden Road, 236, and we carried their stuff there in wheelbarrows for £20. And then they said, Look, we're not moving in just yet, the house needs renovating, if you watch over it for us, like caretakers, you can stay in the basement. We had to pay peppercorn rent: £90 a fortnight. It was the first place that we could kick back in, and the first place that other people started referring to as the Albion Rooms.

It was also where we did our first gig. Steve introduced us to our bassist John Hassall, who lived on the other side of Camden Road in Kentish Town. Steve said, I know this lad, he's got really cool jeans, and he's got his own amps. We were over there like rats up a drainpipe because we were bashing out stuff on acoustic guitars. The idea was we were supposed to be a rock-'n'-roll band, but we never had any amps or guitars.

John was a couple of years younger than Carl and me, and he lived with his mum in this townhouse just off the main drag in Kentish Town. He had a sofa in his bedroom and a mattress on the floor. His mum was really tolerant. She used to restore old masters in the attic for museums. It was a glimpse of a London we'd all fantasised about, a dream life in this townhouse with a laid-back, cool mum who'd bring you cheese toasties while you smoked spliff in your room and played music. In those days, John never really used to speak. He'd been in a band called The Samaritans, who were all older than him and on the gear, and he'd got hooked on heroin, and when he came off gear, he was on a lot of Valium. When he did speak, he used to speak with a kind of Yardie accent, so it was a bit confusing, because he's actually really posh. I played him 'You're My Waterloo' and another new song Carl and me had written, 'Music When the Lights Go Out', and he agreed to do the gig in the basement. I had the music and words for the first verse for 'Music When the Lights Go Out' and Carl put the chorus in and came up with the riff – and we did the rest of the lyrics together.

I remember carrying the amps and stuff across from Kentish Town. John roped in a drummer, Zac, who had a house on the same street and was in a band called Cactus Camel – the name was enough to put you off. Zac did that one gig, and I didn't investigate any further. John had his electric bass, and Carl borrowed one of John's amps and one of John's guitars. I was the only one still on acoustic guitar. Steve was singing. We set up in the corner in front of the basement window. I think we got about fifteen, twenty people in – we were buzzing. All kinds of people claim to have been there that day. Johnny Borrell, future Razorlight front man, was definitely there. He was our support act. He was John's mate – they'd been classmates at Highgate School. Johnny became another character in the mix. I'd sometimes crash at his house with Francesca, this mansion up near Alexandra Palace, where he lived with his mum. He was rocking the *Clockwork Orange* look at the time, eyeliner and a bowler hat.

Sally came back into my life after that first gig. I met her at random on the Camden Road by the Ferodo bridge sign. I shouted out to her, but I could tell she didn't really want to stop. She said, Oh, Peter, I hear

Steve's singing with you now, and I was like, Oh, you know Steve? And she said, I see him at Sasha's. I said, Oh, you're still there? She said, No, but I just see him there sometimes. Steve was always sofa-surfing and bumming about. Then, by sheer coincidence, Carl got off with Sally at some party a few days later. What a bastard! That was my eternal love!

He said she'd told him she was living with Andy Ross, who was running Food Records, Blur's label. So, we went down to the offices in Camden with our guitars and said, We're friends of Sally's, and we've got these songs, can you pay for us to demo them? At the time I was really shocked, and even now it still shocks me a bit – because if a young band comes to the label with guitars, the least you're gonna do is hear two seconds of their songs – but they wouldn't even let us in the building. It didn't occur to me at the time, but I later found out it was purely because of Steve and his reputation from around Camden. I think they used to drink at the Good Mixer, Andy Ross and that lot, so he knew Steve.

I thought, I'll show Food, and recorded two songs on cassette player – a new one called 'Pay the Lady' and 'You're My Waterloo' – and I took the cassette in to Food myself and said, Look, we came the other day, here's the cassette, can you listen to it? I was really buzzing to be inside the building at least, seeing all the piles of records on desks and the posters on the walls of early Blur singles. Years later, I heard some comment Andy Ross made about how he looked back fondly and remembered getting the cassette. But I just remember the way he looked at me – this bloke who actually worked at a record company. He looked right through me. I'll always remember how that felt.

We were desperate to be famous. We'd lie about how successful we were. One time to impress this girl Carl and I told her we were going on tour with Supergrass. I nipped out to a phone box and phoned in to the landline pretending to be the band asking if we'd like to go on tour with them. John actually knew where one of the Supergrass guys lived, and we scuttled past their house on Camden Square pretending to be too cool to be stalking a Britpop band.

Carl and I would have physical fights a lot in the early days, as he got more frustrated with us not getting anywhere. It was usually in front of other people when he was drunk, but one time in the basement it was just me and him, and he pulled a knife. I ended up locking myself in a cupboard with him on the other side of the door saying he was going to kill me. I phoned the police, and it was particularly embarrassing, because when they came Carl had calmed right down: he was pacified and charming. I was still really upset, going, You've got to arrest him, he's a maniac. They asked my name and then, What do you do? I sort of wailed, I'm a poet.

Another time we had a proper nasty falling-out about a leather coat that belonged to Carl, this family heirloom that his dad had entrusted to him. I'd worn this coat out, and I'd promised to look after it, but it had got ripped. He was there on top of the stairs at 236, holding the coat: I asked you one thing, that's all I asked – to look after the coat. He actually wrote this poem called 'Death on the Stairs', which became a song on our debut album, while he was sat there plotting my death. It went 'the tears and the tears in my proud father's coat'.

It does all sounds a bit *Withnail and I*, doesn't it? Funnily enough, I hadn't seen that film at the time. In those days, we didn't have a telly or a video. But that film had been one of the things that had formed the bond between Carl and my sister. When she'd first talked about this fella she'd met at uni, she'd also talked about this film that she'd seen called *Withnail and I*, and it was part of their mythology – they used to quote lines from it. I knew a lot of the lines before I saw it for the first time, which was when I first got with Kate Moss. She was quite big on *Withnail and I* as well, which I was always pleasantly surprised by. But, yeah, when I finally saw it and the Richard E. Grant flamboyant alco-holic character, I thought, Fucking hell, that's Carl.

We stayed in the Albion Rooms for a few months and then they wanted us out, so Steve, Carl and I ended up living at Sasha's. There was this strange scene around that flat. The drummer from a quite well-known indie-rock band used to visit and pay eighty quid to be put in this cage and spat at and poked. We were all really shocked. There was a girl called Pam from Brighton who used to dress up like a panda bear for clients. There was a lot of strange characters coming and going.

Sasha used to keep this pair of drumsticks in her leather cowboy boots, and she actually became The Libertines' drummer. She was obsessed with Carl, but generally she hated men, including me. I remember sitting there sometimes at night, just me and her, she'd be waiting for a client, and she'd say, Yeah, you're never really gonna get anywhere with Sally. I'd be really gutted, just sat there moping.

This was me holding on for dear life, trying to keep the band going and have somewhere to stay. I remember setting up my purple drapes and candlesticks in this room, putting an Aubrey Beardsley print of Oscar Wilde's *Salome* on the wall. I suppose you might say it was studenty, but to me it was the epitome of bohemian finesse. I used to make quite good nests. Francesca taught me that.

NME journalist Steven Wells used to live in the flat below Sasha's with *NME* photographer Roger Sargent, who ended up doing a lot with the band. We tried to get in with Steven Wells. We'd bang on his door and sit in the stairway just haranguing him with our songs, the four or five songs we had, with Sasha playing drumsticks on a biscuit tin. Staying in a brothel with Sasha and having her on drums was tailor-made for the band's self-mythologising, but actually it was awful, quite a terrifying scene that ended in violence.

I'd got a job selling popcorn at the Prince Charles cinema in Leicester Square and talked them into letting us do a gig there – before the first screening on Saturday morning. We managed to get Johnny Borrell in to support us. I think he was called Johnny Borrell and the Hustlers at that point, full cowboy gear. Sasha turned up at the Prince Charles with a pair of scissors trying to stab me, screaming about how I'd stolen her housing-benefit cheques. The Spanish manageress of the Prince Charles called the police – there's this random psycho with a long flapping leather jacket, looking like an alien supermodel, trying to kill a member of staff. It ended up as a massive stand-off outside the Prince Charles.'

VI
The Foundry

1999: Arcadia at the Foundry. Solo performance poetry success.
Meeting Rat Pete. The origins of several tall stories to do
with selling sex. A terrible incident with Francesca. Dealing
speed and squat life. Albion Towers and Steve's final gig.

'The Foundry became our place. I took over from Apu and started presenting my own poetry night there on a Sunday called Arcadia at the Foundry. Organising my own night really set me on fire. It went from poetry to being a sort of cabaret. I got this girl Camille to do these contemporary dance routines, like mime, in her tutu. I was well in love with her. I wrote all these poems dedicated to her.

At first, Carl had to be dragged there kicking and screaming: I don't think at that point he saw a way forward for the band and for the creative songwriting partnership. I usually managed to get Steve and John down there as well in the early days – we'd all get suited and booted, sixties-style. I'd do poetry and we'd play acoustically.

I'd do 'Pay the Lady' with Carl and John planted in the audience, and they'd come up and join me as the song went along. I used to try and do that a lot, say to Carl, Sit in the audience and then come on stage as a surprise. I'd do the standard 'Dream a Little Dream of Me' and, bang, as I'd go into it, Carl would appear from the shadows doing a little tap-dance routine, but he was never that keen, really. He'd sometimes play a bit of piano, and we revived Mr Spaniel and Mr Spaniel. Carl and I would do these really terrible jokes in really strong music-hall vernacular. People were completely bewildered and horrified.

I was actually doing better with the poetry than the band at the time. I was doing solo performance poetry shows two or three times a week. A poet called John Citizen got me involved in this thing called the Paradigm poets, some sort of Arts Council thing. Victoria Mosley was also involved and Francesca Beard. We did a photo shoot at the Groucho Club, and I did something at the ICA, which for me was the pinnacle of my cultural vision at the time. I had this flyer of me in long johns crawling seductively with ruby red lips, pointing towards the camera, supposed to be like a homoerotic take on Your Country Needs You. The flyer looked cool as fuck, but I didn't really have the set. I was trying to do poetry and acoustic songs, but it all went wrong, and people were just talking really loudly, drinking overpriced wine. I ended up slinking out with John Citizen. He invited me to his house. I think I went with the idea I was going to rent a room off him, but that never happened.

I had a regular slot at Finnegan's Wake, a performance-poetry venue in Islington run by this guy Jem Rolls who was a really funny perform-ance poet. Even today John and Carl can still quote some of his poems: 'We won, we won, we won, we won, we won . . . Tony Blair.' I ended up living in the spare room at Jem's council flat on an estate in Dalston, east London. I was desperate to get out from this place in Camden I was staying in after legging it from Sasha's. I'd got it through Rat Pete, who I was chauffeur to for a bit. I met him in a pub. He was drunk, and he asked me if I'd drive him home, because he had a cast on his broken leg. I drove him around for about two weeks, around Camden. His dad was a slum landlord, owned all these buildings in Camden where Rat Pete let people stay. He had this strange speech defect. He'd stretch out all his words – Geeeeeeezaaaaar! Cooooooool! You're shaaaabbbby! You're not in vooooogueeee! He was a very strange character, a white guy with this massive afro haircut, very sinister in a lot of ways. When I was driving for him, I'd go back and forth from the pub to whatever flat he was at with all the party people he'd invited round, mostly foreign birds who were trying to get modelling jobs. He'd let them stay at his dad's flats. He let Francesca stay in one for £20 a week – glorious flat – but then when she went back to Italy for a bit, the rent went up to £100 a week for me.

At the same time I moved into Jem Rolls's, I got a job behind the bar at the King's Head pub in China Town. It was quite a gay scene. Downstairs was the Dive Bar that the Pet Shop Boys wrote 'West End Girls' about – all red walls and candles. The Libertines did our first ever interview with the *NME* in there. The King's Head was quite a dark place, but it was interesting – there was a dramatic air about it. On Fridays there was a Chinese guy called Peter, and the deal was he'd give me a live crab and I'd give him half a pint of Guinness. I'd see his silhouette at the window, and he'd do little claw signs with his hands. I'd slip him a Guinness, and he'd give me the crab. I had about six in the end at Jem Rolls's flat. I didn't really know how to cook 'em.

Helen of Troy, who ran the infamous Troy club in Soho, would come in with her dog for a spritzer at five to eleven as soon as we opened, and there was another regular they called the Queen Mother who was a proper cantankerous queen, absolutely fuming at the world – he was the head waiter at a private members' club in Mayfair. Some of these quite posh old pissheads would offer me money to go to the toilet with them. Even some of the other members of staff offered me money for a hand job. This is a story I'd elaborate on and tell later to the *NME* for dramatic effect, stuff about 'spanking off old queens for

£20'. It's something I would never have done, even for a laugh. I was just inventing these stories that I thought were funny. That's probably the first time I've admitted that, though. I always thought anyone who knew me, my family, would know it was a lie, because I was always making stuff up.

There was actually another story I told the *NME* about robbing a man who had hired me for sex that had an element of truth to it. But if I'm 100 per cent honest with you, I never left the guy tied up in his house. It was quite a well-known poet – spotted on Radio 4 and here and there – and I was actually honoured to be taken back to his Chelsea mews cottage. He had all these busts of Roman emperors. I didn't tie him up at all, and, in fact, I don't think he was particularly pressing for sex. He didn't get it anyway. That's another admission for me, because I fancied myself as this sort of violent dandy at the time – I carried a sharpened umbrella and a paperback copy of *Suedehead*, Richard Allen's pulp classic about a vicious, heavily stylised hooligan and also the title of Morrissey's first solo single.

I was so desperate to make fantasy real that performance was the only way. Carl and I would stage these mock fights on the Tube, and we would have these flights of fancy. We tried to join an escort agency. It was called Aristocrats, and we'd got it into our heads that we'd be taking old ladies out to dinner or the opera. We were like, Yeah, we're skilled in the arts, we'll be good at that. It turned out it wasn't even called Aristocrats as we thought. When we got down there, it was this old bird, proper '60s vibe, slippers and negligée, sweeping the step. We went, Is this Aristocrats? She went, No, love, pointing up. There was no R. It was just 'Aristocats'. The first assignment she had available was to meet some fella in St George's Hotel by the BBC. The story we gave to the *NME* about 'shagging old men in hotel rooms', that was later amplified in the tabloids as 'I was a rent boy', was another fabrication. The end of the real story was we legged it from Aristocats. We did have a laugh with those *NME* interviews. We probably thought we were being shocking. In actual fact, the escort-agency escapade was another dream that was shattered.

Francesca came to live with me at Jem Rolls's flat. One time she was working late at the Italian bookshop, and I was supposed to meet her, but I'd been rehearsing at John's mum's in Kentish Town, so I didn't turn up, and she got attacked at knifepoint walking back through the West End. When she came back to the flat, it was three or four in the morning. I'd been really worried. I'm like, Where the fuck have you been? She didn't say anything. She just got undressed and came to bed. Then she told me what had happened, so I went to phone the police. She ripped the phone out of the wall. I was still determined – it didn't occur to me that she didn't want to report this. I dragged her to Stoke Newington Police Station at four or five in the morning.

Things got really messed up afterwards. I could never speak about it with Francesca, and I buried it for years, never mentioned it, never talked about it – all the guilt around her getting attacked because I didn't pick her up when I said I would. It came up in group therapy sessions when I was in rehab where everything is confidential. A lot of girls would talk about things that had happened to them.

I wrote 'What a Waster', The Libertines' debut single, at Jem Rolls's council flat after Francesca was attacked. It was a slow, tender ballad at the time – the lines 'round the corner where they chased her' and 'when she wakes up in the morning she writes down all her dreams' were about her, and there was stuff Steve said. Steve always thought the song was about him. It wasn't. It was about what my dad thought about me: what a waster. I've never said that before, but I've finally come to that understanding of the song. I went to Germany one Christmas with Francesca, and I was really offended by how he acted – he was shocked that she'd be with me. He said, You're a pretty girl and you seem quite intelligent and nice, what are you doing with him?

There was a housing co-op that a lot of us went to, specialised in finding shared housing for people on the dole. They found me a little Peabody cottage in Tottenham. That's where I met this strange sect of French psychedelic kids who had a cottage on the same estate. There was Davide, who had a long beard, and Sandra, who was this dancer who used to climb out of this plastic egg at squat parties. They played me The Seeds for the first time, and they introduced me to Martin, this old-school biker, who soon had me running round with little wraps of pink speed – in turn, he'd give me a bit of weed.

Martin would say, There's a big rave at this gaff in Dalston, and he'd give me half a plastic football with some pink speed in it, and I'd wrap it up and go down and sell it out of my hat. I didn't really enjoy the music – it was always techno – but I really enjoyed dealing the speed. People at these parties would give me their number, and one of them turned out to be a guy who ran a recording studio around Old Street in Shoreditch, and he wanted speed all the time, so I was basically getting it from Tottenham and taking it to Old Street on a bicycle. I'd maybe cut it a little bit. It was a very easy way to make money. I'd later record in that studio, just before we got signed.

I took speed to Dan Treacy, from the cult band The Television Personalities. Someone said, Just meet this guy at the back of this certain bus – he was sort of sleeping on the bus at the time. I'd also sell speed to the bar staff at the Bricklayer's Arms just off Old Street, a proper trendier-than-thou place – I used to feel a bit intimidated going in there. It was when Old Street was just starting to become very trendy, and the Bricklayers Arm's was full of people with real jobs, the real media. That was why getting signed was so important to me – it was always about trying to fit in, feel like you had some cultural purpose. It wasn't enough to be playing songs for ourselves, writing what we thought were great songs – we needed to have recognition.

Through Sandra and Davide, I started going to this Spanish squat on Church Street, Stoke Newington, that was quite well known, a bit of a cultural hub. They had live music events, poetry events, loads of knees-ups and a half-arsed organic garden. Carl never really got into it because it was a bit too hippiefied for him, but he was into the idea we could get a squat somewhere that was just for us where we could live for free.

Briefly we had the Albion Rooms in a sort of squatted factory that didn't have any power, round the corner from the Church Street squat. We did a gig there. Delvin the wizard, who was in a similar sort of circle to Sandra and Davide, had a generator powered by an exercise bike. We did the cycling, and he let us use the generator. Sandra did a dance while we played. She was absolutely gorgeous – everyone was in love with her. Steve was straight in there. Then we got in a disused cinema in Dalston, but it turned out to not have a roof, so we cancelled that. A couple of months later, we landed on the Empress of Russia pub by Sadler's Wells Theatre in Clerkenwell, and that was the first one that we cracked ourselves. Steve was a big lad, but he went up that drainpipe like a rat up the proverbial. We were a little bit organised that night, all wearing balaclavas, and we had chains, so we locked it all up and made it into a home.

We did a night there, supposed to be an Arcadian cabaret night transported from the Foundry, but the only person to turn up was Johnny Borrell. He turned up in a gas mask and did a folk set with these two black gospel singers he had with him at the time. He was quite good, actually. We played as The Libertines: me, Carl, John, and Steve playing drums. He'd been demoted to drums because he was getting too pissed to sing. He'd get really bad and fuck things up.

I was supposedly left in charge of looking after the Empress of Russia when everyone fucked off to break into Glastonbury. While they were away, I let a few people in who had nowhere to go, and before I knew it there was just shitloads of them. At that time, it was off my radar, but when Steve and the rest came back, they said, Why have you let a load of crackheads into the pub? I didn't see it like that until we tried to get them to leave and we lost. We basically fell victim to a hostile takeover.

Next Steve got into what we called Albion Towers, this strange, dilapidated high-rise building with turrets above Mole Jazz, the specialist record shop, opposite the derelict Scala cinema in King's Cross. The only decent thing we found in there was this old desk. Steve plotted up there, feet on the table, and said, Right, if you want, you can take notes on my life story, but we never got past him working in a chippy in Filey, and hearing the Stooges for the first time, and him and his band robbing an off-licence. He could hardly remember anything. Then Carl wanted this desk. I was like, Let's just all share it, but that was not going happen, and there was a big fight over this desk, and that's when Steve lobbed a monitor out the window and it landed on top of a double-decker bus. No one was hurt, but we had to leg it from there, because the monitor went through the metal roof of the bus, and the police were well on it. When Carl and Steve ended up going at each other, it was awful. After the monitor incident, Steve was up on this wall, and the next thing I look up and Carl's up there doing some weird tai chi move. He booted Steve in the head and then jumped on him and set about him. I had to drag Carl off.

The final Libertines gig we did with Steve was at the Scene club in Soho. I'd done some really cool posters. That was the night Steve did the famous speech, that me, John and Carl can still quote word for word to this day. He was sat in the corner before going on, saying, You don't know what's going on in my head, you don't know what's going on in my head, you don't . . . We went, Yeah, we don't know what's going on in your head. He said, I'm like the fucking Stooges, and you wanna be like The Kinks. This was before the gig. We were like, Look, it's all well and good, Steve, but you're talking bollocks, we're about to play, can we just play. He was like, I'm going to fucking destroy the world. His false tooth kept coming out. Well, just stay on drums, man. No, you don't know what I'm going to do . . .

Then, halfway through the first song, Steve got slung out of the gig, literally got bounced up the basement stairs and battered by a gorilla of a bouncer, this huge Russian guy. It was awful. Sandra was screaming, I'll kill you, I'll kill you, pounding on the chest of the bouncer. I don't even know what Steve had done. I missed it. I was on stage trying to do the gig, and before I knew it Steve was getting punched in the face and – this is the extent to which we'd lost our faith in him – we didn't even stop playing or try to defend our mate. We were just like, Finally, someone's chucked him out the band!'

VII
Filthy's

1999–2000: A little yellow van, a demo and a new drummer. A big-shot manager but no record deal. First review in the NME. *A dream job at Filthy McNasty's Whiskey Café. Meeting Chas & Dave (and Kate Moss, sort of). Alex the aristo introduces us to Banny, a woman who changes The Libertines' lives.*

'This is when my dad stepped up. I convinced Mum to lend me money, and her and Dad did. I was like, Look the band's going well, it's all going good, I've just got to get a van and make a demo and we're away. So, it's an investment, and as soon as we get this multimillion-pound record deal, obviously I'll give you the money back. It was that sort of vibe, and I was sort of right about it, although when I did have money, Mum and Dad would never take any from me, so it was a difficult one to pay back.

I bought a little yellow van for £750 – you can imagine the state it was in. It wasn't a transit van, more like a Robin Reliant, except it had four wheels instead of three. We went to this real ramshackle place called Odessa Studios in Hackney to record the demo. The guy who owned the place, Gwyn Mathias, was always falling asleep or popping home to feed the dog or see the missus, so we'd be there hours and hours and nothing would get done. Within a week of us recording there, the studio basically became free. He couldn't charge us because we hardly got anything done.

One night we were telling Gwyn our tragic drummer history, which he, of course, likened to *Spinal Tap*, because he was always quoting *Spinal Tap*, and he went, I know a drummer, Paul Dufour, he's a classy bloke, he's quite jazzy, he used to play in Fly By Night. Did I tell you about Fly By Night? Yeah, we know about Fly By Night. Gywn had been in this band in the '70s, and he had pictures of them up in the studio. So, two in the morning, Paul Dufour comes down in his Beamer and flat cap. He was a real cockney, getting on for sixty, and he just knocked it out there and then, exactly what we wanted. It took him longer to set up his drum kit than it did to do the take. We nicknamed him Mr Razzcocks, Razzers, and asked him to join the band. We had a lot of skiffle-y/ballad-y songs like 'Music When the Lights Go Out', and Razzers could get this really skiffle-y, jazzy '60s vibe going on the drums. We could rehearse for free at Odessa with Razzers, so that was handy.

Through a girl John met at the Good Mixer, Su Goodacre, we got introduced to Roger Morton, our first proper manager. John said, Su knows famous people, and she's got big knockers. We sound like a right bunch of *Carry On* actors when I think of the things we used to say about girls, but it was a really big deal because John was only eighteen, and Su was a proper little sort in our eyes – a cockney nymphette. She had a band called Superior, all girls, and they were all a bit older and completely filthy. We'd all be round Su's flat, and they'd dress us up in their feather boas and put eyeliner on us. Su would be dancing round in her sparkly knickers, tits out.

Roger was a writer for the *NME* and had this James Bond theme going on, wearing sunglasses at night with this David Bowie haircut and a leather jacket. He also had this cooler-than-thou record collection. Him and Razzers was a terrible dynamic. Roger said, The old man's got to go, boys, it's just not sexy. He reviewed us for the *NME* when we played the Bull & Gate pub in Kentish Town in September 1999. It was on this little toilet-gig circuit, a pay to play sort of vibe, but I might as well have been playing Madison Square Garden, that's how excited I was. I may be wrong, but I like to think it was infectious. Paul gets one mention in Roger's review: 'old guy drummer'. It was obviously going to be a great review, though – he was our manager. My only disappointment was we weren't on the cover. He called us 'the best thing since opium lollipops'.

We presumed because we now had an *NME* writer as our manager, we were going to get a record deal straight away, so we were all buzzing when Roger took us to meet John Waller who'd been managing director at Andrew Lloyd Webber's record company, but he wasn't interested. Then there was just this stasis where we'd always be going round to Roger's house asking him for money and guitars. His strategy was basically to do a gig every three months and invite industry bods in the hope of getting us a deal, but we wanted to play every night. He got us a show at Blow Up at the Wag Club in late 1999. Roger had the gig filmed, and The Libertines put it out on YouTube in 2020 during the first lockdown. He also got us a gig at the Kashmir Klub* supporting I Am Kloot.

Francesca was like the breadwinner at the time. I really needed a job. I was dossing at Odessa, answering the phone for Gwyn, and on Saturday mornings for £5 I'd wash windscreens for the fella who owned the Jag garage across the alleyway. It was where I later went to buy my old Jags. The owner, Tony Smith, was like Big Vern from the *Viz* comic – heavy cockney mobster parody.

---

* In Westminster, another industry hotspot, described by *the Sunday Times* at the time as 'the coolest club in town'.

I worked in this little Soho shop called Ground Zero – £3.50 an hour – selling expensive bits and bobs: cubes that were alarm clocks or coat hangers made out of some strange new durable metal. It was not really my kind of thing. I usually only worked in places that interested me, but I just needed the money. I got sacked after I did a line of speed off the counter – I thought it would add to my worth, but they sent me home and that was that. I also briefly worked at one of those mod shops in Carnaby Street owned by this Pakistani fella and his wife – really strange set-up, but they had the best music: a mixtape they'd been playing since 1990 with the best psychedelic stuff on it. Proper old-school London mods with Charlie George sideburns would come in, and they'd call me a Plastic Mod. I even worked as a road sweeper in King's Cross for a couple of days – that was really hard work.

This is when I got in at Filthy's and the whole Libertines vibe shifted again. I was talking to Su, saying I wanted a job somewhere where I could plot up and write, and she took me into Filthy McNasty's Whiskey Café, which was quite a well-known old Irish place on Amwell Street, near Angel. They did a literary night on Thursday, and Su took me in and said to this Irish fella Dave who ran the place, This is Peter, he's a poet, give him a job, and he did. I got a job as a barman. I opened up in the morning, and I slept upstairs, above the bar, in a room with a couple of mattresses on the floor. I wrote early versions of 'Up the Bracket' and 'Horrorshow' up there, spent hours plinking away on my guitar thinking, This is a good place to write, feeling all the ghosts through the floorboards. The ley lines go right down Amwell Street, under Filthy's down to Exmouth Market to the old Empress of Russia pub and Sadler's Wells. That area is super-charged, there's a psychic consciousness in that part of London – some strange, haunted melodies.

Shane MacGowan had been a regular at Filthy's. Dave had his picture up on the wall alongside photos of Gerry Adams and Johnny Depp when they'd been in. Writers like Will Self and Ken Kesey had done readings there. It had these strong literary ties, but it had a strange mix of punters. It was popular with the well-known Irish Adams family. The younger members of the family would always come in on a Saturday night in their YSL shirts and pay with £50 notes. They'd order a fifteen-quid round, give you a fifty and say, Keep the change, son. I couldn't believe it.

I was also asked to work at a lock-in where Primal Scream and Kate Moss came down. It was as close as I'd ever been to anyone that famous. The next morning, I was saying to some of the regulars, Yeah, that Kate Moss came in last night, and she took me to the toilet and sucked me off. Complete bollocks, completely making it up, this scurrilous story, but it's ironic when you think about it. I said it to Carl, and he went, Oh yeah, I'm sure Francesca would love to hear that. I was like, Oh no, no. Sometimes you'd have film crews coming in and doing little scenes at Filthy's. I was made up when the BBC or Channel 4 came in and did an interview with Chas & Dave there. I was serving behind the bar that day, singing all these old music-hall songs to them.

Filthy's was also where I started putting on nights of my own. I had the keys, so I'd say, Right, Libertines, c'mon, we're going to play a little show in the back room. I'd put up posters around town and get other bands to play. It was like an extension of the Arcadia at the Foundry but finally we were playing our songs. I was getting into putting all these different art bands on. I wanted to create this community of bands that supported each other and played with each other.

It was a great raucous time of having it up around London – moving on through the night to the next place where we could dance and make noise and blag some drinks but all the while looking to meet creative people. Anyone I met who played in a band I was immediately like, What are you doing next Thursday? because I always had an Arcadian cabaret on the bounce, occasionally at the Foundry but mostly now centred on Filthy's.

I shouldn't say it really, but the bar job was all about having access to cash. It was terrible. I used to steal quite a lot. Dave would turn up on his motorbike, drive it into the bar, park up, run upstairs, run downstairs. Doherty, have you cleaned up the fucking dog yet? They had a big Alsatian in the back yard that I was supposed to clean out. Dave was nuts, fucking nuts. I liked that. He'd empty the till, swear under his breath, shout at me and take me down the cellar – which had punch bags and all sorts of paramilitary-looking stuff. We know you're stealing from us, Doherty, just don't let us catch you. It was all a bit of a game.

With the first bit of money I saved, I went down Camden Market and I bought this guitar I was proud of. I thought it was a Gibson, with the F-hole in it. It turned out to be a Givson, an Indian copy. They made the V look like a B. I got completely duped. That happened to me again when I managed to smuggle what I thought was a pukka early '60s Strat out of one of the guitar shops on Denmark Street – I did a switcheroonie with a battered old guitar of mine and walked out with it in my guitar case – all a bit sleazy, really. I thought it was worth a fortune, but John said to me, What are you talking about, this is only worth two or three hundred quid, it's a copy.

There was another barman at Filthy's called Alex Clarke who was quite important in the story of The Libertines. He introduced us to our future manager, Banny Poostchi, who would eventually get us a deal with Rough Trade. I used to do a lot of shifts with Alex, and sometimes he stayed upstairs as well. He was a poet, and everyone said he was the son of a lord who owned half of Scotland. Alex would stand at the end of the bar reading the *Times Literary Supplement* in his tweed suit. To me he was Oscar Wilde, genuinely intellectually stimulating, always writing in his notebook. He had a mate called Lockett who was also supposed be an aristocrat and a poet. Alex and Lockett were actually how I initially got Carl interested in Filthy's. He was always obsessed with the aristocracy. He'd veer from being from a council estate in Basingstoke to having these whispered illegitimate ancestors in the aristocracy. When I'd first said to Carl, You've got to come down Filthy's, it's a real madhouse, he said, No, I've heard that's an IRA pub. I said, It's not any more, it's fine, there's aristocrats here. He was there the next day, and he saw Alex and Lockett and his mouth dropped, Fucking hell, they're real aristocrats. I said, Yeah, man. They were proper plumbed up.

At the time, Alex was completely in love with Banny, this professional woman in her late twenties, a lawyer who'd worked on Oasis's legal stuff while working at the legal firm Simons Muirhead Burton. Alex brought her down to the pub, and she saw us play there one time with Razzers and said, Right, I'm going to manage The Libertines. Everyone was kind of in love with her. She paid for us to do a demo of two new songs, 'Love on the Dole' and 'Breck Road Lover', and she tried to get us signed on the back of that. She was sold on the idea we were like this free band of romantics and poets but in '60s suits. She had just landed this new job as legal and business affairs manager of Warner/Chappell Music Publishing and Warner Music International, and I think maybe she thought of it as this pet project – she'd be like, You're my little urchins, but you've got to get rid of the old man. That was the common theme of that little period.'

Dad was always chucking me and AmyJo about when we were little, throwing us up in the air really high. We loved that.

Peter and AmyJo, Catterick, 1981.
(Courtesy Jackie Doherty)

One of my earliest memories is waking up one morning and finding Dad asleep on the sofa in his boots and uniform. I climbed up on top of him and he woke up and we lay there together watching football on Grandstand.

Peter with England World Cup-winning footballer Martin Peters, 1984.
(Courtesy Jackie Doherty)

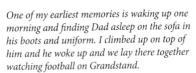

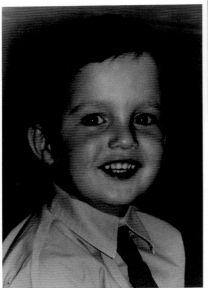

On AmyJo's first day at school I really wanted to go with her. AmyJo was funny as fuck in those days because when she was three/four/five she used to have the old 'gauzy eye' with the patch over one of her thick-rimmed specs.

Peter, aged three and a half, late 1983.
(Courtesy Jackie Doherty)

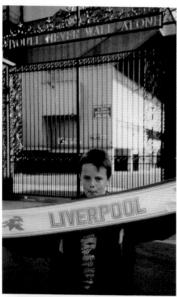

Whenever we went home to Liverpool me and AmyJo would put on a show for the family. At school, in Cyprus or Germany, if there was ever a school play we'd always get the lead roles. I loved it. I loved acting. All us army kids had the same spikey hair at the time.

Clockwise:
At the gates of Anfield, 1987.
Cyprus, 1988.
Germany, 1989.
(All courtesy Jackie Doherty)

As a kid I'd famously put in my nan's false teeth and come parading through the front room.

Acting up, 1992. *(Courtesy Jackie Doherty)*

I really believed that I was going to play professional football. I was skillful, a good player, but I wasn't good enough to play professionally.

1992. *(Courtesy Jackie Doherty)*

Mum says I sang out of tune all the way through to the end of the song.

Singing for the first time in public at a family wedding, 1992. *(Courtesy Jackie Doherty)*

Those army communities are really tight – in a good way and a bad way. Everyone knows everyone. Very, very strange world. You never saw anybody with long hair.

Peter aged sixteen, and friend Cedric, Cyprus, 1995. *(Courtesy Jackie Doherty)*

I got a guitar from a car boot sale. I long for those days. We'd go to a family-run auctioneers every week. I wanted to be an auctioneer for a while because of the patter.

First band, The Peepsters, 1996. *(Courtesy Peter Doherty)*

I'd wander endlessly around the second-hand book shops of Shaftesbury Avenue.

Peter home from uni, Krefeld, Germany, 1998. *(Courtesy Jackie Doherty)*

When we first got down to sitting together with our guitars, I asked if he could play 'This Charming Man', but he started playing the chords to 'I met him in a crowded room', the Blur song, and I was absolutely gutted.

Peter aged nineteen with Carl, Camden, 1998. *(Courtesy Jackie Doherty)*

We loved Gwyn who ran Odessa. He was really important because he had equipment and knowledge of music. In the end, I even started working and living there.

Peter in Odessa Studios, Hackney, with John, 2000. *(Courtesy Peter Doherty)*

Very early in our story, I made out that there was a band called the Luton Libertines who did covers of our songs and sometimes we let them support us. They were this multi-racial cover band with a Pakistani Pete.

Ripped England shirt and Union Jack, 2002.
(Roger Sargent)

The door at Teesdale Street was never the most secure door. It was a door you could kick open without needing a key but it'd still close again – the dream door, really, the portal to Arcadia.

Peter, Carl and Gary with friends in the Albion Rooms, Bethnal Green, 2002.
(Patrick Ford/Redferns/Getty)

We used to go through so many roadies. We'd have guys who we'd fall out with straight away, in the van on the way to the gig, so by the time of the gig they'd detune our instruments.

Walking down the street, 2003. *(Roger Sargent)*

I can feel myself flinching thinking about having to listen to my own voice. With what you hear on the records, I think it really depended on what state of mind I was in at the time.

Libertines in the studio, 2003. *(Roger Sargent)*

We saw Jarvis Cocker in the Rough Trade offices and Carl and me burst in and wanted to give him a red army jacket as a gift. He couldn't get out of the way quick enough – he thought we were trying to attack him. I went to go hug him and he backed away and fell over the desk.

The Libertines, 2002. *(Roger Sargent)*

Thinking back to those days makes me think of that line in the Life of Brian. *What does he say? Eric Idle when he's on the cross? Randy little bugger, up and down like the Assyrian Empire.* And, yeah, I suppose I was really.

The Libertines, 2002. *(Roger Sargent)*

For me and Carl it was always about having a laugh when we did those early interviews.

Peter reading a review, America, 2003. *(Courtesy Peter Doherty)*

VIII
Banny

2000–2001: Dealing Ecstasy. Meeting Wolfman. Visiting Russia with the Foundry. A long stretch on the building site. John leaves the band. Francesca, me and Martin. James Mullord offers a deal. Banny devises Plan A. The Strokes come to town. Steve is back with Bill and Neil. A new line-up and sound.

'I started dealing Ecstasy. Someone would turn up with a Sainsbury's carrier bag full of the fuckers, and they would say, See if you can get rid of these. The idea being if you can get rid of two hundred, they'll give you some more. Alex had this bunch of private-school mates who'd all come down to Filthy's and do pills. They'd all do six or seven pills each and put on weird dance music. Then when Filthy's closed at midnight, we would all go over to Shepherd's Bush where there was an all-night club in a converted public toilet and end up on the tables, E'd up, dancing to really shit techno. We'd be going through to the sun coming up. I used to get this amazing feeling. Sometimes we'd end up in Brighton or Margate, but more often than not we'd end up on the roof of this tower block not far from Filthy's. We'd go up in the lift, everyone lagging and proper chomping their jaws off, and then come down the stairway, twenty-six floors, reading all this trippy graffiti –

twenty-five years of the most creative and obscene graffiti, incredible.

I was working at Filthy's, but I couldn't stay there any more, so I was crashing where I could, always on the lookout. I stayed with this French girl Carole Dubois, who was a poet, a little bit older than me, at this strange pad round the corner from Filthy's. That's where I first encountered Wolfman, Peter Wolfe. His long-time girlfriend Romana lived with Carole. Wolfman was about ten years older than me, and he didn't like me at first, but the fact I worked behind the bar at Filthy's had its advantages, so we sort of became friends by proxy, on the basis I could give him a free glass of wine now and again. Also, I believed in his poetry. I'd get him up to do some for the nights I put on at Filthy's.

I had a very brief thing with Carole – she was another who sold a salacious kiss and tell about me to the tabloids when I was with Kate – but she wound up becoming Jake Fior's girlfriend. Jake was managing Wolfman, and he had a gallery/bookshop near Filthy's where sometimes he'd hire me and Francesca to serve drinks at openings. It was basically the Black Books bookshop, from the cult sitcom, and he was that guy, the grouchy bookshop owner Bernard Black, played by Dylan Moran. Jake looked like him and everything.

Mick Murphy also sometimes let me stay at his council flat close by. He worked behind the bar at Filthy's, a cockney fella who was like a suedehead, jeans down his arse and Stan Smiths, considered himself stylish. For some reason he had to leave the country quickly and went to Lanzarote. I sometimes crashed with Judd the arsonist, another strange character who also lived quite near Filthy's. He was the first person I saw smoking crack. He came in the bar, ordered a pint, drank it and refused to pay, said he knew the owners, and then he lit up a crack pipe at the bar. There was only me and him there. It was eleven in the morning, and he gave me a smoke over the bar. *The Harder They Come* soundtrack was playing, and I suddenly remember feeling really tall, and suddenly really into reggae, actually. It seemed like the sun was shining and everything was all right. I didn't smoke it again for a long, long time. Judd ended up burning down his flat and being locked up.

It was about this time, September into October 2000, that I went to Russia with the Foundry for a short trip. It was part of some cultural exchange. They'd let the equivalent of the Foundry in Russia, called the DOM, take over the Foundry, and now they'd got the funding for what they called 'the return match'. Can you imagine Russia back then? It was bonkers. It was quite a big group of fifty Foundry regulars who went from London. We were all in bunks in one big barracks. The artist Gavin Turk was there. The actor Tam Dean Burn who would always end up getting up in drag and doing a song at my Sunday night poetry nights at the Foundry did that in Russia. My thing was supposed to be doing a version of 'Dirty Old Town' in Russian – that was my show-piece, that was why I was there.

The DOM was like the Foundry times ten. I ended up getting taken to this flat by these two Russian artists, and they locked me in there, like a bunker, and I was trapped there for a day and a half. I think it was some sort of experiment. They were filming me. There was just this disembodied voice coming through a speaker. When I got out, I was wandering around a part of Moscow I didn't know trying to get back to – to be honest, I didn't even know where I was trying to get back to. I was in a bit of a state, a panic, just thinking I was going to get left behind, and there were chickens everywhere on the street. That's my abiding memory of Russia back then – the chickens.

I ended up living in John's house when I got back. It was opposite the job centre in Kentish Town, and on my first visit there they gave me a job on a building site in Chelsea. John's mum would wake me up every morning with a cup of tea. The site was next door to a house that belonged to the drummer from Queen. It was a great laugh. There was one old Irish guy who didn't exactly take me under his wing. He used to call me a plastic Paddy – I was always a plastic something, Plastic Mod, Plastic Paddy – but he'd take me to the pub, and we'd have a Guinness with a drop of port in it. They thought I was bit strange, I had long hair, but I was kind of accepted by the builders – one of the lads who was carpenter was a bedroom DJ, and he used to buy a bit speed off me.

The work was horrible. I was just filling up wheelbarrows with dirt and running it up the plank and tipping it in the skip. That was it, all day, every day. I was on the shop run at lunchtime, four *Daily Stars*, two *Mirrors*, a *Sun* and I'd buy *Dazed & Confused* or something like that. I remember saying to the lads on the site that I played in a band, and they said what sort of music, and I said sort of garage-y but of course garage meant something completely different to everyone on the site. The carpenter lad said, You've got to play the slow songs, innit, you get all the pussy playing the slow songs.

We were still doing the odd gig at that time. We did one at the 12 Bar Club on Denmark Street, otherwise known as Tin Pan Alley, in Soho in early 2001. There's footage of that seventeen-song set. I'm pretty sure Roger Morton organised the filming, so perhaps it was another sort of industry showcase. It had a pay-to-play vibe about it. Roger had started to get really annoyed with me. He would drink in Filthy's, but any gig I organised myself there he wouldn't show up at. He'd play it down, say, No, you can't present this as The Libertines, when I present you, it is going to be with a bang.

The 12 Bar gig was the last one we did with Razzers. He and John were not really into the scene at Filthy's. They felt the band wasn't really going anywhere. Razzers had also stopped wearing his flat cap and had replaced it with a baseball cap. It wasn't on. It was when I was writing 'Time for Heroes', and that's where I got the idea for the line 'There are fewer more distressing sights than that of an Englishman in a baseball cap'. We were sort of falling apart. John actually left the band first. He said, Look this ain't going anywhere, I've got to get a deposit. He'd met Line Thomsen, who he ended up married to and still is. She was working at the same theatre as Carl, and John got a job in the theatres and Carl introduced them. He was just sick of us starting to get a bit heavily battered, really, and he didn't want anything to do with it. That was the death knell for that first version of The Libertines. Roger sort of washed his hands of us. Su linked him up with Johnny Borrell, and that was obviously a better fit.[*]

Francesca was not the first girl I'd slept with, but she was the first girl I had a loving intimate relationship with. She was older than me and more experienced and so sensual, beautiful and poetic, a very skilled writer and artist. She was a real inspiration. I pinched a couple of stonking lines out of her journals for 'Horrorshow'. She used to have these beautifully kept journals, her handwriting was exquisite – a lot of it was in Italian, but more and more it was in English.

We'd visited Italy intermittently over the years. Her mother was really quiet and studious and had this tiny flat in this big tenement block. I remember being there with the light coming through the blinds on these hot afternoons and feeling a sense of peace, that this is how I could live, in an old room in an old stone tenement, writing in the afternoon and then drinking coffee and walking in the mountains. One of her uncles was a labourer in a vineyard, and we'd go and visit him, and he'd sneak us a couple of bottles of wine. These were things that were really alien to me, drinking wine under a tree with this beautiful cheese. The Italian working people had a different quality of life, a different essence – the way they connected to the food and to the land.

At the time, Francesca was working at some art space in London and

[*] Roger Morton would go on to manage Borrell's band Razorlight to international success, circa 2003–2004.

had met this contemporary art duo, Martin Tomlinson and a really strange Australian girl who wore a wig. They'd do these weird installations. I'd go watch them rehearse in the gallery. I tried to organise some parties of my own there, playing '60s records and I'd get Martin and this girl to dance for the night. I actually ended up living in the gallery with Francesca for a bit. I managed to blag them that I could be a live exhibit.

Martin was in a quite well-known band later called Selfish Cunt who I got to support The Libertines now and again, and he came on the road with us very early on doing the merchandise. He was so beautiful, gorgeous. Francesca had a thing with him. When I heard about that, I went to knock him out, but he'd just been attacked on the Tube for being gay by some yobs and had a black eye and bloody nose. As I went to punch him, he was cowering away saying he'd just been attacked – I felt like a real bully, and I couldn't hit him.

After John left the band, I had to get out of his mum's, and I got this place in Whitechapel in east London, 98 Ashfield Street. It wasn't a flat – it was just a room in a sort of industrial unit, and there was an adjacent room with an industrial sink, which served as the toilet and kitchen. Francesca started painting the walls with these fairy creatures. This kaleidoscope collage grew up around the two rooms, and she started drawing on the bricks outside too, making these strange patterns on some of the abandoned buildings in the area. All these little goblins she'd draw, really psychedelic. They were to do with acid trips. I remember staring at them in the midst of an acid comedown, those frozen mornings when you are trying to make sense of coming back to normality from the trip. Those early acid trips for me were really powerful – wondering if I could bridge the gap back to reality and then realising I didn't think I ever would be able to because the stuff I'd done while tripping had been so out there musically for me.

I'd done these demos with Vicki Churchill, who was a singer-song-writer I'd met. Her dad was this Bukowski-type figure. He'd sit in front of the telly watching the racing at his house in High Barnet, and me and Carl would go to Vicki's room to record these weird versions of 'Times for Heroes', a new song called 'I Get Along' and 'Horrorshow', all with drum machines and samples and me recording all these sounds of violence and smashing, pretending I was having a punch-up during the song. Something had really changed in me.

James Mullord, who would later become Babyshambles' first manager, was running a little indie label called High Society Records, and he showed an interest in those demos. He put us into the High Society studio, which was the place in Old Street where I used to deliver the speed – I called it the Speedy Studio – and we did a demo of another new song, 'Through the Looking Glass'. That original version had loads of samples on it – because I knew James Mullord was sold on that – and these skaggy, trippy beats. James offered us a grand to record and release whatever we wanted. He was putting out a lot of experimental music on his little label and always doing some launch party or some DJ night around east London.

He was a bit older than me, a bit distant, but in my mind he was professional – even though he was on the outside of the mainstream industry. He used to smoke a bit of gear, and I used to be turned on by the fact him and his missus, Sarah Churchill, Vicki's sister, smoked it together. Sarah had a band called Cosmetique. I actually did a record-ing with them, playing some country-and-western picking on a version of 'I'm Going Back to Jackson'. They were pals with Jarvis Cocker, and Sarah used to DJ at those weird Sunday club nights Jarvis did down in south London. We'd go along – me and Francesca with Martin, and sometimes Carl, just trying to get a glimpse of Jarvis, who was like a god to us. At the time, he was rumoured to be getting down and dirty on the brown.

This is when Banny came back on the scene. She was saying, No, no, don't sign to High Society for a grand, I can get you a deal with Rough Trade if you sound like this and look like this. It became known as Plan A, the big buzz phrase. We even recorded a song with that title. What was the plan? Get the best-looking people and be as much like The Strokes as possible. That's how it was. It was definitely Banny's vision, but actually that had been my plan all along – there were no Strokes back then, but it was still the same sort of thing: there's a photo of Steve, me, Carl, John and Sandra, the psychedelic dancer, up on Hampstead Heath, and we look like the Stones or the Byrds. That had always been in my head, that we had 'the look'. So, getting the best-looking boys and being as much like The Strokes as possible? Great fucking idea! I was well up for that ... if it worked. I thought The Strokes were brilliant.

I was still working on the building site when I first saw a picture of them – there was a little article in *Dazed & Confused*. All I could see was me, Carl, Steve and John – one of them was even wearing the same T-shirt Steve had been wearing for years. I was thinking, How dare they? Then Francesca brought back one of these Rough Trade triple A-side CDs, *The Modern Age* EP that came out in early 2001. She put it on in the little psychedelic flat in Whitechapel, and I'd never heard anything like it – it sounded like the better-quality rehearsals that we'd had when Steve was on the drums. It sounded like a band having a good time in a room, and the lyrics were amazing.

Steve actually came back into the fold for a little bit, and we started moving towards being a rock-'n'-roll band as opposed to being like a bootleg Beatles or whatever we had been with Razzers. Steve was there during the development of 'Horrowshow' and 'Time for Heroes', which stopped being a folk song and became a punch-up, punk-rock song after I got pepper-sprayed during the May Day riots. I wrote about it and the WOMBLES, a group of anarchists who were sort of the figureheads of the anti-capitalist protests, in the song.

Banny was happy for Steve to be in this new thing we were putting together. Steve also tried to get a drummer called Bill Bones, who I also name-checked in 'Time for Heroes', in the line-up. They turned up for a rehearsal in Whitechapel and that was the first time I tried heroin. We were just smoking a little bit of gear in a one-skin Rizla which they dubbed 'a booner'. Bill was this amazing-looking New York Dolls-y lad from Kent, but Banny just wasn't having him. She was like, He's doing heroin! Steve also brought along a pal of his from Scarborough, a guitarist called Neil Thunders, and he was also rehearsing with this new line-up at these sessions when Carl wouldn't show up. There are demos knocking around from this period with Steve doing vocals on a new song called 'Mocking Bird' and 'Through the Looking Glass'. Carl was a bit disillusioned with it all. It was becoming difficult to get in touch with him. It was a really Strokes-y vibe we had going, me, Steve, Bill and Neil. I just wanted the band to be a band: just lads who were hanging out during the day, mucking about together and up to no good, and Carl was not really part of that at the time.

I got thrown off the building site when this carpenter who I sold speed to robbed it at the weekend and took all the tools. I kind of got the blame as well. They said you must have known about it. But I didn't. I was there five months. I got really buff, really muscly. I'd also got a taste for cocaine, which had been a little too expensive before, but I'd been earning proper wages on the site. For me, it was a really positive discovery. It was part of this new Strokes rush. My life became about going to the 333 club on Old Street, Shoreditch, and the Mother Bar upstairs, and getting battered and listening to the Queens of Noize DJ – Mairead Nash and Tabitha Denholm. They'd end up with their own show on

MTV. They had the run of the 333, and it became our local – you could just go in, you didn't have to pay, and it was open all through the night. I actually painted the outside pink for £25.

Mairead was only nineteen. Steve had a brief thing with her when she ended up shacked up at one of Rat Pete's flats. She was as excited by The Strokes as me and Francesca. I remember her putting on 'Hard to Explain', the lead single from The Strokes' debut album, at 333 and me and Francesca going mad, jumping up on tables and sofas, thinking, This is it, this is our anthem, and the whole world was going to get swept away with it, but no one else was getting it at all, no one else was having it – apart from Mairead, who was going mental behind the record decks. I ended up crashing at her gaff in Dalston. I wrote 'Up the Bracket' there. She became one of The Libertines family.

Tickets were supposed to be like gold dust for The Strokes debut London show, at Heaven in late June 2001. Banny got me one. Francesca managed to get on the guest list after meeting them on the street on the day of the gig. They were going around Camden in a blacked-out minibus and had this chance meeting with Francesca. They stopped her – she used to go round in a short denim skirt and black-and-white knee socks – and they wanted to know where they could score acid. I was back doing shifts at Filthy's, and she came in and said, They've got a big bag of weed in the back and loads of money. It was all really exciting.

Steve managed to get in for free. He used to be able to get into any gig for free. To us the gig was really something, even though the sound at Heaven was a bit swampy and the crowd was just one big swaying mob rather than people going ballistic. We jumped the train and followed them to Liverpool, where they played the next day. It was that gig, which was full of groups of lads in Reebok classics as well as loads of rock-'n'-roll kids all having it, that I thought, Yeah, fuck, maybe it can still happen, you can still ignite something, maybe there can still be another great band.

After the gig we – Francesca, Mairead, Carl and I – tried to get a lift back to London with The Strokes on their tour bus. They spotted us getting into trouble with their road crew – trying to nick their guitar pedals from the side of the stage. These Australian guys nearly battered me senseless. One of The Strokes came over and said, Leave him alone, man, he's got a cool suit on, and that's how we got in their dressing room. I remember being really annoyed there was no music playing, and I thought, If I ever have a dressing room, I'm going to have record player in it, playing the Ronettes or something.

We explained to them we'd jumped the train from London and didn't have any money. At that point they were sort of half entertaining the idea of giving us a ride back to London. They said, Listen, we want to get some traditional English food, and we said we'd get some fish and chips for them, and they pulled out this wad of money. Will this be enough? They gave us a couple of fifties. Yeah, yeah, that'll do nicely. We disappeared with the money, and by the time we got back they were all piling on their bus with these exotic-looking twins, these two Afro Caribbean twins. I thought, We're not getting on the bus, and Mairead was gutted – they just swished past us, they'd moved on.'

IX
Rough Trade

2001–2002: Writing songs that sound like The Strokes. Gary Powell on drums. Getting a deal with Rough Trade. A new Albion Rooms. Having money. Dad's reaction to 'What a Waster'. Wolfman plots up and Alan Wass moves in. Carl gets the hump.

'Banny said she wanted five songs that sounded like The Strokes. She had this lovely flat in King's Cross, where I crashed quite a lot because it was walking distance from Filthy's, and she also had this incredible flat on the South Bank. I remember being at her kitchen table there with Carl, making the chorus to 'Up the Bracket' really driving, really Strokes-y – as opposed to The Smith's rip-off it sort of started out as. The chords for the chorus of 'Up the Bracket' – 'And it's just like he's in another world, doesn't see the danger on show' – I took direct from 'I Want the One I Can't Have' by The Smiths.

'Up the Bracket' was a song about standing up to someone when you're getting mugged, that's how I saw it. Someone's asking for your money, and you just say, No – you've had enough of people taking from you. It was influenced by a line in 'Hard to Explain': 'Was an honest man, asked me for the phone, tried to take control, oh, I don't see it that way'. My song – it's a bit of a strange lyric actually – 'He said he'd pay me for your address' and then I say, 'you see these two cold fingers'. There's also a religious line in that song, 'Joseph bloody in a hole'. You know the story of Joseph and his Technicolour Dreamcoat? His brothers beat the shit out of him and threw him in a hole. Carl actually came up with that line.

I'd managed to get Carl back interested now there was this deal with Rough Trade being talked about. I always knew in my heart Carl could be wooed by the trappings of the industry, wooed by a little bit of money in the bank, a bit of fame – I knew that would be enough to hold him. But Carl was not keen on having Steve around. It was a bit of a him-or-me-type situation. Then Banny introduced us to Gary Powell. He was dating a secretary in Banny's office at Warner and in another band at the time that were supposedly on the verge of getting a deal.

The first time Gary rehearsed with us – just me, Carl and him – I had this feeling like we were a proper rock-'n'-roll band. I'd never played with a drummer that fucking powerful. He was ten years older than me and Carl and a lot more experienced – he'd played with Eddy Grant. Some of those early rehearsals with Gary took me somewhere else. I'd never made a sound like that before. He didn't even have a full drum kit in them days – it was whatever was to hand, so he played a pared-down drum kit, and we had a dirty rhythm guitar and a bass and screamy vocals. It was a whole new rush. I can feel it now, getting tingles thinking of that rehearsal room near Shepherd's Bush Underground.

My heart was completely in it. In the same way I was a true believer in Jesus and how the love of God could save your soul when I was fourteen, now I was sold on rock 'n' roll and The Stooges, 'Search and Destroy' – these big lines, almost biblical lines: 'Honey got to help me please, somebody's got to save my soul'. Steve was always in to Iggy Pop, but I'd never dared to envisage myself as one of the disciples, but then as I got more and more into the electric sound, the punk sound, I felt I could be. A Molotov cocktail in one hand and an electric guitar in the other – that's how I saw myself.

We loved Gary off the bat – we wanted him to join the fucking band: he liked a bit of The Ramones and The Stooges. We took him down to Filthy's quite a lot after rehearsals, but he was hedging his bets. The Rough Trade thing wasn't in the bag. Banny had Rough Trade A&R man James Endeacott come watch us rehearse, but she gave him a demo of the stuff I'd done for High Society, and he said he was really disappointed with it – just loads of Hancock samples and strange beats and not the great rock-'n'-roll band he'd heard in rehearsal. Banny was determined, though. She was a mate of Gordon Raphael, who had produced The Strokes debut album *Is This It*, which was a huge hit at the time, and she used that to keep blagging Endeacott, and in the end he agreed to come see us play live, even though he didn't like the demo.

He came to a gig at the Rhythm Factory, a tiny venue on Whitechapel Road, just off Brick Lane, which became the place for our stock cele-brations. Basically, Arcadia at the Foundry begat Arcadia at Filthy's begat Arcadia at the Rhythm Factory, but it wasn't an arts scene any more – it was pure sticky backroom rock 'n' roll. That first gig there was my baptism of fire into the world of music promotions – the cash-in-hand, thrill-a-minute of promoting local bands. There were so many – and the more bands I could get to play, the bigger the crowd would be for The Libertines.

It was packed the night Endeacott came to see us. It was still just me, Carl and Gary on stage, with me and Carl swapping bass and electric guitar between songs. We didn't do that many songs, just the ones that were the most Strokes-y. Endeacott loved it. He put us in to do demos at Nomis in Hammersmith. Both Carl and I were sofa-surfing, both quite a bit in debt, so we were both completely reliant on this deal happening. So, when Banny said Rough Trade owners Jeannette Lee and Geoff Travis liked the demo and wanted to sign us, it was . . . I can't describe it. Just pure joy.

Banny told Gary we wanted him to sign the deal with us – as opposed to him just being a paid member of the band. And he didn't want to do it. He wanted to keep his options open to be able to play with other bands. Nowadays when Gary wants to go equal on live splits, we always go back to that moment, and we say, Look, we offered you it all in at the beginning. But these days it is a bit more egalitarian.

Then Carl said, Look, we're going to have to call John and get him back, and I went, No fucking way, not in a million years. He left. I don't want John in the band. We did need a bass player, though. I was phoning Jai from school and saying, Look, you've got to come down and play bass. I wanted someone I loved and wanted to have it up with. But Jai had started playing football semi-professionally and wanted to stick with that, so in the end John was the only choice, but on a wage and the proviso he could not write songs or do any interviews.

That Christmas, I went home. I missed my flight and had a real struggle trying to hitchhike from Dover to Düsseldorf with an over-sized bag. Mum and Dad were still in Germany, at Krefeld. I'd seen them once in a blue moon over the past five years. I'll never forget, I was sat on the green sofa, explaining to Dad how it was all sewn up, we had a deal and this lawyer manager who knew the industry, ticking all the boxes for him. And he said, OK, play us some of the songs that you're going to conquer the world with, and I played him 'What a Waster', which was going to be our first single, and he said it was shit. Yeah, he said it was awful. I was gutted.

Then the following Christmas, after it'd been released as a single, and after the *NME* had put us on the cover a couple of times, he said that 'What a Waster' was great, had me going round to the neighbours' houses playing it! I was really bitter about that. I think it was a case of, when I was growing up, he always said whatever you're going to be, whether you join the army or whether you're a street sweeper, just make sure you're the best at it, that was always his thing. So, for him the backing of the *NME* was evidence that maybe we were half decent because we were getting recognition within the industry. If you read my mum's book, that was also the Christmas where I went to the dinner table on Christmas day in my vest, looking really pale, and she wrote that it was the last time she saw me as she knew me. I had a bit of gear in my guitar case. It wasn't like I was banging up or anything, just smoking a little bit off foil. I think there was an imminent sense of catastrophe in my mum's heart then.

We needed a place to live. I said that to Rough Trade immediately. That was a priority. We didn't have anywhere to live! We were proper Hawaii Five-O sofa-surfing, had got it down to an art form. So, Rough Trade found us 112a Teesdale Street, Bethnal Green – the final Albion Rooms. My bedroom had faded '70s wallpaper and a big old brass bed, my dream bed.

I think out of the fifty grand we got from Rough Trade, Carl and I shared forty. We also got money from signing the publishing deal with EMI. I don't really know any more details regarding The Libertines' business in those days. Banny knew what she was doing. It was all set up beforehand: we signed with Rough Trade, we signed with EMI, we had people who were going to do the press, people to do the accounts, all Banny's people. She had it all worked out.

Carl and I took most of our share from the Rough Trade advance from the bank on the first day, and we had it in big piles of fifties at the Albion Rooms. Why? That's what we'd always said we'd do. I went straight down Denmark Street to Andy's Guitars and bought the original 'heavy horse', an Epiphone Coronet – I've still got it, and it's worth thousands now, but at the time you got them for £250 or £300. People presumed 'heavy horse' was a heroin reference, but it dated back to my school days when I used to go to a record stall in the Birmingham Bullring on a Saturday that sold bootlegs. 'Heavy Horse' was the title of a Smiths live bootleg. That's also where I got the title of 'The Last of the English Roses', my first solo single. It was either the title of a Smiths bootleg or a Smiths fanzine that I bought from that record stall.

We gave those shops on Denmark Street a lot of good business. Carl got a Melody Maker, and he's still got that too. That's what our dreams were made of: rare, vintage guitars and the best old amps, Selmars and old Vox AC30s. We kept all this stuff at Teesdale Street, and considering what went on, I can tell you only one guitar ever got nicked from there – the big metal one I bought. We bought it just to do lines off. It was like a big steel country guitar. It sounded awful, but we took the strings off and turned it on its back. It was about two grand of vintage guitar. We bought a few of them, but that first one went walkies.

A dealer called Dollarman began to make a daily appearance at Teesdale Street. Carl was bang into the cocaine, but he made Dollarman promise he'd never sell crack or heroin to anyone on the scene. So, it was a blizzard of cocaine. I remember having a chat with Dollarman, saying, Can't we start buying in bulk off you, Dollarman? No, mate, I've got to keep you boys rationed so you keep it under control. I did like cocaine, but I preferred smoking it in rocks.

Carl says that the first time he saw me smoke crack was at the Nomis demo sessions we were doing in early 2002, after getting signed, just banging out demo after demo after demo. My closest friends at the time were Amah-Rose and Hannah Bays. They basically moved in. We were the same age – we were always hanging out. They loved Carl, but he was never part of my rock-smoking and ketamine thing in the Albion Rooms – he couldn't bear to see it, but I was well away, longs nights drifting in and out. Hannah was a very talented artist, a Royal Academy of Arts graduate who would design a number of future Libertines and Babyshambles record sleeves. Amah-Rose was a black girl who was from a literary Islington family. I think she does some sort of journalism now – I saw her reviewing something in *The Times*. At the time, she did some poetry – all three of us used to write poetry, a lot of it on the walls in the Albion Rooms.

Hannah – and this is long before Amy Winehouse – was always done up in a beehive and denim skirts. All those years we were hanging out I never met Hannah's boyfriend, but it turned out it was Blake Fielder-Civil, later Amy's husband who bragged about introducing her to crack and heroin. Amah-Rose had a bit of a beehive as well. We were all into The Smiths. Not long after we got signed, the three of us walked down to Soho from Bethnal Green and got our first tattoos. Amah-Rose got a star on the back of her neck that she instantly regretted, and Hannah got a stiletto on her shoulder. I got a love heart with an arrow through it on my shoulder.

At that time, I also liked to smoke a bit of heroin in a roll-up. When I first started dallying with gear, people like Carl and Francesca and AmyJo couldn't get their head around it. There was no attempt at understanding – it was just, It's wrong. There was no discussion about it. It didn't go down well. Heroin was the next logical step for me. Well, alcohol's all right, but it doesn't really suit me. Carl was always calling me a lightweight, and boozing would inevitably end in a punch-up with him, whereas I found a different vibe really with the people I was using heroin with in those very early days of getting into it. No one would hold them up as upright moral characters, but with people like Wolfman, it was always about writing, about literature. Wolfman turned me on to some really good writers.

Once I got signed, Wolfman went from hating me to loving me. He became a familiar face at Teesdale Street. He tried to explain to me how he was mates with Shane MacGowan, how he'd been known as Pete Nice, the subject of a Channel 4 show called *The Greatest Unknown*

Rock 'n' Roll Star, but the world had just forgotten him. Another one of his claims to fame was that he'd been on the front page of the *Sun* because he'd survived a shotgun incident where a bouncer turned up accusing him of sleeping with his missus while he was in prison and fired a shotgun point-blank at him.

He was a very unstable character – there were rumours about how he'd tried to kill himself three times. He also had loads of these strange accidents. Once I saw him get hit by a bus, and he literally flew up in the air over a Mini, a cartoon spiral, landed on his head, and then he just got up and went into Filthy's. But I thought he had a raw and rare talent once you scraped away some of the grime and some of the bitterness, and he was just funny as fuck as well, a really comic character in the Dickensian, nay the Dostoevskian, mould – a fallen figure. And for all his dark atmospherics, Wolfman was actually quite sedate a lot of the time. It was Wolfman who banged me up for the first time. It was horrible. He did it deliberately . . . gave me a proper nasty shot of something, and I was fucked in the bathtub. I thought, Fuck this, I'm never going to inject again, and then a month later, OK, I'll do it again, but just a little bit this time.

During those early days at Teesdale Street, there was a real sense of overlapping worlds and overlapping understandings of what was going on – quite a trippy time, really. Steve was hanging around a lot, so was Su Goodacre, and Alan Wass, the drummer in a band called Left Hand, moved in. He became one of my best pals, and we stayed close right until he died. Rat Pete also reappeared. Alan had been staying in one of his houses. I said to Alan, Why you hanging round with him? You wanna be careful. He went, I heard you used to be his chauffeur? Yeah, but he's not nice. Alan would be like, Ah, he's funny as fuck, listen to him talk, Geeeeeeezaaaaar!

Alan was just a kid of about eighteen or nineteen, in an all-white Adidas tracksuit, a proper Rude Boy. His dad was a bit of an underworld figure. Alan thought I was this great guitarist. I tried to explain to him that I was more the lead singer and Carl was more the guitarist, but Alan never really got this into his head, and he was always really dismissive of Carl – he used to call him Pablo. I went, His name's Carlos not Pablo. I used to call Carl Carlos. Carl hated Alan calling him Pablo. Alan always used to give people nicknames. I became Elvis, which is a great nickname. Scarborough Steve was known as the hippy, and Johnny Borrell was known as Johnny Two-step. Everyone got a really bad nickname except me.

He had this weird thing he'd say: Yeah, for the boys, Pete, for the boys, we're the nuts, we're the nuts, we understand. In the early days of Teesdale Street, Carl, Alan and me went on a proper night out and ended up at some Hollywood actress's London apartment. We were all in her room, and she was all over Alan. Carl and I were really annoyed, but Alan was like, Nah, nah, I'm not into it, babe, it's all about the boys, it's for the boys. Carl and me were like, Ah, we're not about the boys, you can shag us if you want to.

Basically, I was bringing drug addicts to the flat and plotting up there, doing songwriting with Wolfman and songwriting with other people, loads of girls knocking about, and it wound Carl up. But it'd be all right for Carl to go mental in those very first weeks. Carl would turn up with shitloads of different people wanting to party, and I'd be like, No, we've got to write more songs, so that was the dichotomy. Yes, I was writing songs with these other junkies, but at least I was writing songs – that's what I was doing. I wasn't just throwing it all away on drugs, whereas Carl would just come back battered, and he can't really work when he's on drugs.

Carl gives a fair appraisal of those early days at Teesdale Street in his book.[*] I'd be in my dressing gown wanting to work on songs, and he'd

* *Threepenny Memoir: The Lives of a Libertine* (Fourth Estate, 2010).

been out coked up and pissed up with a shitload of cunts who I didn't know who he'd met at some party, and I would drive them all out the house, to have Carl to myself to do some songwriting, but inevitably I'd drive Carl out as well. Sad, really.

But there was such a celebratory feeling in those early days. We were both having it right up in different ways. We spent the lot. I went mad buying really expensive records, and I probably kept some of those antique dealers down Brick Lane market in business. I loved it down there, bought all sorts of stuff. I also found this amazing vintage-military-attire shop, selling flags and uniforms, down in the West End. My dad would have loved it in there. He used to collect old military cap badges. I really got into my military jackets, especially the ones worn by the army bands, as they tended to have the patterns and decorative stuff on them. I bought these amazing red ones for the band to wear. It was very important, very important, how we looked, in those days. I also got a great Red Cross original medical band from the Crimean War from there. I used to wrap that round the upper arm of my leather jacket. For as long as I had it, I used to wear that.*

* Eagle-eyed readers will recall Peter's mother was an army nurse.

X
Up the Bracket

2002: Recording 'What a Waster' with Bernard Butler. Supporting the Sex Pistols. Pissing off The Strokes. Mick Jones produces the debut album. A regular supply of heroin and crack.

'There was talk of Gordon Raphael producing us. He recorded some stuff live, and we did bits of recording in Teesdale Street with him. He stayed over a few times and insisted on sleeping under this pedal organ we had in the corner. In the end, Rough Trade got Suede guitarist Bernard Butler to produce our first single. He turned up while we were doing the Nomis demos. Carl didn't really know about all the mythology side of Bernard, how he was hailed as the greatest guitarist of his generation but quit Suede after their first album. In fact, he didn't know who he was at all. He said to me, Who's this weird bloke in the Lord Anthony parka mooching over the amp in the corner?

I had some close moments with Bernard. He'd play old Smiths songs, telling me how him and his brother, when they were growing up, loved The Smiths, and I grew to love him in a way, but the personal relationship was a bit strained. Maybe he'd grown out of some of the shenanigans I was enjoying. We went to his house one time, and his wife was not happy at all – we felt like we had invaded someone's sanctuary, but we were just up there to have a laugh, let's go out and have some bevvies. Bernard was a melancholy soul, really. We recorded 'What a Waster' at RAK studios in St John's Wood, with me and Carl sharing the lead vocals. When I listened to a finished copy on vinyl at Teesdale Street, I was deflated. I thought it was a bit shouty, really . . . it felt a bit in your face.

To get us ready to go out and play live, Rough Trade put us in one of the small rooms at the big industry rehearsal space the Depot on Brewery Road just by Pentonville prison. We were there three months. Oasis were rehearsing in one of the big rooms. As the years went by, we'd always go back to The Depot to rehearse, but each time we went back we always had a better room until when we did the rehearsal for The Libertines reunion at Hyde Park in 2014, we were in the room that Oasis were in when we first sneaked in like little urchins and sat on the floor watching them. Liam squinting at us, like, Who the fuck's that?

It was while we were at the Depot that Mick Jones out of The Clash showed up. He came in pissed and fell asleep. When he woke up, he asked us to play the songs again. After that, we all went down the Albion pub round the corner from the Depot, amazing gaff. Gary and John never used to come in, but Alan Wass always did. Mick Jones loved Alan and Left Hand. In fact, he agreed to produce Left Hand as well as The Libertines. Mick was a friend of Jeannette at Rough Trade. Everyone thought the bank robber that The Clash wrote the song about was based on her dad. Mick was also a lifelong QPR fan, so that was an instant bond, but I'd never really listened to The Clash.

I stayed up all night and watched *The Filth and the Fury*, the documentary about the Sex Pistols, and *Westway to the World*, the Clash documentary, back to back. The next morning I felt completely rejuvenated with this whole new idea of myself and music and London and everything we were doing with Mick. *The Filth and the Fury*, especially, blew my mind. I'm always hypnotised by old footage of the Pistols. John Lydon had this image of being a bit rotten, vicious, but actually he was a really intelligent, sensitive kid. There's footage of him walking around London and some hod-carrier shouts at him across the street, Oi, Lydon, you mug! And he turns around, and you see him quite timid for the first time. And he goes, Yeah, I always was, wasn't I? I think he's amazing. There's footage of Julie Burchill sat at the feet of the Pistols interviewing them. John was saying, When I do these shows up North, I always talk to the people. I say, So, what's life like for you, y'know. Basic stuff. Love that quote. I don't have any heroes, they're all useless. That's another belter.

Jeannette had also done some stuff with John's post-Pistols band Public Image Ltd, and she got us a slot with the Pistols at their come-back show at Crystal Palace Sports Arena, not long after we got signed. I'd heard Lydon liked *Steptoe and Son*, so I had the intro music on loop on my little tape recorder. I was playing it really loudly in the dressing room next to theirs trying to get his attention. Then he was there in his jumpsuit with pounds signs all over it, like an old prison uniform with arrows on it. I think it was at the time of having a vote on whether to join the Euro. We were just bouncing after him. Lend us a quid, John, lend us a quid. He was going, You Spice Girls are getting too much. We said, Are you gonna watch us play, John? I don't miss a trick, he said. I was happy with a friendly comment from him, really, without the venom.

It was still a bit sparse when we went on, but I was determined to put on a show for the Pistols. Half the crowd was absolutely pissed already, and we were lucky not to get our skulls cracked with bottles flying everywhere. Everyone was singing 'Yellow Submarine' at us, because we were wearing our matching red army jackets. We did feel like we were at war that day, the people booing and chucking stuff at us – it was hilarious. You sort of thrive on that at that stage, and all the songs were super-charged. Because we'd been rehearsing so heavily, it was pretty ferocious, I think – it was all about getting your fingers to bleed on stage. If you didn't come off with blood on your fingers, then you hadn't played properly.

At the after-show party, I was trying to get John to score for us, and he was really accommodating. He did some hand gestures to some bloke in the corner, put one finger on one nostril and went, Dave! Libertines, sort them out. I was really buzzing. I felt like the people he was with backstage were cool. It was a bit like Glastonbury, like a dance festival – I didn't really expect that. It was just good fun. Loved it.

We were put in them situations a lot early on. Our whole career was essentially being orchestrated by Rough Trade, and over time that really started to bother me. I wanted more fluidity and chaos. But in that first burst, they got us support gigs with Morrissey, The Strokes and The Vines. There was never any strong camaraderie – it wasn't really like we were being invited into their domain by the bands them-selves. In fact, there was quite a bit of animosity between us and The Strokes.

It started when we were all down at Trash, which by then had moved to The End, off New Oxford Street, to see the Yeah Yeah Yeahs. It was their first ever show in London, and I was really out of my nut. Karen O came on stage with a can of lager and was tipping lager on the crowd, so I was grabbing random pints and chucking them back at her, and I might have got up on stage. I got flung out anyway, but I managed to get back in later with a guitar, and that was the last thing The Strokes wanted. They were sat round trying to pull, and I had this guitar out. Johnny Borrell was there too. It was a lock-in after Trash. Carl got the guitar and was trying to play Julian Casablancas his songs, and Julian said, Why do you always want to play guitar, man? Put the fucking guitar down, and Carl was really offended. In a book about The Strokes,[*] Nick Valensi, their guitarist, remembers me from that night, and basically he said I was a pimp, and I had these two dodgy birds with me and was trying to get him back for a foursome at a hotel. Nice story but not how I remember it.

When we supported them, Julian wanted some gear, he wanted some coke. I just had some rocks, so I said, I've just got this, and he went, Are you trying to give me crack, Peter? Really off. Another gig, when I did have some coke, he sniffed the lot out of my tin and then fucked off. Carl and Wolfman didn't rate him at all. Alan Wass came to the gig and was just shouting out in the middle of the crowd, They're shit, Pete, you're better than this lot. And Alan ended up having a big fight with the same Australian security guards who'd had a go at me up in Liverpool that time. Julian said to me, Why do you like to hang out with people who fight, man? I took that as a compliment. I remember Alan bending down into their faces backstage and going, Are you from New York? He was being really obnoxious, so everyone got chucked out.

Recording the first album at RAK studios didn't take that long. I'm thinking two or three weeks – really quite quick. Mick Jones really believed in it, and he put a lot of trust in us, sort of challenged us to believe in ourselves, and we really did. We set up the songs just exactly as they needed to be. It was a real sculptured selection of songs that we'd put together from scratch basically, me and Carl. It was exciting to be finally recording them but stressful as well. It happens a lot in the studio with us – we really get our heads too into the songs. We'd proper get it on in the studio, evolving the songs, especially the lyrics, and

---

[*] *Meet Me in the Bathroom: Rebirth and Rock and Roll in New York City 2001–2011* by Lizzy Goodman (Faber & Faber, 2017).

pushing each other to the limit, and it'd always end on a crescendo with the vocal take.

We grafted on the recording, put a lot of our hearts and souls into it. There was a feeling like it was working while we were recording it, the band was working, but it took years for people to get them songs. It didn't sell a great deal at the time. It never really hit home. It did eventually, but I'm talking the first year. When I look back, I think it's probably one of the best things we did. The production is ace, really muddy.

I had Wolfman come in and do this rap on this really dirty garagey song called 'Wolfman'. It was quite dark, and it didn't really work – no one really dug Wolfman's vibe in the studio. It was a bit bleak for people. I thought it was brilliant. Mick Jones turned round to me and said, He's not like you boys, is he? He's not very nice. Nothing really came of that song, but we used to do it live with Babyshambles, and we still do with the Puta Madres sometimes. 'Begging' was one of my favourite songs on the album, especially the intro. That was another one I wrote when I was staying at Mairead's. 'The Boy Looked at Johnny', with the line 'don't you know who I think I am', was named after the Tony Parsons and Julie Burchill book of the same name that I'd dreamed about owning for a long time. I finally found a copy of it in the Music & Video Exchange in Notting Hill, cost me £12, which was a fortune for a book. People think it was about Johnny Borrell, and it was, I suppose.

Carl and I were supposedly still living together, but that was just a media thing rather than the reality. He'd already had enough of Teesdale Street. I say that because I remember while we were doing the album Carl asked me to set him up with this girl who used to call herself Wolfman's secretary, and he ended up spending the night with Wolfman and this secretary. I was at home in Teesdale Street. We had the studio in the morning, so I got some kip – yeah, watch out – and the next morning Carl didn't turn up until a couple of hours into the session, and when he did, he was completely fucked.

I said, What you been doing? He said, I went to Wolfman's, and I wanted him to get some coke, but he couldn't, he could only get brown or rocks. So I said, So, you've been doing brown and white all night, and he said, Yeah. And I said, Oh, that's all right. I've written this new song called 'Skag & Bone Man', and we did it there and then. There's loads of messing around before it crashes into the solo . . . he was chasing me round the recording studio. That song didn't end up on the album, but it ended up as a B-side to 'Up the Bracket'. I remember saying, Look, you see, if he gets fucked, everyone thinks it's hilarious – which everyone did, everyone thought it was really funny he was so out of it – but if I do it, it's, Oh, Peter needs to go to rehab. Later that day, when Carl was still fucked, we did the album track 'Radio America', and you can hear him passing out at the end, the sound of his head cracking against the microphone. 'Radio America' was an old song from way back, slow and gentle, because sometimes I really did want to slow it down, even though it was so manic a lot of the time.

Paul Ro, Paul Roundhill, was my first reliable source of half-decent-quality crack and heroin. One of our first social meetings was at Teesdale Street. Hannah and Amah-Rose were there. We played chess and had a little session, and he insisted for every piece that was taken off the board, you had to take off an item of clothing. He was tiny and bespectacled, in his mid-forties, but a randy old goat. I was horrified by this suggestion, and he was going, You're not really a libertine.

His claim to fame was he scored for Nico when she came to London. He was also tied up in some big to-do with Boy George and the gear in the mid-'80s. I know he came out of it badly in the Boy

George book.* When I met him, it was £20 deals, so I'd go to his flat in Whitechapel, which was only a couple of streets away from the Rhythm Factory, with £80 and get two of each – two white, two brown, two rocks of crack and a bit of gear. He was infamous for the Paul Ro tax – he'd take a little bit, so you had to try and negotiate, but it was so easy, you'd be guaranteed to score. He had a million Bangladeshi kids on speed dial.

In those early days, after we did gigs at the Rhythm Factory, I'd always go to Paul's with a big old gang. Those are great memories of the sun coming up over the rooftops of Whitechapel, seeing it through to the dawn at Paul's and dancing in his front room – he had a massive collection of reggae seven inches, a huge collection. A lot of the time, though, when we went round to his flat it would just be Paul holding court in his string vest and a pair of denim shorts and sandals. Once he'd had a pipe he could just talk for hours on any subject. He'd just rant.

I used to take Steve round there. Steve might have even lived there for a bit, but Carl and Paul never connected. I took Carl round to Paul's once, and that was awful because Carl didn't want any rocks, he wanted powder – much to Paul's consternation. I think Carl had his trumpet with him that day. Carl called it his bugle, which was also a slang term for cocaine – that was his joke. Well, he had two bugle jokes. One was he'd shout fire in the hotel and blow his bugle, and the second one was 'anyone for bugle' and then he'd blow really hard on the trumpet. He had a couple more in his armoury that didn't really work. Those two were the stickers – guaranteed hilarity.

You could meet anyone at Paul's flat. He had quite a large network going through his flat. Douglas Hart became quite a good mate over

* *Take It Like a Man* (Sidgwick & Jackson, 1995). Roundhill is referred to as 'Paul Cod' and labelled 'a pond-life dealer and junkie'.

the years, the bass player for The Jesus and Mary Chain – he made the video for 'For Lovers'. Initially, Douglas was just a figure who'd be in the shadows at Paul's who didn't want anyone to see him there. He'd dash in and out, like a lot of people did.

Paul would refer to the flat as 'the salon' – as in the literary tradition – and he'd play the part of the inspiring host. He called himself the 'professor of smack'.'

XI

On the Road

*2002–2003: Early hype and a new pair of brogues. The chaos
of the first UK tour. Release of the first Libertines album. A
parting of the ways with Carl. Drag with Wolfman. The first
live TV show. Recording 'For Lovers'. A trip to France.*

'We got a lot of press attention early on. We actually got our first *NME*
front cover before the first single came out. Somehow Rough Trade
and our press guy Tony Linkin, the boss at Coalition PR who also
handled The Strokes, had it under lock with the music press. Even
though the vibe was you're not touching these boys unless you're going
to give us a good write-up, we did get some bad reviews early on –
proper nasty, some of the stuff they wrote. Carl and I used to be of the
opinion, right, if you don't like the music, don't fucking write about it,
and if you're going to get personal, we're going to come and find you.
We had murders with Tony about getting the addresses of journalists.

Carl and I went with Banny to Paris to do some press, and she treated
us to some proper expensive London brogues – matching brown
brogues. They became part of the look for a long time – jeans, leather
jackets and the brogues. We'd give them a bit of scuffing, switch the
laces around. We'd always swap laces, so I'd have his and he'd have mine,

and then maybe we'd get a Japanese kid to write their name in Japanese – always looks cool, bit of ink on the brogues. But a lot of the press we got used a shot of us in our matching little red military jackets. Our first French magazine cover used that picture, and the headline was 'Danger, Branleurs!' I asked, What does that mean? because we were carrying them round, big piles of them, our first magazine cover abroad, anywhere probably – maybe even before the *NME* – and it was 'Danger, Wankers!'

We soon discovered there is only so much that hype can do when we started touring on our own. We had quite a lot of static audiences, which is not what we thought it was all about. It wasn't the same as when you're putting on your own gig in a back room somewhere where people can just have a good time, just let themselves go. It was a forced environment, and it actually just made us more agitated, and we'd play more violently to all these crowds that didn't really seem to know what was going on, didn't really care about the songs either way. We were all deranged and hopped up on the punk vibe and completely smashed it.

It was such a huge buzz going out in the splitter van on our first UK tour – we'd only played outside of London once before, and that was with Razzers at some summer fete near John's granny's village in Oxfordshire. In my mind, it was always going to be wide open, like a psychedelic parade – nothing was going to change. We were still going to be a messy performance poetry bandit band. I managed to blag it so that either Martin or the Queens of Noize were always with us doing the merchandise. The first band T-shirt was such good quality, hand-stitched, on a blue background with a stencil of a silhouette of Francesca's face with 'Horrowshow' written on it in Gothic letters. They were hard for me to get hold of, and I was in the band.

Tabitha and Mairead used to fling themselves everywhere at the gigs – they were our only moshers for a long time. Tabitha did this thing – you know the old-fashioned way of jumping into a swimming pool, feet first, holding your nose. She'd stand on the edge of the stage, hold her nose and then backflip. Her and Mairead often got up on stage with us, crashing into amps – there was a lot of crashing about. Wolfman came along as a support act and invariably Amah-Rose would come along as well – it was all about trying to have these amazing knees-ups all round Albion. We were always dragging everyone back to some poor kid's place, who'd said you can have a party at mine, or dragging people onto the bus. There were loads of pills about, loads of cheap drugs, especially when you went up north, Manchester or Leeds, Scotland as well.

Wolfman tended to be in a perpetual state of solitude and doom, or he'd just suddenly freak out and jump out of the bus and disappear for days. I found him one time shivering in a hedge in a Nottingham hotel car park. What have you done to me? That was one of his favourite lines, What have you done to me? Get me home! Where's home? I don't have a fucking home! Steve was often knocking about – he'd get himself in a right state too. There was a gig we did in Brighton when Carl battered him with his guitar – I think Steve thought he was back in the band again and had got up on the stage. It was messy, but it was still the honeymoon period in terms of heroin and crack.

Kill City came on tour with us too. That's when I met Lisa Moorish, the band's singer, and it must have been when she got pregnant. We had a son together, Astile, born July 2003. We also took Alan and Left Hand on tour, the 'infamous' Left Hand – the *NME* was running weekly bulletins on the bad behaviour on tour, and that included Left Hand urinating in Carl's shoes. It was a strange mentality Left Hand had – they were always fighting with the world, and Carl couldn't understand that mentality. He said, Why can't we all just be on the same side? I didn't know what was going to happen with Left Hand.

James Endeacott showed up with a box full of *Up the Bracket* CDs at Oxford Zodiac on that first tour. It was the first time we'd seen the album. I'd done the artwork. I did the artwork for all the early singles and the tour posters – managed to get my foot in the door and block any idea that Rough Trade were going to do it. Well, it's supposed to be that way, isn't it? The band should do their own covers. The actual picture on the cover of the album, of police squaring up to protesters, came from some bad civil unrest in Argentina at the time. Mick Jones had found the photo, and I put a few collage-y bits on it using black gaffer tape.

That was also the night I met Nadine and her twin sister Davina – last seen getting on The Strokes tour bus. I really fell for Nadine – head over heels. I think I asked if she wanted to do the merch – that was my chat-up line. We were together on and off for a few years. She became like a comrade in arms.

At those early gigs, Carl used to have a tremendous, weird psychotic state he'd go in after he'd come off stage. He'd sit in the dressing room curled up, foetal almost, and it would have to be half an hour, forty minutes before we'd go out on the lash, all celebrating. I used to be quite protective of him in those moments. I could see how fragile he was – going on stage really mangled his head. He was obsessed with being an actor and a performer all his life, and we were both obsessed with being famous, and when it finally looked like it could happen, it turned him inside out. I could really feel his anguish.

I was always on at him to rehearse set-pieces for gigs. I'd say, Look, I'll crack you round the back of your head with my guitar on stage, and he'd say, No, no, no, I'm not doing that, I'm *never* doing that, and I'd really get the hump. The few genuine fights we did have on stage were terrifying – I thought he was going to fucking kill me. One of those early Reading or Leeds festivals we did in 2002, I gave him a gentle heel up the posterior, and that escalated pretty quick, got nasty. Whenever it reached that point, I'd think, Oh no, fuck, he's snapped.

We were already going in different directions. When we did a second *NME* front cover late in 2002,[*] I looked pretty fucked up, and there was a mention of my heroin use and the tension building in the group over drugs. I predicted then it was going to turn sour. Carl never took on the crack and smack thing. He didn't like it. There had been moments, once or twice, where Carl felt compelled to do heroin, out of desperation really, to try and get on my wavelength, trying to be sociable in the context of his friendship with me, where I was telling him it was all right, it was safe. That sounds quite dodgy on my part, but we'd always been that way, and it had gone both ways with drugs and alcohol. He was a ferocious drinker and had a gargantuan consumption of other things, mostly uppers. I have a fond memory of being sat in bed with Carl in Paris watching an old DVD of *Casablanca* smoking brown. It must have been when we were first doing gigs and promo trips in Europe. We were in a flat that belonged to one of the girls at the record company, and it was when we wrote 'Don't Look Back into the Sun'. It was the chords from 'Don't Look Back in Anger' by Oasis mixed with 'Ride into the Sun' by The Velvet Underground, hence 'Don't Look Back into the Sun' – and we both knew we had a good one with that.

Carl had become mates with Supergrass drummer Danny Goffey after we toured with them around Europe in late 2002. Even though we'd smashed a few barriers, got a bit of acclaim, we weren't famous. Supergrass were like tabloid material – legends, really. People would say I looked like Julian Casablancas, but I thought I looked a little bit like Danny Goffey, so when I was hearing these rumours about Carl getting up to all these truly Libertine-esque adventures I was awfully jealous. It was like, Why can't I be mates with them? I suppose I was just jealous of Carl meeting new people, really.

* 'The Libertines: Scrapping, screwing & getting trashed with Britain's most f***ed-up band'.

At the Rough Trade-organised party to celebrate the launch of *Up the Bracket*, I left in tears. It was an industry affair, at some bar in King's Cross. Danny was there with Carl, and I'd been at Wolfman's flat beforehand. I remember first of all they didn't want to let me in, and then when I got in, they wouldn't let me smoke crack inside. I got really upset and left, went back to Wolfman's. Wolfman was thrilled that I was so upset. Then I wore a skirt at an album-signing session at HMV on Oxford Street, and Carl didn't see the funny side of that. It was just a traditional working-class thing: get dressed up in ladies' clothes for a laugh. Wolfman and I used to do a tribute to the Queens of Noize where we'd get done up in drag, in horrible wigs, sunglasses, denim skirts, fishnets, and we'd DJ. Well, I think we got kicked out of a few clubs trying to DJ! We called ourselves Fru and Shel. All right, Fru. Hiya, Shel. People really did think we were two pissed-up birds – we had nice legs. I'd brought a denim skirt for Carl to wear, à la Wolfman, but alas he didn't dig it.

We still had this chemistry on stage. You can see it on the first TV show we did, *Later . . . with Jools Holland*. We did 'Up the Bracket', our second single. Tabitha and Mairead were in the audience going bonkers. It was an ace performance, dark and grimy. I was surprised by how good we were! Katie Bapples was there too, wearing this sado-masochistic outfit, proper Catwoman-style. A few years later, she sold a crazy story to the tabloids claiming I'd got her addicted to heroin and how we'd cut each other up with razor blades. She also said I'd forced her into a threesome with Carl and that she'd seen me in the shower with another man. Well, maybe she saw me in the shower with Wolfman once at Teesdale Street, but that doesn't mean anything. I'm not gonna shag Wolfman.

There was one night around then with razor blades, but not with her. It was when we recorded 'For Lovers' in this studio that was two little rooms above a shop somewhere, and Jake Fior had his fingers on the dials. I did the vocal in one take. I'd tried to get Carl to come along to the recording, but he refused. Afterwards, Jake put his hand in his pocket, gave us £250, and me and Wolfman had a proper session. Wolfman knew the best dealers all over London, and we sat up in south London somewhere and got all cut up. I'm looking now at my chest, and it's covered in scars from that night.

'For Lovers' was a great song, and it turned out to be a really good recording, but Rough Trade just didn't want to know. It was recorded in 2002, but it took so long for it to come out . . . over a year and a half. It was murder getting it out. Jake took credit for the arrangement and production, which was fair enough, but he bought a lot of Wolfman's writing credits. We were in a pub in Angel, really skint, and he gave Wolfman, I think it was £700, which was a lot of money, but still, when you think about how successful that song became, it's tuppence for what that percentage of the song came to be worth. I think it's not too self-congratulatory to say I brought things out of Wolfman, just by pushing him or by putting a guitar in his hands or recording stuff. He didn't get out of the house a lot. If it wasn't for me, a lot of this wouldn't have happened with Wolfman – it'd just have been dark mumblings from under the blanket. I did my best to get him recognition, and a lot of time it was hard – Rough Trade didn't want to know. I wanted to share Wolfman with the world.

Back then I think Carl or Rough Trade thought I was pretending these songs were written by Wolfman just to piss them off. I can't think why else it'd be such a struggle to get recognition or get them released. Everything was moving so fast with The Libertines, and there was so much out of my control. I just wanted to record as much as I could in the way I felt most comfortable.

One of the final straws for Carl, before I got kicked out for the first time, was when I dragged him to France. Somewhere along the way we'd met these two French guys who had this little label called Dialectik, and they said do you want to come and do some recording? I made a list of things we wanted: a Vox AC30, vintage guitars, and £10k of heroin and £10k of coke, and they agreed, but of course none of it materialised. They just sent a minibus over and Alan Wass, Carl and me went with these French fellas. Alan was going to produce the tracks, which he ended up doing. At that time, Alan had changed. He'd gone from someone who swore he'd never do hard drugs or wear ripped jeans, being so proud of going to Glastonbury and not getting any mud on his all-white Adidas tracksuit, to suddenly being Clint Eastwood – jeans, a poncho and massive leather boots. I was in a newsagent in Camden Town one night, two in the morning, and I was a bit drunk and got into some argument with these five Somali lads, and they started attacking me, and Alan came out of nowhere – he had a big hat on, long coat, swept them all up in his arms and put them through the window of this all-night shop.

We ended up in this studio, Garage Hermetique, in a suburb of Nantes, and did these songs without Gary and John. It didn't matter to me that they hadn't come along – they were great songs, brilliant songs. We did 'Narcissist' and 'The Ha-Ha Wall' that both ended up on The Libertines' second album – and they needed to be recorded. I think we did them amazing justice with Alan on drums. There's a little seven inch knocking about, a really cool one, released in 2007. Rough Trade wouldn't let Dialectik release the stuff at the time.

Carl definitely switched on that trip. We were in this cheap Formule 1 hotel, twenty euros a night, and Alan and I were smoking brown on the bottom bunk. Carl got the hump. To be fair to him, he'd had years of chaos, and he was starting to enjoy things being organised, sound-checks and riders, but for me it was the other way round. That was horrible for me, to be in that system, someone else organising the recordings and gigs. I sort of even became allergic to setlists. Anything organised or industry-orientated began to wind me up. I remember I was late for some video shoot, and James Endeacott came round to get me, but I refused to come – and they shot the video without me. Bastards. It was a pretty crap video anyway, for 'I Get Along', which Rough Trade had some plan to release as a single in America.

I was still putting on my own shows at the Rhythm Factory, and they were always quite messy affairs with a lot of the gang there – this glorious Arcadian rabble I had and a load of new, young unsigned bands – The Paddingtons from Hull, Martin had started Selfish Cunt, Dominic Masters had The Others, Johnny had Razorlight, Steve had The IVs. We were in and out of each other's radar system. Ben Bailey from Thee Unstrung helped me out of a few tight corners. I think I felt like I'd almost managed to put the Arcadian cabaret of old into existence. That is what I wanted, whereas Carl wanted to keep on the grindstone for a bit. We'd never really had an alternative before to the ramshackle way, because without me booking the gigs in these wonderful and strange places there wouldn't have been any fucking gigs. Whereas now we had people lining up to give us gigs.

I wouldn't say I had hostility towards Rough Trade. I just felt we deserved something a bit more maverick. I wanted something a bit more out there and forceful in regard to the Arcadian dream, the trippy-ness of what I wanted to be doing rather than the conveyor-belt vibe. I had a real belief in poetry and the otherworldliness of music and culture being able to save the world. I was on a strong anti-capitalism kick at that time and had been for a few years – I was all for social revolution or a revolution of any kind. I was just desperate to channel my energies into something worthwhile, really, full of revolutionary spirit. I wanted to make it as explosive as possible – that's how I was feeling at the time: a bit explosive, a bit combustible. Everything was coming to a head. We were finally booked to appear on *Top of the*

Pops in January 2003 with 'Time for Heroes' sort of scraping into the top twenty. I felt it was an important time, and I was really revved up. I really believed in what I was doing, and I sensed at the time Rough Trade weren't full believers in the Arcadian dream, so I needed to push that little bit harder.'

XII
America

2003 (part one): Top of the Pops *debut. The guerrilla gigs at the Albion Rooms. Bad behaviour at the* NME *awards. Being booted out of the band. An addict in Japan. Abandoned by Iggy Pop. American TV debut and a sudden urge to record – the Babyshambles Session.*

'I had a wicked French military jacket that I'd nicked from Portobello Road for that first *Top of the Pops*. I thought I looked great, and my vocals were live, but the crowd they had in didn't really seem to be 'Time for Heroes' aficionados. I had to work really hard to get, through the camera, to whoever was watching out there who was going to be susceptible to its charms. Looking back, it was probably the start of a series of anti-climaxes, or disappointments, frustrations, I had with the band that led to me getting booted out.

After we were on *Top of the Pops*, we got mobbed outside a venue for the first time. We were headlining the Astoria in London, the biggest show we'd done at the time, and Carl and I looked at each other as we were signing things. We'd been after that superficial buzz for a while, people mobbing you, wanting a photo of you, or wanting you to sign something, but it didn't really fulfil me. I remember there was a homeless guy standing back from the crowd watching us, and I made eye contact with him as if to say, Can you score for me? Just the old eye-brow raised, and I nipped off down Old Compton Street with him and picked up a couple of rocks. I had this pang of sadness as I got the bus back to Whitechapel to carry on the session as opposed to hanging out with Carl, who was going out and partying on that Rough Trade industry vibe.

There was still positive stuff when you feel like you're shooting upwards into something glorious, but then you realise you've got to do it all again the next night. When you become part of the industry, you've got to perform, you're almost whipped into it. It was all tour managers and regimes: it was the industrialisation of The Libertines. At the gigs we were doing around the UK in early 2003, I got really into getting fans on stage. That became a real feature. I had this idea in my mind, I used to talk about it in interviews, of breaking down the barriers – which involved getting as many kids as possible onto the tour bus or onto the stage. Again, this would piss everyone off. There was always someone standing on a guitar tuner, cutting the line or something, but it was all good fun, all part of it for me.

This was where the internet was a godsend. I was able to reach out to people directly on a newfound platform – our website Libertines.org that a couple of fans had set up. On the first day I logged onto the chat forum I pretended to be a couple of people. They were the very first posts on the fansite, stuff like, I'm sure I saw one of The Libertines sitting on a wall, trying to generate a bit of engagement. I felt a bit silly for doing that. Mainly I used the forum to advertise spontaneous gigs. I'd just put a notice up in the morning and do the gig in the afternoon or evening at home in Teesdale Street. I didn't call these spontaneous happenings 'guerrilla gigs' – the press started calling them that. They were a great way to have it up, to try new song ideas as well get a bit of cash in hand. I was also really into meeting the kids that came. I wanted to find out who would buy a ticket for £10. It was often young teenage kids who'd grown up in London with parents that let them out all night, how I wished I'd grown up.

The guerrilla gigs were always a proper buzz for me. I loved it, really enjoyed it, but Carl, John and Gary were really against them. The problem for them was we started getting lots of press about it. Journalists loved the idea – they were like, This is great, The Libertines giving back to their fans. So, they went along with it in the press – Carl's no mug, he could see it was creating a legend, a myth – but it was their idea of a proper grim nightmare. I'm not saying that to be nasty, that's just how it was – a complete anathema to them. They hated it. It was always through dodgy amps, there was no one to change the guitar strings, no soundcheck, just setting up and playing in the front room. Carl was happy to take the praise in the press, but he never wanted to do these gigs – used to rile me up intensely. Carl would also question where the money was going, but I was the one who'd gone down to the internet café and put the advert up. I'd done the legwork! And I'd do the show if Carl played or not.

The *NME* awards when The Libertines won Best New Band set the tone for about the next ten years of my life. I remember Geoff Travis saying how it was so horrible seeing me so out of it and how getting an award seemed ironic to him, but I was imbued with this sense of chaos, added to mischievousness. I just wanted to liven things up a bit. I think I threw a few firecrackers among the silver tables set up for bands and industry figures. It was all a bit weird and bland, these self-congratulatory awards with everyone sat at these tables without indulging in any kind of food fight or anything. I felt almost obliged.

It wasn't long after that I got kicked out of the band. They went to Germany for a gig without me. Absolutely outrageous! I was doing a little run around King's Cross to score while the tour bus was parked up, and when I got back forty minutes later, they were gone. It was pretty disturbing. Whatever elements of my behaviour outraged Carl, there was definitely some things that he did that shocked and confused me, upset me, and that would have been one of them. It was unfathomable even if ultimately it wasn't his decision. I can see myself now, sat on the verge by the bridge on the Caledonian Road in my ripped jeans, thinking maybe it was joke, that they'd parked round the corner or something. The gig in Germany was supposed to be the beginning of a European tour and that got cancelled. Very disappointing.

I was brought back in a few weeks later to do gigs in Japan and America. It was actually when we were in Tokyo that it first dawned on me I was a heroin addict. When we first got to the country, I had plenty with me in my guitar case, but that soon ran out, and it's a tricky place to score, Japan. I'd never had to go without it for a few days. As a budding addict you're aware of this idea of withdrawal, but it doesn't really hit you until the first time. It was always pretty bad, psychologically especially. At this gig we did in Tokyo, I smashed up the drum kit and kicked John's amp over, and Gary and John left the stage. I was on stage on my own, and I said to the crowd, This is better, isn't it, you know what I mean? It was a bold venture to take the band in a new direction. I think Carl might have come on and played drums for a bit. Then I ran across to a bar opposite the venue, and, this is true, there was a blind guy playing darts, and suddenly I remember being really focused on that. I ran back to get Carl and everyone, saying, Look, look at this, there's a blind guy playing darts, but everyone was a little bit sullen.

I was really raw, feeling a bit constrained with the framework of The Libertines as it was. I just really wanted to lash out at the band. I wanted the lads to be part of the chaos and the fun, and everyone was reining it in a bit, and I was really reining it out, if that's an expression. At another gig in Japan, I made one of my first attempts at stage diving, and the crowd just parted, and I cracked my skull on the dancefloor: I was lying there half unconscious, got carted off in an ambulance.

I told my mum I was taking heroin at my Nanny Liverpool's funeral. I had to fly home early from Japan to be there. I just presumed she'd be really understanding about it. I was saying, Yeah, I've taken it, but it's all right, it's quite nice, and it all kicked off and went downhill from there, really, with Mum and Dad. I just thought because I was starting to make it as a professional musician, for want of a better word, that I was then justified in making completely independent decisions about everything, and taking heroin didn't seem like a big thing, but it didn't really go down well at all. Mum and Dad drove me back to London from the funeral. It was the night before the flight to America, and I got them to drop me off at Paul Ro's, and I spent the night there.

I felt like I was going to explode in America – it was the perfect place to really go for it. Part of me wanted to be the most fucked-up person in the world. I remember as soon as I arrived, I was in a bush with a bottle of whiskey at Coachella Festival in California, and Iggy Pop actually appeared – Iggy Pop and The Stooges were a main attraction that year – but he was jogging. He stopped and said something like, I've been there, but now I'm into jogging, and he was drinking through a straw from a bottle of water. So, even Iggy Pop had abandoned me. Then the power got cut quite early on while we were on stage. I think there was a curfew and the day's schedule had overrun. We tried to play acoustically but got escorted off by security. Set the tone, really.

When we arrived in New York, I felt compelled, driven to record. I was carrying an acoustic guitar with me the whole time, just plotting up outside cafés, playing and writing. I tried to get Rough Trade to pay for a studio and they wouldn't. I was in the Rough Trade offices at the Chelsea Hotel, and something really annoyed me about the fact they were wearing shorts in the office. I don't know why, wouldn't annoy me now, but at the time it really pissed me off. I think I shouted at them, I am Rough Trade! That was my embarrassing moment. Alison Mosshart from The Kills was knocking about the Chelsea Hotel. I asked her to marry me. I really liked her. I recognised her from about five years before when me and Carl had answered an advert in *Loot* looking for a room and this suicidal Goth girl had shown us round this flat in south London somewhere. She ran away from me in the Chelsea Hotel.

We had hotel apartments on Rivington Street in Manhattan, on the Lower East Side, where we were all plotted up – we all had a nice suite each. Well, Carl and I had a nice suite each. I was going round with a girl called Nancy who had stayed at Teesdale Street for a while. She was a photographer and filmmaker and a bit of a scenester, seemed to know a lot of people. She was good fun. We were on the same sort of wavelength. We were on top of the apartment building in the sunlight one time, working on some songs, and Carl came along, and she was telling him to stay out of it, saying he was interfering in our creative process. Carl got the right hump with her.

I was scoring crack from a homeless guy called Chris, looked like George Floyd. I'd seen him picking up fag ends off the street, and he came up to me and said, You got a real cigarette? We formed a firm friendship that lasted about four days. I actually got him to join the band. I'd been working on a new song called 'That Bowery Song', and I got him to sing along at the apartment, and it was sounding great. So, I got him on stage when we did the Bowery Ballroom, and it was a disaster. He completely froze, fell apart, lost his nerve. One of the reviews said it looked like I'd just dragged some crack bum onto the stage

– quite an accurate view. Chris switched on me at some point, and he wouldn't get out of my apartment. He put the fear of God into me – I think he might have had a gun. Carl chased him off for me, managed to avert danger. It was all a bit on top, and Chris threatened to come back and burn the hotel down and shoot everyone.

Damon Albarn turned up at that Bowery Ballroom gig, and that accentuated the divide in the band, really, because he was all over Carl. There was a party after the show, and it was a Rough Trade organised one, and I was really against the whole thing. In the end, I ran off into the night to score, and Carl ended up going off into the night with Damon.

We also played CBGBs while we were in New York and were on a few cool magazine covers. I've seen footage online of a fourth gig we did, in Philadelphia at The North Star Bar, and it's amazing, but you can tell Carl's heart is not really in it. After the gig, I went to this basketball court to score some rocks off these huge black guys. One of the lads in the support band took me. Then we drove back to New York in a minibus: me, James Endeacott, Banny and the boys. It was the only time I was that in your face with the rest of them about crack. I was smoking it in the back seat of the bus and blowing it in everyone else's faces. They were all silent, seething. Maybe I was looking for a reaction, but I also just wanted to show them you could relax on it. It was a different vibe, the crack in America. It wasn't as digi as the stuff in London, where you might get prang or uptight smoking it, as opposed to emanating good vibes. In America it seemed a lot smoother, sweeter. I was smoking it through this glass flume. That's one thing Chris had passed on to me – they all smoked it through these little glass flumes.

I was feeling a lot of resentment towards Carl. I felt certain songs that were being credited to us both were mine, and I always made a point of saying, Carl sings that song, I sing these songs. I do cherish my creative partnership with him, and we have written a load of shit-hot stuff together, and even the stuff that's not written together we've recorded together and we've both carried each other along in the belief the song was great, but – and this is bit of a harsh thing to say – some of those songs were really all mine. I felt back then I was giving Carl a lot even by letting him sing certain songs, like the way we did 'I Get Along' on *The Late Show* with David Letterman. He took that song on as his own by singing it, and he did write the chorus, the 'I Get Along' bit, but the verses were mine, so I could easily have sung that one.

We were all really excited to be playing on American telly. It was a real moment of pride and celebration for everyone, but Carl was really worried about me playing up, and it's almost like I went too far the other way – even to the point of stopping playing to prevent the microphone falling over after I fell into it during the guitar solo bit. That was really, really odd, really strange.

Things were really starting to fragment. I had this childish urge, basically, to assert myself as the lead songwriter – to declare with strong evidence that I was the creative force and that The Libertines were just a show band for the industry, which, again, might be a little bit harsh, but that's really the way I saw them. So, I found this really cool studio, Sorcerer Sound on Mercer Street where Lou Reed, Run DMC and John Cage had all recorded, and I went in, and I was playing for hours and hours – just press record. Mostly it was just me playing acoustic and this drummer I'd known from the mod days in London – Spiky Phil. He'd been a bit of a face on the scene and now he was a tailor in New York.

I recorded not just the bedrock of the second Libertines album but also the bedrock of the first Babyshambles album plus loads of amazing songs that I'd record later solo and some great covers too of stuff I was into then – The Coral, The La's, The Smiths, Morrissey, Ocean Colour Scene and Ian Brown. Rough Trade must have got wind of it, because after the first session Carl and John came down, sort of half-heartedly. John played keyboards at some point on something. There was quite a cool version of 'Don't Look Back into the Sun' that Carl played trumpet on. Adam Green from the band Moldy Peaches also came down. He'd been at the party after the Bowery Ballroom show. He did a version of 'What a Waster', and we did a version of Moldy Peaches' 'Who's Got the Crack', where you can hear Carl and me having a little back and forth about smoking white. The relationship with Carl was as strained as it had been at any time in the past. He was having serious doubts about the future of the band.

So, I had all these wicked songs newly recorded, and I remember suddenly thinking it'd be a good idea to put them all online for free – not thinking specifically to get up everybody's noses, but thinking I was going to die any minute, so I wanted to get the songs out. I advertised on the Libertines.org fansite for someone who had the wherewithal to whack it online, and I had this clandestine meeting with this Asian American girl at the Chelsea Hotel, and I gave her the files in a brown paper envelope. Then there was a really tense couple of days as I waited for them to go up.

They went online as the *Babyshambles Session*, a three-CD set of approximately fifty songs. The name Babyshambles actually came from Tabitha, her pet name for me. Hard-core fans got hold of it, but it didn't have the combustible effect I'd hoped for, like, Oh, here's all these amazing songs. Wow, we were wrong, Peter is not such a fucked-up drug addict. That proved to me it wasn't about the songs or the music for Rough Trade. For them it was more about how they could coordinate or harness the energy in a neatly packaged way. The *NME* didn't even pick up on it, no one picked up on it! Whereas for me it was like apocalypse-type stuff. I was thinking it was going to be this great celebration of all these amazing songs, and it wasn't like that at all. It proved to me that it needed to be all nice and packaged and shiny and released by a label for people to know whether or not they could like the music.'

XIII
Burglar

2003 (part two): Recording 'Don't Look Back into the Sun'. Alone on the Whitechapel roof. Out of The Libertines again. A descent to rock bottom. Trying to start a new version of The Libertines. The birth of Babyshambles and a son. A first visit to rehab. The burglary of Carl's flat.

'When I got back from New York, I got The Paddingtons to do a guerrilla gig with me at Wolfman's basement flat on Gunter Grove in Chelsea. While I'd been in New York, there were rumours Wolfman had died, but rumours of Wolfman's death were always greatly exaggerated. He's died and come back at least six times to my knowledge. Jake Fior had found him this flat, but within two weeks we'd trashed it. Of course, the gig filtered back to Rough Trade and to Carl, and, compounded by the fact the Babyshambles Sessions were now up online, they felt I was out of control, but I was on a mission to do what I wanted. It sounds a bit corny, but I felt I was perfectly expressing myself as an artist. But it wasn't running parallel to the professional career. The two things seemed completely disconnected to me: Rough Trade and the industry machine and being a songwriter and artist didn't seem compatible. Not only that, the situation I was in with The

Libertines wasn't compatible with my songwriting or with how I was feeling about performing. I felt I was really hitting my stride as an artist and songwriter, and somehow The Libertines wasn't conducive to that stride.

I did turn up at RAK Studios to record 'Don't Look Back into the Sun' at the start of summer, but I was with Wolfman, and Bernard Butler, who Rough Trade had decided to book to produce the band, wouldn't have him in the studio. We had a big argument on the pavement outside. Gary came out and said something to Wolfman that stuck in my mind. He said, Wolfman, Peter's got to take care of business, man. I was like, Oh no, fuck this, and I went off smoking crack with Wolfman. The band didn't seem genuine to me, and my heart wasn't in it. I did eventually wander in for a few hours. I could hear them warming up without me, and I was so upset. I was a bit of a mess emotionally, in a general state of mental flux. It was hard to face Carl, and pretty quickly Bernard and I started shouting at each other, kicking things about. I offered him out: Say that again, and I'll smash you in the fucking face. In his mind, I was so out of it. He did my guitar parts on 'Don't Look Back into the Sun' when I wasn't there. Bastard. What made it even more annoying, weirdly, was the fact you couldn't tell it wasn't me. I listened for little flourishes that weren't Doherty stock standard notes but there weren't any – which was almost more painful. They fixed it up and whacked all that piano on at the end.

The guerrilla gig on the Whitechapel roof was the kiss of death. I'd organised it with some artist who had a studio – a lovely space – and advertised it as me and Carl playing acoustic. People turned up, and we had cups of lemonade and a PA system, all good family fun. I really thought he was going to show up, but it was the day of his birthday, and his sister and all his other mates had organised some karaoke party for him that I wasn't invited to and didn't really know about. His argument was he never was going to show up, but he'd said he would – otherwise I wouldn't have advertised the gig online.

Then they went off to tour Europe without me. Carl called me from the cross-Channel ferry to tell me I was surplus to requirements. Banny had left me a message saying, Don't come to the shows, but I said I wanted to hear it from him. I thought if he doesn't want me in the band, that's enough – so that was it, really. They put out a statement saying the split was temporary and blamed my 'current condition', adding 'Peter is unwell'.

After Europe, they did a UK tour without me too. I tried to get into the gig they did at Kentish Town Forum with this Irish lad Owen, but it all kicked off. Alan Wass was with us, and he got bounced down the road outside the Forum – it was horrible. Alan got a proper kicking. Owen ran a crackhouse from his council flat in Kentish Town. I was staying there with Nadine, really scraping the bottom of the barrel. I'd been kicked out of Teesdale Street and had nowhere to go, but I needed a steady supply of crack and heroin. Owen was part of a whole new world of people who really knew a fifty-quid shakedown when they saw one. I was on the street with him one time, feeling this real dark energy, and he said I had to prove myself. So, I snatched a phone off this bloke on a bike at the traffic lights, and then I had to go out and do it again and get a better phone. It was as low as I'd been.

Jeannette Lee got me to go to rehab. I told her I was looking to put a new band together, and she said there was somebody she wanted me to meet, a keyboard player, but she wouldn't tell me which band he was in. I still don't know, might have been Elastica. He tried to talk to me about drug use, and then the next thing I was being whisked off to a hotel somewhere in the countryside that Rough Trade had fixed up – Farm Place in Surrey, reputedly 'Britain's answer to the Betty Ford

Clinic'. I wasn't into it – you have to stop taking drugs for a start, and that really hit me like a hammer blow to the head, and the idea of having to do group therapy absolutely appalled me. I refused to have anything to do with group therapy . . . just the idea of it was complete anathema to me.

I thought I'd settle in for a few days, write a few posts for Libertines. org and then do a self-publicised breakout. That cycle went on for years, really. It was never a heartfelt commitment to getting clean when I went to rehab, not until more recent times where I've done rehab for months at a time and got into the swing of sobriety a bit more. I'd always dramatise those first few rehabs when I wrote the blog posts. I'd have myself on the operating table with loads of IVs of various descriptions – normally it was just something they used to take your pulse with, put two stickers on your nipples and your belly. Every time I went, I'd get a box of Converse All Stars off Rough Trade and a novel from Jeannette: *Moby Dick* or *Crime and Punishment*, some great books – in fact, they kept me in rehab longer than the treatment most times – then I was off on my way in my new All Stars.

That first time I was sat around talking about drugs at this place in the country, and it just made me ache to use again. I did a week, then someone told me Katie Bapples was getting married to Wolfman, so I got the train back to London and ended up back at Filthy's. Of course, the wedding turned out to be a complete lie. Someone said afterwards it was just Wolfman's way of getting me out of rehab so I could pay for him to get a fix. I know he comes across as a bit of a bastard a lot of the time, but he was. Completely. He won't deny that. And in the years after this, I'll probably describe a lot of times where he's been even more of a bastard.

Will play for bed and breakfast was one of my slogans at the time. I started staying with a friend of Wolfman's called Marcus who had this

Edwardian terrace in Shepherd's Bush, quite close to Wormwood Scrubs. I used to call Marcus's place the pirate ship, but it was just a big mess of drugs and music. I was sort of collecting these old sailor tattoos. I got Gladys, the mermaid, on my forearm – at that time the only vein I used to go in was just on the tail of the mermaid. At first, it was me, Nadine and these twins from Preston shacked up at Marcus's. They were two teenage girls, fifteen or sixteen, who'd come to Libertines gigs up north and then one day turned up in London. They were really geeky and bespectacled, but they could play all Carl's guitar parts, all the really complicated parts, like the 'Don't Look Back into the Sun' solo. I thought, If they're going to carry on without me as The Libertines, I've got as much right to carry on as The Libertines too – that's the way I saw it, and that's where these twins came in, briefly, until it occurred to me to just admit defeat on that front, because Rough Trade had such a tight hold on the name, or the idea of the name.

Then Neil Thunders and Steve moved in, and they brought Max, who had been the drummer in The China Dolls, Steve's goth metal band in Scarborough when he was a teenager. So, I was toying with T'Libertines – Max, Neil and Steve all being Yorkshiremen – or Thee Libertines . . . two Es. Then, fuck it, Babyshambles. We all got Babyshambles tattoos, and we holed up to rehearse at this crackhouse on Gascony Avenue in Kilburn that Marcus had introduced me to. This mad old woman ran the place. She said she was the daughter of a Persian diplomat, but she was now shacked up with some pisshead in this makeshift crackhouse in an old Victorian townhouse. She ran it with an iron fist, Paul Ro style – had a proper taxation system going.

I wrote 'Lamentable Ballad of Gascony Avenue' on the Puta Madres album about the place. Lisa Moorish came round to Gascony Avenue one time, and we had a massive row on the steps. I think it was the day she was going into hospital to have our baby, and I was supposed to drive her there, but I was in no fit state to do that. But I was there for the birth of Astile at the UCL hospital.

Babyshambles recorded a demo at Gascony Avenue, and I stuck it online. The girls who'd set up Libertines.org had now set up Babyshambles.com for me. It occurred to me that if the songs were good – which I believed they were – then whether or not I made any money from selling the music wouldn't matter because people would love the songs and therefore come and see me play – that was my reasoning. We did a load of demos that I put online for free. The songs were getting really dark, and the atmosphere was really dark a lot of the time in these various hideouts.

For all the sorrow and slummy-ness of my existence, those songs elevated me to a place in my heart that was beyond reproach. I longed to be able to play my songs to people who wanted to hear them, not even for money or drugs, just for peace of mind, and it was like I was in this raging war against the industry to prove I could do it that way – I could get music out there and make a living from it and not have to play by their rules of having to go to rehab.

But those early Babyshambles gigs were always chaos. We got booked to do a gig at the Tap N Tin in Medway, Kent, through this kid Dean Fragile who ran the legendary Friday-night indie knees-up there. I think it was around the time The Libertines were doing Glastonbury without me, and I bought this old black Beamer off this fella who lived across the road from Marcus for £150 so we could get out to Kent, but it didn't even get us out of London – it broke down. Then when we did get there, midway through the gig, Neil Thunders wandered off stage.

Neil drove me to Carl's in this red Ford Fiesta he'd borrowed off a junkie couple he knew who were visiting from Scarborough. I hadn't gone there to rob Carl. I wanted to see if it was true what I'd heard – that they'd gone to Japan without me for a festival date at Fuji Rock. It turned out to be true, but when I got to Carl's door, I thought he was actually there inside in the flat. I'd been up for a few days, and I thought I saw shadows through the frosted glass, and I started shouting and then I booted the door in.

It was a lovely basement flat on Harley Street, Marylebone. I remember being so choked up when I got in there. I was in tears. He had a collection of photos from over the years and a poster his mum had made to celebrate some Libertines gig or something that I hadn't been to – my first instinct was to burn them all, but I left all that stuff alone and just took the little items of value, the DVD player, a guitar that I recognised as being Danny Goffey's, a harmonica, just stupid stuff, a laptop and a bit of cash, and just literally put it in the car outside the flat and that was that – off to Gascony Avenue. A bit naughty, really.

The next morning, Saturday, I panicked and thought, Fuck, I need to put the stuff back, and then literally the next thing I knew the Flying Squad turned up and nicked me. I'd told Lisa what I'd done and she thought she was doing the right thing by me, that I needed to be dealt a short sharp shock for my own good before things got worse. It was the most bungled burglary ever, if you want to call it that – very unprofessional and unpremeditated. Exhibit A was a photograph of a Reebok Classic print on the face of the door – in the interview, they had it measured out in the digital imagery, my trainer print. The Flying Squad were over the moon – they mustn't get such easy nickings very often, so they capitalised. There was some ham in the fridge at Carl's that I stole, and it was out of date. I got my comeuppance there as well. I missed my first court appearance due to food poisoning. I eventually pleaded guilty to burglary at Horseferry Magistrates on 11 August with a date set for sentencing a month later.

I got bailed to Marcus's and given probation. I went to my probation report in Shepherd's Bush in readiness for the trial, and my probation officer said to me, Look, say you're doing crack and heroin, just play up your drug use, and you'll get off with a court order. I did this interview with the *Evening Standard*, really going to town on my crippling heroin and crack addition and genuine regret over the burglary, apologising to Carl. The idea of going to the nick didn't ever really occur to me. I think once I started injecting and was still breathing, I thought I'd pretty much averted all danger. And I was injecting frequently. I think I thought I was untouchable. And I was told by all sources I wouldn't get a custodial sentence – that my first robbery offence really didn't warrant a sentence. No one thought I'd get sent to prison, certainly not Lisa or Carl.

I've read in some retellings of this infamous incident that Carl's sister Lucie was in the flat when I booted the door down. She wasn't there, but they were sharing the flat, and Carl maintains I went through her underwear drawer. That's what got him when he heard the news. He was told I went through her underwear drawer, but I definitely didn't. I maybe opened it, and once I realised it was underwear, I closed it. Carl didn't know anything about the burglary until I was nicked. He didn't know the stuff was sat outside in the car for twenty-four hours – the items were still in the car when the police came. I hadn't nicked the stuff and taken it off to sell it. I'd done it as a sort of wild act of madness. We've discussed it since. I know there's also been things said about him grassing me up but he didn't. Not at all. And there was never an option for him to drop the charges.'

XIV
Wandsworth

2003 (part three): A deep cut on The Libertines
tattoo. A disastrous London debut for Babyshambles
following a suicide attempt. Sentenced to six months
in Wandsworth – the grime of what actually happened
inside. A reunion with Carl at the 'Freedom gig'.

'Things ended horribly at Marcus's. I felt the honour of these Arcadian disciples was at stake and ended up having a big row with Marcus that threatened to get violent – basically all kinds of carnage kicked off. A nightmare. I went back to crash at Jake Fior's spare flat. That's where I was when I watched them do 'Don't Look Back into the Sun' on *Top of the Pops*. I was with Nadine – we had a mattress on the floor and a little telly on a chair. It was with their new guitarist, American Anthony Rossamando, who looked like a lame version of The Strokes, but they made him put his hair over his eyes so you can't even see it's someone taking my place necessarily. I cut myself quite deeply, opened up the Libertines tattoo quite profoundly that night. I was very upset – more deranged, actually, I suppose.

While I was on probation, Wolfman and I ended up trashing a room at this hotel in Clapham Common, the Windmill Hotel. We were nicked and taken to Brixton Police Station, but even then I didn't think I'd be sent down when I got to court. I'd hide out sometimes with Steve, who had started squatting at Wolfman's old place on Gunter Grove with his missus Stephanie, this American girl who was a model. One night Lisa came over with Astile, and we left Steve and his missus to babysit. Lisa and I went out into the night, went into loads of clubs. The sun was coming up by the time we got over to Gascony Avenue, and she went off to get the car while I ran off to score. Somehow this deal went wrong, and someone grabbed me in a doorway and pulled a knife. I thought I was going to get stabbed, but Lisa came belting up in her little Jeep, jumped out and came wading in, screaming at this guy, punched him, grabbed me and threw me into the Jeep, and we drove off into the dawn – really dramatic. She basically saved my life was the way I saw it. We got back to Gunter Grove, and Steve and Stephanie were in complete shock because Astile hadn't stopped crying for the seven hours we'd been away.

This is when Babyshambles played at the Troubadour club, in Earl's Court in late August 2003. The place had a bit of reputation as an artistic and cultural hub – Dylan was supposed to have played there, and it really had a vibe about it. It was meant to be our big London debut show, and both Wolfman and I had shaved our heads as a way to signify this new beginning, but it was doomed. On the afternoon of the gig, Neil Thunders tried to hang himself from a cherry tree at Gunter Grove. He came wandering up the road with his long woollen scarf that he'd used to hang himself still connected to the branch that had snapped. It's not funny, but it became a comic anecdote. This is my bass player for that night's gig, wandering down Gunter Grove with this long scarf attached to a branch after an unsuccessful suicide attempt.

My mum also turned up for that gig with my Nanny Doll. Mum was living in Holland, where Dad was now posted, and came to meet me beforehand and was trying to get me to go back to rehab. She recalled us walking through a cemetery and me throwing myself to the ground, crying or something, saying, Mum, just forget about me. That sounds like me: I think that's a solid foundation of my character, prone to despair or melancholy. I was definitely battling the demons. I know I was wearing a wicked Burberry mac that day – it was absolutely the nuts – and a straw hat. It was my look at the time, with a maroon Fred Perry, scuffed brogues and jeans.

It was a shocking gig – one review called it 'too painful for words'. Each member of the band would start up different songs at the same time. The idea was, as in the early days of The Libertines, that I'd be the songwriting powerhouse and Steve would be the elegant frontman – but his memory for lyrics hadn't improved, so it was all a bit messy. My nan had brought Pandy to the gig, a teddy bear I'd had since the day I was born that AmyJo gave to me. Nanny Doll and my mum took a taxi back to Cricklewood halfway through the gig. My nan came on stage with Pandy, said, Got to go now, Pete, gave me a kiss and walked off stage. She and my mum thought it was a fantastic gig! Meanwhile, Wolfman and Scarborough Steve are fighting over bags of gear behind the amp. Scarborough Steve was fighting a lot that night. Alan McGee, who was interested in managing Babyshambles, was at that gig with Lisa. I think my mum had a word with her. She had a habit of having a word with any girlfriend of mine she met, Nadine or anyone. They'd tell me afterwards, Oh, your mum took me aside and said, Run while you've got the chance. That was the recurring theme. She'd always say, Get yourself away from him, you're just a nice kid, he'll drag you down. My mum was serious in those moments when she could see I was using. I think that Troubadour gig ended with Wolfman getting punched by Steve, and then I ran off sick into the night, had a bad hit or something, staggered all the way to Regent's Park with Amah-Rose.

Jake Fior took me to Horseferry Magistrates Court on 8 September for sentencing for the burglary. I don't recall anybody from the management or record company or band being there, but I had this troupe of Arcadian apostles in the gallery, and my nan was there holding my straw hat and Pandy. Uncle John, my dad's younger brother, had brought her. My mum and dad were in Holland. It was Mum's fiftieth birthday. I sort of swanned in, expecting a slap on the wrist, and the magistrate turned round and had a right pop at me for being a drug user and sent me away without a flinch. I was absolutely dumbfounded. There was an element of shock. It was the maximum sentence he could give me as a magistrate for a single offence – six months.

When I got to HMP Wandsworth, Category B, the first cellmate I had, said, Eh, what you in for, Doherty? Burglary. He asked me how old I was. I said I was twenty-four. He said, Oh, I've just heard on the radio about a twenty-four year old who's been done for burglary on his mate, he's in a band or something. That was quite funny. I was quite pleased at that. I felt that familiarity immediately. I didn't tell him it was me. I think it also got a few small columns in the tabloids – that was a rarity for me at the time. I wasn't really that famous at the time, sort of a minor rock-'n'-roll figure.

I was in that cell for just one night, but all that night this guy was going on about all the crimes he'd committed – it was just horrendous. He was getting really excited, sat on the top bunk, his legs swinging up and down constantly, saying to me, What's your favourite weapon, then? Do you like this? Do you like that? talking about all these different weapons. I knew he just wanted me to ask him. So I said, What's your favourite weapon? And he smiled, big grin. He jumped down off the top bunk, and with immaculate timing, not deliberately comic, he landed and said, Mace! All day long, mate. All day long. He was in for moving into a Barratt show home, and when they tried to get him out, he'd defended his newfound territory with a couple of machetes – not his favourite weapon of choice, obviously. I never saw that bloke again.

Next I was put in a cell on my own in A-wing on the ground floor, must have been the induction wing, and that first morning I was woken up by this fella banging on my cell window going, Oi, Donnargy. He called me Donnargy, this bloke. He went, Donnargy, look, and he was holding up a dead rat by its tail. He was cleaning outside in the bit between the barbed wire and the cell window. He was this fucking huge skinhead geezer from Sutton, and he kind of took me under his wing. He was only twenty-two – he'd been in for three years already, and he was in for seven more. He was only a kid, really, but he was much bigger than me and more sort of prison-wise, although there was something really innocent about him. He said we had an affinity because he was into rock 'n' roll. It turned out he wasn't actually. It was just that his brother liked Linkin Park. He got me a job cleaning and sort of protected me. We had this agreement he was going to be my security when he got out. He'd get us a bit of gear, tiny little bits smuggled in where you'd have what he called a 'Ready Brek glow'.

There was some sort of massive heatwave at the time – it was like the hottest summer on record since 1540 – and as the day wore on there were real problems with people collapsing because of the heat, water problems . . . it was all a bit Dickensian.

This might sound a bit sick, but I enjoyed the uniform – it really captured something militaristic and nostalgic for me, everyone in the grey tracksuits or red tracksuits and you had to wear the pin-striped shirt with the HMP logo on it. That feeling slowly disappeared during – and I can't believe I'm saying this – the subsequent times I went back to prison. In Wandsworth that first time, I was just a twenty-four-year-old lad with a shaved head, just kept my head down, completely anonymous really. I'd say I was in for burglary, and people would ask how many did you get away with that day, how many had you got away with before that? When they learnt I got six months for my first burglary, they were really shocked, genuinely shocked – horrified! They were like you've got to sue the government. I didn't realise how bad my luck was.

I met Will Brown when I was moved from the induction wing and placed in a different cell. It was just me in there at first, and I was looking round, and there was a picture of Mecca on the wall, and in the cupboard was a shitload of potatoes with all fungus growing out of them – someone had been keeping their potatoes from dinner and putting them in this cupboard. I'm stood there with my bag of stuff, and suddenly this wiry Muslim kid, screaming and shouting in Arabic, is thrown in the cell by two screws. The screws said, We'll be back in a minute – we'll get reinforcements. Someone jumped up to the window at this point, shouting, Heart of a Lion, heart of a Lion, and banging his chest. I think this Muslim lad had knocked out a screw or something in the yard. The reinforcements arrived, four or five of them, and dragged him away.

I'm left alone in this cell, and that's when Will Brown turned up, this bouncy, jaunty, ginger-haired cockney. He comes in the cell and literally his jaw dropped. He saw the potatoes, saw the picture of Mecca, and went, What the fuck's going on in here? I went, I don't know, it's not my potatoes, I've just been put in here myself. He went, Well, I hope so. He got all the potatoes, picture of Mecca, all this kid's dirty clothes, and threw them in the bin, and then he started saying, You see that fucking . . . full-on racist, and then he ripped a bed sheet, strapped his ghetto blaster to the window with the material and put up pictures of his kids, and within an hour he was promising to kill Carl.

Someone had cut out and posted me an *NME* article – the headline was 'The Decline and Fall of the Albion Empire'. It had an amazing picture of me with a shaved head and a Fred Perry, but once I got to actually reading it, I got more than a little bit upset – it really came down heavy on the addiction side of things. Will Brown put his arm around me and said, What's the matter, Pete? Don't let these cunts get you down. At the time I was blaming Carl for everything and I said something about Carl and Will suddenly got really sinister. He said, I'll have him wrapped up, stuck in a boot and dealt with. Will actually lived with me for a bit when he got out.

It was different being in that part of the prison. A load of older white south London blokes were running things – they were all with this family that did the failed 2000 Millennium Dome jewel heist. One bloke showed me this file photo of him with a postman or security guard tied up and a big pile of money. He was giving me gear, and I didn't pay for it.

I got transferred to HMP Standford Hill on the Isle of Sheppey. I didn't know I was going – they just came and took me. I was out of my depth at Sheppey. It was a Category D open prison. The rigid discipline and hardship of a Victorian slum prison suited me a bit more than the kind of looseness of the system at Sheppey. It was a bit on top. You had your own room, your own cell, but there were no toilets in the cells. Everything was communal, the toilets and the showers, and there was a communal hall at the end with a pool table with no balls. It was Saturday night when I got there, and I remember someone saying, It's Saturday night in Brixton, and they put on some really loud horrible dance music, on this crappy ghetto blaster, and things turned really dark and weird. Three guys came in my cell, giving me tobacco, and I thought they were being really friendly. One of them was from Dover, this horrible old geezer, and he really put it on me. He was basically saying, What can you do for us if we get you gear? They were genuinely shocked when I told them I wasn't up for business. I wasn't gay or anything. They were like, Oh, we've been told you were up for a bit of business – if you suck me off, I'll give you this and that. It was kind of matter of fact.

There was a black guy, a good lad from Lambeth, who I got chatting to in the showers, and within minutes of talking to him, he said, You need gear, blah, blah, blah . . . take this number, take this code, you get your man to meet my man on the outside, and I'll have it in your room as soon as it's made. So, I made a call to Dean Fragile, and he can remember going down to make the drop in Lambeth and doing the deal in an alleyway, and then it was all phoned through, bang, bang, bang. So, I got a nice bit of gear pretty much straight away. It was the first proper bit of gear I'd had since being inside, and it knocked me sideways. I collapsed in the dinner queue. Everyone thought I was throwing a moody because the big thing was to get in the hospital wing. I passed out and fell down face first, and it was only because some bloke caught the back of my collar that I didn't smash my face on the floor. He's held my collar and then put me down gently, and then I've woken up and gone, I'm all right, I'm all right, I'm fine, and then five, six seconds later, exactly the same thing – I passed out.

Lisa brought Astile to visit while I was in Sheppey. I was begging her to give me twenty quid, and she was like, You're supposed to give me fucking money. My mum wrote to the chaplain – every time I went to prison, she'd write to the chaplain. It'd just be a matter of time before there was a knock on whatever cell I was in, and it'd be the chaplain with a crucifix and a bible, and he'd say, I got a letter from your mum. It was fine if I was in the cell on my own, but if I was with a cellmate, it'd generally lead to confusion – they'd find it hilarious, Your mum wrote to the chaplain?

The chaplain in Sheppey gave me this guitar that had four strings, and he let me sit down with it for ten minutes on my own. I was sitting on a patch of grass outside this ugly stone chapel playing 'Don't Look

Back into the Sun' and 'Back from the Dead', a song I'd written with Wolfman, and I just completely broke down for the first time in the whole process. I'm getting a bit upset thinking about it now, because it was this huge wave of half relief and half I don't know what – just heavy, heaving sobs. I hadn't played a guitar for weeks, and I realised that's what I did and that's who I was, and I had a notion, albeit momentarily, that music was enough on its own without drugs.

It was always a strange experience going to the chapel in prison. A lot of people went just to get out of their cell, and there was shitloads of dealing going on in there. In Sheppey, there was supposed to be a hymn sung, but no one would sing to this automated music coming through the speakers. I started getting this huge emotional surge again, wanting to sing, so I did, and everyone else is looking at me like this is completely weird, and because I knew the words to the hymn from childhood, it was even weirder.

Carl came to visit. I'd been sent back to Wandsworth at that point because of the overdose thing in the queue. Seems like I was in Sheppey weeks, but I was only there a couple of days. When I got back, I had to deal with the fella who thought I'd done a runner owing him all this money. It was only fifty quid, but that was big money inside. But it turned out OK. He actually ended up helping me when this big bloke came swinging at me with a load of nuts and bolts from the bunk bed in a sock. I'd accidentally wandered into somewhere I shouldn't have and looked at someone the wrong way. He was only a little bloke – with glasses – and he just levelled this big bloke, proper weighed him in, horrible crack. Then he said to me . . . I won't actually tell you what he said, because it's not nice, and I don't want to be seen to be glorifying racial slurs, so he said, We'll call it even for that so-and-so, and for the money you owe me, if, when you get out, you take a card to my wife in Lewisham – she's dying of cancer. I'd told him AmyJo was a primary-school teacher in Lewisham. I think I lost the piece of paper with the address on it when I got out, and for years that used to sit in the back of my mind – one day I was going to get a crack on the jaw for not respecting this guy.

The whole experience of being in prison was pretty grimy, all in all – grimy for everyone, but people adapt, don't they? Twenty-eight days I did in the end. There was an appeal hearing where they reduced my sentence. As a leaving gift, the guy who called me Donnargy, I can't even remember his name, he never did security for me, gave me his HMP donkey jacket. I had to smuggle it out in the big clear plastic HMP possessions bag. I'd got quite a bit of fan mail and books sent in, so I folded it up and hid it among all this stuff. It was a proper treasured item.

When you come out, there's nothing ceremonial about it – it's just basically you get out and this massive metal gate slams behind you. I stood there, and I couldn't see anyone at all, and then I turned round and saw up the road *NME* photographer Roger Sargent's bulky frame silhouetted in the morning sunlight, and then Carl in an old Burberry mac and brown brogues. It was quite a tearful moment. It had been a long time since we'd spoken – so much had happened . . . it felt like years, really, like centuries.

That night we did the 'Freedom gig' at the Tap N Tin. I needed some bunce when I got out – I wasn't even really living anywhere – so the Freedom gig was just going to be a solo show, but it turned into a Libertines reunion gig.

After a few drinkies with Carl in the afternoon, I obviously needed to score – fucking hell, I'd just got out of prison. I'd held it together quite well with Carl, and it was lovely to see him, and it was all very emotional and almost spiritual, the Albion getting back together never to part, but I actually really needed a bit of brown and a pipe so, of course, Paul Ro's was the next stop. In my head, I would have felt I was getting myself together, but I guess from everyone else's point of view I was getting myself warped.

I went with Paul Ro to the Tap N Tin, and when we got there, Paul wasn't allowed in the venue, and there was a massive punch-up. Carl, I suppose, must have been at the bottom of the decision not to let him in. Paul was like, How dare you, I got him here. Paul could be a bit tasty when it comes on top, but he ended up getting picked up by the scruff of his neck by a bouncer, swinging his arms around, like a cartoon coyote. It was awful, and it all came flooding back to me, Aaaah, this is why we split up, this is why the band couldn't function, because crack and heroin aren't allowed. That was it, really – it was all downhill from there.

I think Carl was struggling with hard drugs as well from what I can understand. I wouldn't say he was ever banging up, but there are hints that he was heavily into cocaine, taking it all the way, when the band was in Japan and touring America and Canada without me, which, when I look back, kind of hurts even more, really, when you think that's what I was being vilified for – drug use. He was also drinking like a complete manic. He did a bottle of Jameson on his own every night.

We did do an amazing wee set – I think we even threw in 'What Katie Did', which up to then had been a controversial number, because it was my song, a Babyshambles song, the only obvious pop classic that Babyshambles had at the time. This was The Libertines moving in on it – the shadow of Mordor fell over the song, and from then on it was classed as a Libertines song.'

XV
McGee

2003–2004: A new manager. A songwriting session that ends
with Carl in hospital. The truth about that night. A new flat
in Whitechapel. Writing 'Can't Stand Me Now'. The return
of James Mullord. Recording the debut Babyshambles single.
Three nights at Kentish Town Forum with The Libertines.

'Banny was no longer managing us, and one day when I was at AmyJo's
house in Lewisham Alan McGee made this proposition to me: he said he
thought The Libertines were the greatest rock-'n'-roll band in the world
and he wanted to be our manager. I just said, Look can you get me a flat?
And he said, Aye, we'll get you somewhere to live. I was like, Right, you're
in as far as I'm concerned. He thinks we're the best, he can get me a flat,
he's our man – of course, it did occur to me, having managed Oasis, he
would also be able to make us huge.

I'd seen at that point how messy it could get trying to run a band – I'd
done my best, really, to get Babyshambles together as a functioning
band, and it wasn't happening at all. The effect of drugs on someone's
creativity and ability to play can be almost negligible, but the effects on
your ability to steer the ship businesswise and organisationally is just
huge – you can't do it. So, we needed someone to represent The

Libertines and Babyshambles. At that point, I wasn't really sure which way it was going to go. I'd really enjoyed that taste of absolute freedom I'd had with Babyshambles – no pushing and pulling in different directions, all on the same trajectory. That was so magic.

There was still a sense in Carl's heart that I could stay clean. That felt dangerous to me, because I knew in my heart I couldn't do it – no way I wanted to do it. McGee wanted me and Carl to try and write new songs together, and we went to his mansion in Hay-on-Wye in the Welsh hills and sat down together with our guitars, alone for the first time in what felt like for ever, literally in the wilderness. There was no one in the way, no interruptions and 'What Became of the Likely Lads' came out immediately, and a couple of other good ideas. Then in the midst of this drunken songwriting session, Carl said the weirdest thing to me, and it led to this massive argument. He was lying in the bathtub, it was empty, he had his clobber on, and he was really drunk and . . . God, it's just awful even to think about.

He said, When Annalisa visited you in Scarborough, did you get together, what did you do? It was just such a weird thing for him to ask me. All our years of being entwined in each other's lives we'd never really discussed the details of our sex lives. Annalisa Astarita was this ballerina who we'd met on tour in Nottingham in early 2003. She was from Preston. She'd gone with me on the bus, but I remember Carl taking me aside the next day and saying, Look, you don't like her, I really like her, and he nicked my phone, copied her number down and then chucked my phone away. Basically, we'd both been a bit taken with her, but she'd ended up going with him, and then I'd seen her in Scarborough when I'd gone up there with Wolfman to see Steve about starting Babyshambles. Then, while I was in prison, her and Carl had been going out.

When he asked what we'd done in Scarborough, I couldn't remember specifically what had happened. I'd had some sort of bad trip, acid or ketamine, freaked out. I'd thought she was a policewoman, in uniform and everything, and I threw her out of the house and threw all her clothes out of the window.

Carl wasn't happy with these vague memories of what had or hadn't happened in Scarborough and completely freaked out, said we could never be in a band again. We had this big argument and then he fell into a stupor, unconscious. I took a bucket of water and threw it on him and left the bathroom and went to my bedroom. The next thing I knew, there was a loud crash. I just presumed he'd got out of the bath and slipped on the water and crashed into something. He hadn't. He'd tried to kill himself, this bizarre suicide attempt.

The next morning, McGee woke me up, demanding, Did you do this? I was in this little old-fashioned brass bed in one of the rooms. Did you do this? It was like, What the fuck's going on here? He had Carl by the arm, and Carl had his Crombie on up round his face, and his whole face was battered. It was just a pulp of blood and flesh. Did you do this? It was horrible. There was blood dripping down from Carl's mashed face onto the floorboards. It looked like a Halloween mask he had on. McGee has since said he had to force Carl's eye – which was hanging out on its optical nerve – back into its socket. I sat up in bed not knowing what was going on. I had heard this crash in the middle of the night, but I didn't know he'd fucking hurt himself that badly. There'd been a crash, but I'd gone back to sleep. What he'd done was he'd cut himself — there was an initial fracture from the smash, but then he'd taken loads of smashed glass and stabbed it into his own face while screaming at himself in the mirror ... proper, horrific self-mutilation.

McGee took him to a hospital in Wales and left orders that I wasn't to be let in. They thought I'd done it. Carl knew in his heart it wasn't me, but he didn't tell them it wasn't me, so people just presumed it was. It was all a bit fucked up, really. I texted Annalisa and said, Look, I know there's things to discuss, I haven't seen you since I went to prison, but I'm not bothered about that, can I see Carl? She said, Look at your actions, you're no friend of his . . . blah, blah, blah. After that it was all off my radar . . . he had to go to a surgeon in London, ended up having hundreds of stitches in his face and the bone reset in his cheek. He ended up needing a metal plate put in his head.

The flat McGee got me was in Whitechapel on a council estate. It was quite compact, but I managed to get a few guerrilla gigs in there. There's footage online of the first one, a housewarming gig on Bonfire Night: my little bed pushed up against the wall, already loads of writing on the wall – lyrics, ideas for new songs – and about fifteen to twenty kids crammed in. Mo, a Bangladeshi guy who I owed some money to, did the door for that gig. Mo Diddley I used to call him, this Bangla Boy, one of the Brick Lane massive, he used to deal shots.* I think I owed him £80, and he just hung around until eight people came and paid. When I advertised that gig, I said people could get in free if they brought an instrument, and it turned out to be a great night – I was doing Chas & Dave songs and all sorts. There was a kid's play park on the estate where the flat was, and we ended up spilling out onto there – someone had a banjo, someone had a violin – and we did a version of Albion walking around the playground.

Mark Keds, aka Mark Hammerton, lived just round the corner. He'd been in a band called The Senseless Things, and he was a great guitarist. He was also into heroin. I wrote 'Can't Stand Me Now' at Mark's flat. He was knocking these chords about – something to do with Blondie – and it all came together: 'If you wanna try, if you wanna try, there's no worse you can do, can't take me anywhere, I'll take you anywhere'. I wrote that song as a kitchen-sink drama, the idea being that me and

* Crack cocaine.

Carl would have a verse each. I was turned on by the thought of putting words in Carl's mouth. When the time came, I presented it to Carl like that: Right, we're going to sing to each other. He changed a few lyrics, and we all shared a songwriting credit. Mark died quite recently, having struggled with his addiction for years.

It was tricky, really, thinking how you could get a band to function at the same time as being in active addiction. The only way to do that obviously is to be working with someone who can tolerate that, which means someone very open-minded or another addict. What I really needed was someone managerial with business acumen who could put up with the drugs, and I thought that might be McGee, but it turned out James Mullord was to be that man, and he would guide us on our mutual trajectory for the next couple of years.

I'd known him since he'd battled with Banny for the soul of The Libertines, and one of his High Society Records bands, White Sport, had supported The Libertines a few times, but it was only when I got a beautiful and poetic text from him that I started to see him as a bit of a visionary. He then started coming over to the flat in Whitechapel, and I really liked his attitude. He had a wicked old car as well and wore this cool brown leather jacket. We hatched a plan to record a single. I just wanted to put stuff out. I didn't want a year-long process of recording and mixing or whatever. I wanted to go in, whack down a brilliant song and put it out, and I wanted to do that once a month. That was the plan Mullord and I had – we were going to release a single a month. It became impossible, but Mullord was up for that; he was up for rene-gade tactics, which was what I wanted.

He really believed in me. He sat me down and said, You're a brilliant songwriter and your lyrics are brilliant and I want to record you, I don't give a shit what else you do. I so needed to hear that. I'd never heard that from anyone before, not from Carl, nor the other Libertines or

McGee. It was always, like, Oh, yeah, the song's good but . . . Mullord was like, The most important thing is the fucking music and the energy. He saw something in me that outshone the darkness that was perceived as being there by everyone else.

He organised Pat Walden from White Sport to play bass on the single we recorded at the Speedy Studio on Old Street. That was the session where Wolfman fell face first into a plate-glass table. Seb Rochford played drums. He knew Pat, but it was all to do with James's connections. We did three songs: 'Babyshambles', 'Flophouse' and 'What Katie Did'. There was a lot of drugs involved. James threw himself into it. 'Raging Jim' was James Mullord's alter ego after three days up – he would start running through the streets in his bathrobe, gnashing his teeth.

He lived on the Marquess Estate in Islington in this strange flat like a bunker – it was really hard to find his front door. The estate was like a post-war vision of what the future of London was going to be, but it had just become a warren of crime. Inside he used to have quite a lot of doctor's equipment, screens and plastic-surgery outfits. Just across the road was the Duke of Clarence pub. It was pure darkness, half IRA and half dealers. The bar didn't open until ten o'clock at night. I promoted this gig there in November when we had Babyshambles featuring Pat Walden and Seb Rochford, The Libertines with Razzers on drums and The Libertines with Gary on drums all playing on the same night. Carl played with a bandana covering one eye.

It's weird to think The Libertines ever played again after the sudden re-emergence of complications because of bad feelings over Annalisa, but McGee was still trying to put together a new supersize Libertines. He had booked three nights for us at the Kentish Town Forum at Christmas, and they'd sold out. The Libertines were really starting to bring in the punters, but in my heart – and it's sad to say it, really, from today's vantage point – I wasn't connected with the band at all. Those gigs were a real struggle for me. I was getting ripped apart on stage – my heart was just in tatters.

I insisted Chas & Dave support us, and I went on stage with Chas & Dave and did proper old music-hall songs. We had to go through them beforehand because they couldn't remember some of them. I remember they were very concerned about my drug use, and they wrote me a song, 'Why Don't You Have a Cheese Sandwich Instead, Pete Doherty?' That was almost the ultimate accolade for me, to have Chas & Dave write me a song. There's a wicked Douglas Hart-directed video for 'Can't Stand Me Now' which used footage from that final night at the Kentish Town Forum where you can see me pulling people up, really agitated, desperate to get people up, waving them up and then pulling them up by their hands, even if they didn't want to, dragging them over, leading to a huge stage invasion.

My mum and dad came to visit me at my flat in Whitechapel that Christmas with Emily and AmyJo. I don't remember my dad being there. Everyone was a bit on a knife's edge about the drug thing, really. It was hard for people to accept that's what I'd become, but I was so bang into it, right in the middle of it. I wanted to be alone that Christmas. I was saying, I'm going to spend my Christmas wrapped up in foil, and I did get myself wrapped up in foil, like a piece of ham.'

XVI
The Libertines

2004 (part 1): Mission aborted in Paris. Three nights at the Brixton Academy and one razor-blade incident. A damp squib meeting with Liam Gallagher. Recording the second Libertines album after a fight with Carl. A hair-raising performance of 'Can't Stand Me Now'. Moving in with Peter Perrett and getting his sons to join Babyshambles.

'We were in Paris, Carl, me and McGee, on another doomed attempt to write new songs. Carl was intent on having a big breakthrough song like Franz Ferdinand, who had just released 'Take Me Out', whereas to me I felt like we'd already written the songs that were good enough to win people over. Maybe they hadn't connected in the way they might do in your dreams, but we'd already done it. Even if it took twenty years for people to fall in love with them, I knew it would happen sooner or later, and I was right! So, I wanted to carry on in the same vein, really. Carl was always after being as big as we can get, but I don't know if it works like that. I don't know if you can train yourself to write a massive song. I didn't particularly want to try.

We didn't do any writing in Paris anyway. He couldn't be in a room with me when I was using, and I was using all the time. The appropriately titled Hotel France Albion, close to Montmartre, was where McGee had booked rooms. Then Carl had to leg it back to London. His sister was in some sort of trouble. I stayed on at the Albion, and we made the 'For Lovers' video with Douglas Hart. McGee really loved the song and had persuaded Rough Trade it could be a single. I was in quite a state in Paris – I ran up a tab at the bar next to the Albion and played a little set there so I could pay it off. Then I asked Rini – Irina Lazareanu – to run away with me. She was in the same modelling agency as Steve's missus and was now living in Paris. She already had a fiancé, though, so I got a train to Brescia near Milan and I found Francesca. I said, I've come to get married, and she was like, I've been looking at what you're doing from afar, and you're just a soap opera now. She really blew me out, so I wound up back in London with Nadine.

Sadly, I don't remember too much about the bigger gigs that came next. McGee had booked a tour of major UK venues, finishing off with three nights at the Brixton Academy. I know it was hard work getting on stage, like running a gauntlet, very uncomfortable. Something was really pulling apart. Just before that tour started, I turned up for the *NME* awards, where The Libertines won the Best British Band award, really fucked. I was all over the place. I'd disappeared up my own arse. I was really nervous. That's when Carl and I recited Siegfried Sassoon's 'Suicide in the Trenches' poem.

I was an extrovert, I've always enjoyed performing, but there's part of my character that succumbs to severe anxiety. I don't seek outsider status, but sometimes with severe anxiety comes a sense of solitude and doom.

I wanted to play big gigs, but I was struggling. Partly it was to do with a lot of the lyrics I was singing, written in that time when I was just dallying in heroin. By now, I was fully immersed in it, so getting my head round songs like 'Horrorshow' was a bit skewed. It's weird. I always used to think that people would be able to see from looking at me that I was a gibbering wreck inside, but in the footage online it doesn't come over like that. That's the beauty of rock 'n' roll, I suppose – that's why it suits gibbering wrecks, because you can just pile everything in, especially when you've got a guitar.

I also wanted to do some slower, mellower songs on stage, because if you're spending half your time smacked up, you're obviously feeling mellow, aren't you? Whereas with everyone else it was a ferocious one-hundred-miles-an-hour, million-miles-an-hour, rock-'n'-roll show. It was chaos on my little heart.

I do remember The Bandits playing with us one night on that tour at Manchester Academy, and one of them came to the dressing room and said, Liam Gallagher's downstairs, he says he's gonna knock you out if he sees you. I thought, Wicked, I'll have a bit of that. Astile was growing up in St John's Wood with Lisa, his mum, and his sister Mollie, who was Liam's 'secret love child' – the fact had not made the press yet. I saw Astile quite regularly, and Mollie and I got on really well, she was a great kid. So, I went down to see Liam, and I was expecting him to come swinging for me, but he didn't. He just went, All right, I'm all right, everyone's all right.

Hats off to Alan McGee for stepping in and trying to make a go of things and getting them gigs done. He'd hired these two six-foot-six-inch twins to look after me and Carl, make sure we behaved: Mutt (Michael) and Jeff. They'd done security for Iron Maiden for twenty years. Mutt came to pick me up from the Whitechapel flat for one of the nights at Brixton. I was with Neil Thunders and some girls, and I said, They're all coming with me, and he said, No, they're not. I said, What you talking about? It's my gig. He said, Look, I'm getting paid to take you, and he carried me down out of the flat, into the car and into the venue.

Halfway through the set, I thought, Na, that's not right, and I started cutting myself up on stage – I had a razor blade in my pocket – and then I kicked over John's amp, ran off the stage and out the venue and legged it down Brixton High Street. Daft. I made it to Stockwell Park Road, past the skateboard park, and then Michael, who was chasing after me, caught up. He picked me up and said, If you don't finish the gig, we've been told we don't get paid, put me under his arm, carried me back to the venue and put me back on stage.

I had this feeling the people in the crowd would understand how I was feeling, automatically, telepathically – so when I got back on, I was like, Do you understand what I mean? It's my gig, I can invite who I want. Thousands of people were just shouting stuff and throwing things.

Carl and I were both assigned one of the twins to pick us up in the mornings for the sessions for the new album. I remember sitting in the car from Whitechapel over to west London to Metropolis, getting myself together, making sure that I wasn't going to be a mess. I was in the studio ready to go and then it all kicked off. I said to Carl, Look, I've got this digital eight-track, can we set it up in your flat and work on ideas for the album. He went, What, the flat that you burgled? I went, Oh come on, man, let's put that behind us. And he said, No, my sister won't let you in the flat. It really upset me. I remember saying to myself, Don't let him see you cry, sort of thing, biting my lip. Mick Jones, who was back producing us, had a spliff in one hand and his brogues on, and he came over and said, What's the matter, Pete? And Carl went, Oh nothing, he just can't handle the drugs. I completely lost it, and I thought for the first time in all these years I'm actually going to stand up to him, and I went to batter him. I jumped across this glass table, and Michael caught me in mid-air by the scruff of my neck. That was it, really – the whole thing fell apart.

The next day we just piled through all the songs, and then I washed my hands of it. We did nine songs in the first two days, and in the end there were fourteen on the album. I think I went in three times after those first two days, sort of intermittently over the next two months. It was always really fraught. I was in the studio the barest minimum. Geoff Travis later said the album was 'crafted out of the scraps' I gave them. I wrote or co-wrote thirteen of the songs.

The guitar part on 'Narcissist', the song which Carl had written on his own, I did on the first day – in one take – and then I really had trouble getting in there and pulling my head out of my arse to do the backing vocals. 'Tomblands' was a tune – 'In the land of the gauching skiving sun there's bodies in the room lad' and 'Yo ho ho he was the mini Martell man'. I loved those lyrics and was gutted that Carl got to sing that song. Carl put in the middle eight, bridge part of the song: 'I didn't want to be the one to tell yer, she was only fourteen, we sussed out your sordid little scene', which was a great lyric, but because he wrote that bit, he took it upon himself to do the lead vocal. I ended up a bit twisted about that.

Overall, I felt disconnected from the recordings. But I did get one over on Carl and Geoff Travis with 'Last Post on the Bugle' – you should have seen their faces when they finally heard the original song I'd nicked it from. They only twigged once it was too late to do anything about it – 'If I have to go, I will be thinking of you when . . .' – it's a song from the '60s called 'War or Hands of Time' by The Masters Apprentices, an Australian psychedelic band. I'd heard it on this Nuggets compilation box set I bought when we were in America, and I just thought it was the most beautiful song. I was absolutely buzzing that I managed to slip that through the gap. No one had a fucking clue.*

---

* 'Last Post on the Bugle' was credited to Doherty, Barât and 'War or Hands of Time' songwriter Michael Bower.

One of the final nails in the coffin for me was the artwork I knocked up for the album cover. I turned up at the studio one day at random with the artwork, which everyone had been going on at me about for weeks, and I presented it to Mick Jones, and he gave his approval, and I thought that was enough. Then the next thing I knew they're using the junkie photo taken by Roger Sargent at the Freedom gig. My cover was more like an old cigarette-tin vibe, a patchwork of images – I'm sure the old Hammersmith coat of arms, which is the original QPR badge, would have been in there because of Mick Jones. I think I had my face and the boys' faces in the crest on each corner.

The one song that was absolutely spot on from those sessions was 'Can't Stand Me Now'. We knew we'd written a monster. It's still to this day probably our biggest song, really – it's the one that gets everyone going at gigs. We did it on *Friday Night with Jonathan Ross* just after recording it, in March, months before it came out as a single. We were so excited about it – we just had to do it. That was the best performance ever. I was made up with my hairdo that day – it was proper Jesus and Mary Chain. I remember being in the make-up room, and they managed to make it stick up, and it stayed up, as opposed to it staying up for the first three bars and then the sweat glues it to your face.

I got sort of friendly with Peter Perrett, the singer from The Only Ones. He was another heroin addict. I took him into the studio, and we did a version of his big hit, which I loved, 'Another Girl, Another Planet'. We played it at the Rhythm Factory that night at a gig I'd organised. The Libertines sort of reluctantly came along – they couldn't back out because of Peter Perrett. Even though Carl had never heard of him, he realised he was a legend, so he had to get involved. Perret was a bit of a recluse and hadn't been on stage in years. It was one of those ramshackle strange gigs where you sense things are not as they should be with the band, but people were so happy to see us together, playing together.

There was now this real sense that it was maybe going to be the last time we played together every time we played.

I took Nadine and a few other girls over to Peter Perrett's house in south London when it was his missus's birthday. It got really dodgy. He sat me down and showed me loads of home videos of her when she was younger. Him and his missus didn't leave their bed apart from to score. I lived there for a bit. It was a good hideaway, somewhere Mutt and Jeff couldn't find me. I used to share the bed with them, this bed covered in tin foil and homemade crack pipes.

His kids, Peter Jr and Jamie, had a band called The Cunts, and I tried them out in an early line-up of Babyshambles with Pat Walden. Pat was working part-time on the cash register, selling plectrums and drinks at the Rooz recording and rehearsal studios in east London, and he roped in Gemma Clarke on drums. Her dad, Graham, ran Rooz. We actually did a few gigs with that line-up – very early, proper mental gigs. There was one in Stafford where I threw the money we'd got from the door, about three and a half grand, into the crowd. This one bloke, this punk fella, was right in my face going, We don't want your money, we want the music, and he was throwing the money back at me. One of the Peter Perrett boys was going, Look, they don't want the money, we'll keep the money, and he was picking it up off the floor. That same gig I threw myself off a speaker stack into this mosh pit that was full of skinheads, proper having it. We were just making a racket. There was lots of fighting that night, and the Perrett boys ended up sheltering behind an amp whilst Gemma was fighting people off with a drum stool. I remember thinking, Na, them boys aren't cut out for a life in the Shambles . . . one of them stayed on bass for a little while, and Pat replaced his brother on guitar full time.

This was when the 'Babyshambles' single came out on Mullord's High Society Records. Mullord had problems with Rough Trade, but eventually he got permission to bang it out as a limited edition.

Everyone calls it the first Babyshambles single. It was a one-off that got everyone going. We did 'What Katie Did' on The Libertines album, and Carl sort of owned it, really – he sang the lead vocals, even though I wrote it – but I got the song out first on that single as a B-side. It was one of the reasons I whacked that out. It was being presented as if Doherty and Barât were still this great songwriting partnership, and I wanted to lift the curtain.

I knew that would hurt Carl, but with Babyshambles there was no way I was going to do 'Don't Look Back into the Sun', or 'The Ha-Ha Wall', or 'Can't Stand Me Now'. I wouldn't do that to him. But really and truly a lot of those early Babyshambles songs should have been on *The Libertines* album, like 'Back from the Dead'. Carl actually came down and whacked out quite a good guitar part on that, and he was now going, Well, why didn't you get me to play on 'For Lovers', because McGee was saying it was going to be such a big hit. We did ask at the time!'

XVII
For Lovers

2004 (part 2): 'For Lovers' on Top of the Pops. *Rehab in Thailand
– projectile vomiting and mystical incantations. Lost in Bangkok, a
death, two transvestites and a 'superfan' benefactor. Herr Flicky. A
new addition to Babyshambles. Sacked again from The Libertines.*

'My nan came to *Top of the Pops* with Pandy when I did 'For Lovers'. It
was me and Wolfman's band, The Side-Effects. Rough Trade had asked
Jake Fior to sort it so that Wolfman wasn't involved, but the BBC
banned him anyway – they said he was too demonic. That's a real thing.
Too demonic for the BBC – which of course he loved. Truth be told, he
wasn't actually that interested in doing *Top of the Pops*. So I was there
in a really nice little skinny tight suit doing a really great version of 'For
Lovers'. The band mimed, but I did the vocal live with Wolfman's backing singer Frankie, who had sung with Marvin Gaye one time. I really
enjoyed it.

For all the sadness and anxiety to do with The Libertines, there was
a lot of hilarity and comedy and enjoyment and adventure in my life. I
was proper off my rocker. I didn't feel like I was spiralling out of control
– half the time I felt like I was shooting up really high. Somehow in
amongst it all there was always a self-pumped-up football of an ego just

to keep me rolling. Like that moment when my dad was punch drunk and pretending to be Sugar Ray Leonard, there was a lot of that in my spirit at the time – of being in a complete stupor, whether it be alcohol or drugs, really riding a wave of trying to have as good a time as I could have. But for McGee and the boys it was just a point-blank we cannot function as a band with you using. There was no give and take on either side, so it was an impasse. They were still trying to finish recording the album, but McGee was planning summer festival dates and a huge world tour to coincide with when the album did come out.

I agreed to go to rehab at the Priory Hospital in southwest London to show willing. It was another of those rehab places where they give you medication, lithium, to sleep. After two or three days, I came round, and I got out. I left on the day Millwall played Man United in the FA Cup final and went over to east London to see Paul Ro. The band were pissed off, and McGee cancelled some big gigs.* It was a mess. I was skint, and I gave *The Sun* an exclusive interview announcing I was quitting the band. I told them 'I felt trapped in a cage'. It was a cry for help more than anything.

About a week later, I went back to the Priory, which rekindled hopes we might play Glastonbury that year. Rini came to visit with a lovely gilded cigarette case. Carl brought me a brand new QPR shirt. Then my mum came, and she insisted she be allowed to search my room for the doctors. Apparently, she went in and said, Have you searched his room? and they went, Yeah, yeah, but she knew me better, and she went under the tiles in the ceiling and found a bag of weed and loads of other drugs, including heroin. She insisted on standing on a chair with a broom – it was unbelievable. I was fuming. I was all set for a comfy stay in rehab. I checked myself out after a week.

---

* Morrissey's Meltdown Festival, the Isle of Wight Festival, a Rock Against Racism gig in Finsbury Park and the Wireless Festival in Hyde Park.

McGee then paid Jeff to take me to this clinic in Thailand. The evening before the flight I went to Carl's new club night called the Dirty Pretty Things that he was running with Annalisa, and the band was there and we played a few songs. That was the last time we played together in that era, although there was a lot of goodwill about me committing to go to rehab in Thailand. I wouldn't say they tricked me into going to Thailand, but I didn't know what I was getting into. I was yet to try opium or China-white heroin, so the whole idea of getting over to Thailand was quite exciting. I remember being at Heathrow Airport and not exactly thinking I was cool but thinking I was hot stuff for openly smoking crack in the departure lounge. I really had this sense of being untouchable – I'm going to Thailand and I'm smoking crack at the airport and the world's my oyster sort of vibe. But within eighteen hours Jeff had just dumped me in this monastery, taken a selfie with me in my new pyjamas and then fucked off.

Then it suddenly dawned on me I wasn't with a shotgun in a Land Rover going off to find the golden triangle with a big empty sack for the opium – I was stuck in pink pyjamas in a monastery, Wat Tham Krabok, with no phone, no computer, no real knowledge of detox. Any time I'd been in rehab, they'd given you medication. There was none of that – you just had to cluck through it. I wanted to get out within the first ten minutes of being there, but McGee had given specific instructions that my passport was to be put in the safe by the head monk.

There were sixteen bunk beds in this one room for the international clientele – seemed to be a lot of Dutch and Scandinavian people there, and one lad from Manchester called Lee, more of whom later – and then there were these 'cages' where they put the locals who were addicted to jabba, this really psychotic, very cheap, form of meth, a leftover from meth production, that was rampaging through the country. Loads of kids rocking back and forth manically.

The place was famous for bringing out the goodness of the human spirit and the idea of addiction being like a poison, not just the substance but also the behaviour. They had this projectile-vomiting ritual. Years ago, in the '50s and '60s, this monk had developed this potion from something like seven hundred different varieties of bark and herb and soil and crushed insects that when swallowed was supposed to bring out any toxins from your body. You swallowed this mixture that tastes absolutely foul, and they force feed you a bucket of water, and then you have to projectile vomit three times – and you have to do that procedure three times. Supposedly, once you've done that, you've exorcised the demons and the poisons from your body, and you're left to recover as a shattered heap of bones.

There was no money at the place – it wasn't a spa. They'd stick us all in the sauna and lock the door. I passed out in there, and afterwards I went to the head monk to complain. He assured me that me passing out in the sauna was a good thing because it meant I could get the positive effects of the sauna without all the complaining that everyone else who couldn't get out had been doing. He said I should go to private prayers with him at night.

The meals were absolutely god-awful. We went down to this kind of a sweet stand that had Fanta and cola in plastic bags, and they were frying really dodgy-looking sausages in this big rusty pan, and that was breakfast. But you weren't encouraged to eat. You were just encouraged to drink this lemon tea and water in preparation for the projectile vomiting – you had to have gone three days without eating to do so.

I had a guitar with me, and I remember singing 'Don't Look Back into the Sun' and Lee being really intrigued. He'd done his three projectile vomitings. I told him I wanted to get on my toes, and he said, Don't do the ceremony, then.

Before you do the projectile vomiting, you have to make an oath, swear on your life to the gods of this particular monastery – there were massive carvings of them – that you will never take drugs or drink alcohol again, ever. The monks took it really seriously. If you do three projectile vomitings after taking the vow, you will die if you drink or take drugs again, there's no two ways about it.

Then I sort of began to feel the serenity of the place. I got really excited by these conversations I had with this black American ex-soldier who was now a monk and had lived in this monastery in the jungle since the Vietnam War – he'd been so horrified by his own actions during the war he'd given his soul over to the spiritual. He was telling me all the tales of all the people he'd seen there. He said, Oh, I saw you didn't eat those vegetarian black sausages, but that's all part of your new life now – you won't eat sugar again or drink alcohol, you're just going to get in the robes and sandal about the jungle. He said, We need lots of hands for building the new temple.

I was like, Yeah, I could do that. I got caught up in the mystique of it all, the cult of Buddhism, with the shaved heads and the colours and the incense – there was an element of falling into the magic. So, I did my vows. I can remember it now, the incense and the bells and the ceremony, and I had to repeat in Thai what the guy said, and there was a little pamphlet that gave you translations – it basically said I sacrifice my life on the vow that I will never drink or take drugs again. Afterwards, I really felt it, like, Fuck, I've done it, I've done it, I can't drink or take drugs again.

But it's not as simple as that. You've now got to do the projectile vomiting. All I can say about that is you really do feel the darkness coming out of you – whatever things had been rotting away in my stomach in London, to do with Carl, The Libertines and Carl's face, and all the trouble over girls and money and theft and burglary and jail, all the poisonous stuff that was breaking up the band and was rotting me, I felt it coming out of my stomach in this black bile. It proper comes out as well – you drink the poisoned mixture and then drink a bucket of water and this stuff flies out.

That night I was just lying on my bunk kind of proud I'd done it, but I was a gibbering, snotting, crying wreck, and I was bit embarrassed about that. Lee was laughing, and I was thinking, Fucking hell, what have I done. We're lying on the bunk, and there was one of those massive Thai electrical storms overhead, and I said to Lee, Look, I don't really fancy doing this projectile vomiting again, and he went, Let's have it away on our toes, c'mon, you're Pete Doherty, I've seen you in the paper – someone had sent a fax of a *Sun* article that had a cartoon of me in a cell with bars, and they said Pete Doherty is being held in a monastery jail cell being hit with bamboo sticks, because that's what they thought they did to the Thai people.

So, Lee and I decide we're going to break out, but the problem is the passports are in the safe. So, basically, Lee, really ballsy guy, storms the office and threatens this old monk. He proper kicked off, and he started giving it, We're fucking British citizens, her majesty impels you to give us freedom to move and pass without let or hindrance. The monk said to him, I don't know what you're going on about, you can have your passport, we don't want you, but we've been told we're the official guardians of this one, pointing at me. Lee went, Well, he wants to fucking leave, he's a grown man, aren't you, Peter? I went, That's right. He then threw a statue across the office, turned over the desk, did something threatening with an umbrella, and we got our passports. He said, That's how we do it in Manchester, Peter.

We were in this forest, and I remember thinking, We're just stuck in the middle of nowhere now, but Lee showed me his backpack, and he had shitloads of money in it – loads of American dollars and ridiculous amounts of this really colourful, beautiful-looking Thai money, purple and blues and pinks. He stopped this minivan, some bloke driving through the forest, and offered him a shitload of money to drive us to Bangkok, where he knew some bird. She worked in one of them ping-pong clubs, one of those weird places where you basically sit on a barrel and put your cock in a hole and there's someone sat in the barrel who you can't see sucking you off, proper sleazy. It was a really weird scene in Bangkok – police cars were coming round with trunks full of mari-juana, and there were rickshaw drivers with really good China-white heroin. I didn't really want to try the jabba, but that's what Lee went straight for.

Then he disappeared from his hotel room. They pulled me over, the hotel, and asked me, Where is Lee? I went to the room – all this money was on the bed, hanging out of his backpack, and his passport was there. Two or three days went by, and he still hadn't turned up. I had this horrible, eerie feeling that he'd gone for good. When we left, the monk said to Lee, If you go to Bangkok, you will die. I went through his bag, and he had a couple of hundred quid, so I just started spending his money. In the end, I had about fifteen girls in my room, and boys – it was hard to tell which was which. There was nothing sexual going on – we were doing drugs. These two really tall Vietnamese transvestites just moved in and wouldn't move out. They followed me home from the corner shop.

I went to the internet café and got in touch with Rough Trade and McGee. I tried to explain what had happened, but to them it was just gibberish. I was saying, I've left the place, I'm being intimidated by these transvestites who won't get out of my room, my mate's died, I've spent all his money and this dealer has let me build up a massive debt, and I don't have any money, and I can't pay for my hotel room either.

So, I contacted Mya, who worked at the *Bangkok Post* and had writ-ten me a letter while I was at the monastery asking if I was OK and could she come down and do an exposé. She must have seen the article in *The Sun*. I told her I wanted to do some concerts to raise some dough, so she took me to this really clinical, clean, overpriced bar for professional westerners. She wasn't part of the sleazy underworld of drugs and sex workers. She was this plump little Thai girl obsessed with English music and journalism. I got a bit drunk and tried to do a song at random, and they asked us to leave. She thought it was really funny. Then she took me to a radio station, and I did 'Back from the Dead' and Don't Look Back into the Sun' live on the radio. I was trying to get money out of Mya, and she wasn't having any of it. No, I'm not going to give you money for drugs. I was like, You don't understand, I've got no money left. Can I come and live with you? No, you can't. I think it was because the transvestites followed me everywhere.

It was on top. I was in trouble, and I was fucked. As well as having no money, I also had a massive China-white habit. I was in bits. It was carnage in my hotel room. I got in touch with Gill Samworth online. That's when Gill really pulled it out the bag, bought my plane ticket home. She was there for me, and no one else was. Gill was a Pete fan. The *NME* called her a 'middle-aged superfan'. She was at every gig. Turns out in the early days, when we didn't know who she was, she was at every gig as well. At the Freedom gig, Carl was absolutely slaughtered and fell over and cracked his chin, blood everywhere, and Gill had scooped up his lifeless body and put it in her car and drove off with it into the night. No one knew what the fuck was going on. When Carl came to, he was in the back of her car going down the motorway, and he just saw Gill turn round smiling at him, saying, It's gonna be all right. It was like *Misery*, the film where the stalker captures the writer. That's not fair. I'm joking. She took him to the hospital. She was absolutely genuine, Gill, loved the music.

The plane ticket was like a thousand quid. I was sat on the kerb trying to work out how to get my stuff out of the hotel and get to the airport quick because this flight Gill had booked was not refundable. In the end, Mya helped me escape in a big laundry basket. We stopped off on the way to the airport, and I got a tattoo so I could say thank you to her. I've still got it – it's supposed to be the letter of her name, an M, but it looks like an H, and I've been told by the few Thai people I've shown it to it was not only her initial but it also means horse.

Gill picked me up from Heathrow with Wolfman, and we headed over to her place in Hackney, the infamous Pink House, a two-storey flat on the bottom floor of a tower block in Homerton – the outside painted a garish pink. Gill was a bit of a cat woman – she ended up with twenty-six cats in the Pink House. It was a merry old place, a proper bandit's hideout. It was pink inside as well. I was officially given my own room there. It was great – it was so clean and seemed so luxurious to how I'd been living. Wolfman ended up plotting up there permanently. When it all collapsed, when the whole Babyshambles dream collapsed in on itself, as it did most mornings, and you needed somewhere to bang up ketamine, Gill's was the place. She kept the home fires burning. I'd plot up there on and off for years.

It was when we were coming back from the airport, in Gill's old Vauxhall Cavalier, that I got arrested. I don't want to say, but Gill went through a fucking red light, and we got pulled over. My first words to them were, I've just come out of rehab from Bangkok, as if they were just going to whistle us on. They went, Yeah? I said, I'm a musician, maybe you've heard of me? Peter Doherty, I'm doing really well now, just back from the airport, and they just proceeded to go through the whole car. I had a flick knife in my luggage. It was actually a present I'd brought back for Carl to replace the one he'd had taken off him in Norway.

He'd picked up this knife on an early European tour with The Libertines, decided it was German and christened it Herr Flicky. He was always whipping it out and pretending to cut my throat. He used to do this routine about Herr Flicky in an Irish accent: And then at

Christmas time the turkey goes gobble, gobble, gobble and gets his little throat cut. We were on the tour bus, and I woke him up and said, It's Norwegian customs, and he said, I don't care about their local traditions, I'm trying to sleep, and that was the last Herr Flicky was seen. So, I thought I'd bring him back a flick knife from Bangkok, thinking that maybe this gift would mean all would be forgiven for me having sacked rehab, and I got nicked for it. That really didn't bode well for the healing of our relationship. I was taken to Bethnal Green Police Station, charged with possession of a flick knife and bailed.

McGee called this so-called emergency meeting when they knew I was back. Rough Trade and McGee had completely left me in the lurch – that was my grievance: I felt they fucking left me to rot in Thailand. I went and had a rehearsal at Rooz instead – me, Pat and Gemma. That was the night me and Pat wrote 'Fuck Forever'. Playing with Pat was a whole new thing. He was proper into his Dinosaur Jnr and Sonic Youth, a much dirtier sound, but there was also a Hendrix/Zeppelin element to him. The only thing I could do really was to throw myself into writing music, and I did, headlong at that point. It was a very fertile time. I was going over to Pat's flat in Ponders End a lot. He was like Carl, very private, and it was sometimes difficult to get on a creative wavelength with him, but when we did, it just worked. 'Killamangiro' is a good example of song that was already there, and Pat kind of took the instrumental part and made it his own. I was leaning in quite heavily to Pat's heroin addiction as well. We were enabling each other. He was already deep into drugs when we met. There were rumours he'd been sectioned, and he actually passed out on stage at one White Sport gig at the Rhythm Factory and got taken to Whitechapel General.

I felt disenfranchised from The Libertines, from my own creation. Instead of playing Glastonbury at the end of June with The Libertines, I did a gig at the Rhythm Factory with Babyshambles. Drew McConnell turned up at Rooz on the afternoon of the gig and rehearsed six or seven hours, and he played bass that night. He knew Pat somehow. I was really impressed by his spirit – getting involved at short notice. I knew we were on to a winner there. Drew slotted in perfectly, he was well up for the ramshackle vibe and he obeyed orders. I'd say, Look, we've got to have shirts off for this gig, and he did it. I was happy as well we had a bass player who was as good-looking as John. That was very important. I felt I was coming close to my peak. I was writing some of the best music of my life, and I was doing some of the best perform- ances of my life as well. The Rhythm Factory gig was a portent of things to come – it was shockingly good, in a much darker way than The Libertines had ever been.

On the same day I was up in court charged with possessing an offen- sive weapon, The Libertines announced they had sacked me due to 'well-known addiction problems specifically with crack cocaine and heroin'. They were going to continue without me. In the statement the band made, Carl said, 'The other members of the band – Gary, John and myself – have come to this conclusion after three recent failed rehab attempts, all of which Libertines have funded'. Like before, they left it open-ended, saying that once I'd quit drugs, I could be back in the band.

It was heartbreaking to be exiled from Carl's life, but I'd become a bit more hard-headed by then. I'd given up trying to pretend I was going to get clean. I had absolutely no interest in getting clean. I had a great deal of interest in – I wouldn't say getting dirty, but I had this vision of drugs eventually just being made legal. I felt it was society's lack of vision that was criminalising this thing. There was a part of me trying to prove you could remain a functioning member of society and be a crack and heroin addict . . . that was a pet project of mine. It really was a case of popping up on a whole new plane. The chaos and camaraderie and circus atmosphere that I wanted for The Libertines, but which wasn't being embraced by the band or the structure we had around us, I had with Babyshambles. We were a gang that was well up for the ride – lots of amazing characters around us, lots of people who had lots of stuff to prove. We really fucking went for it from the word go. We just thought, Right, we're going to do this, and it's going to have to be exceptional.'

XVIII
Babyshambles

2004 (part 3): Lots of bad press. Much talk of death. A ray of sunshine, Dot Allison. The Libertines go to number one. Desperate attempts to get clean end in failure. Babyshambles hit the road and chaos ensues. Mullord's money-making schemes. 'Killamangiro' is a hit. Temazepam ruins the show. The Libertines split.

'People started to sell pictures of me or stories about me in this period. The awful Katie Bapples thing ran in the *Daily Mirror*, and, although it was all bollocks, it looked bad. It also came out that Lisa was mother to children by both me and Liam Gallagher, and Liam said something in *The Sun* about keeping 'that burglar and crack addict away from my child'. The *Guardian* ran an article that had a picture of me smoking a crack pipe with the headline, 'Annihilation beckons the doomed star of rock', but I don't think that annihilation was really in my head at the time. I didn't really feel I was 'spiralling towards the classic rock 'n' roll ending, ravaged by heroin and dropped by the band', as the *Guardian* wrote. I think at that point I thought I might have come through the worst of it. In a way, the drug world blankets you a little bit, not just from normal reality but from the fame side of things as well. You know you have a bit of a wall around you – you are in places no sane-minded reporter or paparazzo will ever be able to enter. I loved being out of it in obscure places – whether that was at the Pink Tower, Paul Ro's or the Thai jungle.

I actually suggested to the *NME* when they did that special-edition Libertines split story with two front covers, me on one and Carl on the other, that I review The Libertines at T in the Park, and I was not even joking. I thought having been in the band I'd be perfectly placed – would give me as righteous and as justified a platform as anyone to comment on the show. I also thought I could maybe sidle on from the side of the stage for the encore, and we could all live happy ever after. I was completely shocked and frustrated by everyone's reaction – the preposterousness of that idea as it was received, I couldn't understand it. Apparently, there was someone on the VIP entry to the festivals they did that summer who was told specifically to keep me out.

If I look back now at the press from that time it's all a bit unhealthy, really, all those mentions of death and dying. I told the *NME*, 'When they play without me, I'm gonna die, it means so much to me I'm gonna die.' I actually didn't do many interviews, but I did one with the *Evening Standard* in exchange for cash, and I also talked of 'ending it all' in that. I also predicted Carl was going to kill himself! I'd heard mention of him sitting at the back of the bus surrounded by broken bottles absolutely battered, people whispering in his ear that he needed to carry on without me, he couldn't not do these gigs, couldn't cancel these festivals, couldn't cancel the tours McGee had booked in Europe and America. I think he felt an enormous sense of responsibility. In his eyes, part of him felt like he was doing the right thing, keeping the band going – the other part might have missed his old pal. I sent him this message via Babyshambles.com: 'Do not fool yourself into fooling yourself. You are not The Libertines now.'

To be honest, the image that springs to mind is just being broken at that point, actually. That's how I see it now – just being really broken. I can taste right now in my mouth the atmosphere at the Pink Tower and it being very dark. I did try and kill myself: it was Wolfman's birthday, 3 August, and he said jokingly that for his birthday present he wanted me to die. He couldn't have known, but I was in a particularly bad way that night and didn't make it to his gig at the Scala as advertised and apparently it was a right disaster. The wind used to really gather around that tower, as it does around the bottom of tower blocks, and it blew the front-room window in. Wolfman was stood there like the devil with his arms up, like Dracula, with his tailcoat flapping and all the windows blown in. He said if I pissed on the lamp the electricity would go up the piss and kill me, but it didn't – it just blew out all the fuses on Gill's ground-floor maisonette.

There were moments when our tracks would cross in London, me and the band. I turned up for the opening night of Roger Sargent's exhibition of Libertines photos at Proud Galleries in Westminster much to everyone's surprise and annoyance. There was shock, really. I was wandering round the gallery with a guitar. I think the band was supposed to play, and I ended up getting up and doing something. That was where, for the first time in a public domain, I remember feeling like the kids, or the fans, were on my side a bit. The band was trying to make me out as the villain, but when I got there, the kids were really happy to see me with a guitar.

Dot Allison was someone who Paul Ro put on my radar. She was the former singer in One Dove, and was now solo, writing material for Massive Attack and Death in Vegas. Paul knew her brother Ian, who ran a local east London literary magazine, *Full Moon Empty Sports Bag*, which was great, incredible. I'd generally have a poem or two in there – things I'd knock up at Paul's. He used to have one of those little old square BBC computers, and he'd insist I had to write something before he let me use. I was always trying to write fiction. Anyone who wasn't a raging addict really couldn't see anything good in Paul, but I saw the creative side in him. He'd helped me write the song 'The Saga' on The Libertines' second album. That was another battle with the industry – to get him properly credited. He was so disliked by Carl and Rough Trade. I also thank him for putting me in touch with Dot.

We started doing a few strange gigs together around east London – in matching T-shirts with rainbows on the front, Sonny and Cher vibe. It was when 'Can't Stand Me Now' came out and was a massive hit, and we did a version of it live with Dot playing the lead on xylophone. We actually did a few Libertines songs with her playing Carl's part on the xylophone. I shacked up with her at her house for a bit. We were sort of together. We were supposed to be living together, but she wouldn't let me have a key to the flat. She was really against the addiction. She let me use her bathroom initially. I'd not had a bath in ages, and she ran me a lovely bath with candles, but I was smoking crack in the bath, and she got a bit upset. I was in love with Dot, but the drugs threw a spanner in the works. This was just before I met Kate Moss, because Dot later said the last time she saw me I was going out to buy some fags and then the next time she saw me I was on the front of the paper saying I was getting married to Kate Moss.

The Libertines' second album went to number one on the day I appeared at Thames Magistrates Court, at the beginning of September. I got a four-month sentence suspended for a year for possession of a dangerous weapon, the flick knife. I arrived at court with James Mullord in a battered old car singing an Oasis song out of the sun roof. There were quite a few TV crews and reporters waiting. I thought I put on a good show for them that day. I was wearing a wicked grey suit, but then all the reports were about me being 'drug-haunted' or the 'doomed star of a tabloid tragedy'.

I was reconciled now to the fact I wasn't going to be allowed back into The Libertines. There was no way. It was not going to happen. So, James Mullord sorted the first proper Babyshambles UK tour, twenty-odd dates. We called it the *Stone Me What a Life* tour and had these amazing giant posters of Tony Hancock sat over a cup of tea knocked up. It was a phrase Hancock used to express exasperation, but in relation to me obviously took on a double meaning. I was determined to show The Libertines I *was* fit for purpose, even more so than them, because I was now super driven to show that I was going to take off.

In preparation for the tour, I tried to go cold turkey on the army barracks where my mum and dad were now stationed, Blandford Camp in Dorset, the same army barracks I'd lived on as a kid. We must have done 100,000 sales of the *Up the Bracket* album by that time, because I took the gold disc home, and they put it in the toilet. But I was basically on my deathbed, clucking like a motherfucker, vomit bucket by my bed, my mum coming in and putting all the needles in the sin bin. There was a lot of my childhood stuff in the room I was in, stuff they'd kept, all my QPR VHS tapes. Dad was coming in and feeding me whisky, trying to get me through it. I think he actually had to carry me to my bed at one point.

I realised I wasn't going to be able to do it, and I was going to have to find a way out. In the end, we got Gill to meet us at a service station somewhere between London and Blandford. She came down with some bits, and my mum and dad handed me over to Gill. My dad kept 'heavy horse', the guitar, looked after it for years, thank God! It's now a treasured possession, but that would have gone, been sold to get cash for drugs, if my dad had not taken it off me. In my head, when I think of that episode, I'm so much younger, but I was actually twenty-five then. I was completely battered, completely run down, trying to get clean but really struggling. It was a bit of disaster, bit of a sad time, really. My dad couldn't cope with it. I know I broke my mum's heart too, but she tried to deal with it. Dad was just against drugs, and he really made his feelings clear about how he felt about me, how I was 'crack-piping [myself] to death', how 'wretched' I was – he even said I represented everything he hated about humanity, that I was 'a liar, a thief and a junkie'.

The tour was absolutely bonkers, incredible. Babyshambles really came into our own then, just literally riots everywhere. The two nights we did at London's Scala were as mad as I'd ever seen a crowd, which was what I was pushing for all along – to make something more mental than The Libertines. That was always in my heart and in my sights – to show Babyshambles could generate as powerful a reaction as The Libertines. The people who came were different. It wasn't just Libertines fans who were switching – it was a slightly more mental breed of fan, a new generation.

Being on stage was cathartic. There was a lot of crying in pain, screaming, on '8 Dead Boys' in particular, with the repeat of 'when it suits you, you're a friend of mine', and diving into mosh pits. I got the rush I wanted from The Libertines but felt I'd been denied by the mechanisms of the industry and the management system at Rough Trade. They were always creating this distance between the nutters and the gig, where I wanted it to be one big celebration, one big riot – that's what I was after. I wanted to see the raw energy. I wanted to see the scenes I'd seen in footage of the Pistols and The Clash, mental kids right in your face while you're playing and diving in and fighting with the crowd, and it all came to be.

There was a gig we did at the Shepherd's Bush Empire – Primal Scream and Supergrass also played – and that was actually the first time I met Kate Moss to talk to, in one of the celebrity rooms. We just ended up face to face on the stairs, and she said to me, Oh, your little boy gets on with my little girl, something like that. Quite a strange meeting, because I didn't know what she was on about. I had no idea that Lisa Moorish and Kate actually had this close relationship, had been really good mates for years. They both had a black love heart tattooed on the same finger, and they were both born on the same day – twisted sisters they called themselves

'What Became of the Likely Lads' was another hit when it was released in October, but money came from the gigs. Money didn't come from having hit albums or songs in the top ten – there was no money in that, as far as I remember. So, James Mullord was always looking for ways to make money. He would have all these money-making schemes. One of them was *Celebrity Big Brother*. They were going to give me £100,000, but we were asking for them to give me fifteen minutes three times a day off camera sort of thing, so it never happened. His schemes generally always ended in disaster, like with the guy who offered us money to make a documentary, Max Carlish. Dot was around when Max was there. She hated him, everyone hated him, everyone just thought he was weird, but Mullord thought we were getting a million quid off Channel 4 – so that's how he got let into the fold.

He was filming when Babyshambles recorded 'Killamangiro', with Paul Epworth producing. It was one of those visiting Liverpool jokes we had growing up. My mum always used to say, What's the name of the mountain range in Liverpool? Kill a Man for His Giro. A Doherty standard: stood the test of time, really, but I wasn't very comfortable recording that. I think I did it Libertines-style – just did my part and then took drugs out the back. Paul Epworth was not someone I wanted to work with particularly – I had no concept of him, really.[*] I like things to be on a personal level – you get to know someone and then you do the music. In this instance, I think Drew decided Epworth was cool and should do the record. I was a bit uppity and frustrated at those sessions, disconnected, leaving it to Drew.

We did a few TV shows around that time to promote the 'Killamangiro' single. I remember a Sky One show because I asked out the *EastEnders* actress with freckles, Patsy Palmer, but her boyfriend was stood right next to her, so it was a bit embarrassing. We also got thrown out of *Top of the Pops*. Someone in the crowd shouted crackhead as we were preparing to do the main take, and we dived in and started fighting with him. Luckily, we'd already done the run-through, so they used that as the actual televised bit. I had my top on inside out. This was when the *NME* called me the 'Cool Icon' of 2004, and straight away there was loads of backlash about me being jailed and sacked and a junkie, and what a terrible man I was. I don't want to blow my own trumpet, but despite what was being written in the press about me, I think I'm right in saying I actually had the most top-ten hits of anyone in 2004.

That was certainly one hell of an autumn/winter. We did another big Babyshambles tour that was monumentally messy and ended in absolute disaster. The Libertines were also touring the UK at the same time. There was actually a full-on riot in Aberdeen after one Babyshambles show was cancelled. I passed out on the bus because of this temazepam we had got hold of, and they couldn't get me off the bus to do the gig. All the kids were shaking the bus, literally trying to push the tour bus over; the band's equipment nearly got destroyed. The cops came and loads of kids got arrested.

* Producer of bands such as Bloc Party, The Futureheads and Maximo Park.

I think that was one of the worst times of my whole musical career, waking up on a farm in Aberdeen, everyone fuming with me because I'd been out cold. It turned out my aunty had been at the gig, and she'd managed to get the bus to drive out to the farm. She was a Scottish woman who'd married my uncle Phil when I was a kid.

I was completely temazepamed on that tour. The gig we did at Blackpool Empress Ballroom, I was singing everything in half-time, wandering around on stage battered. Pat threw his guitar down, and Gemma and Drew left the stage with him. That was the gig where Johnny Headlock, Johnny Jeannevol, got his nickname. He put me in headlock to get me off stage. He was this hip-hop geezer from Hackney who Pat got involved, doing security and humping stuff about. Johnny was only about five feet ten inches, but he was a very intimidating character in the flesh. On that tour I got attacked in the street by some proper lumps. They were like, Hey, crackhead, and they got hold of me and were pushing me about. I thought I was about to get pummelled, and Johnny just stepped in, and he fronted them with his goggly eyeball, and they all just backed down instantly. He had one eye that went and did what it wanted.

But that Blackpool gig was shocking, I thought that was about as hard-core as it got, but the Christmas gig at the Astoria was worse – that *was* as bad as it got. It was 17 December, the night Carl announced The Libertines were splitting up for good after a one-off show they did in Paris. I failed to show for the Astoria gig, and the crowd went mental, wrecking the stage and equipment. The security turned the metal whips on them.

I was upset about The Libertines. I actually tried to get this taxi driver to take me to Paris that night so I could talk to Carl, but it turned out his son had tickets to the Babyshambles gig, so he started taking me to the Astoria instead. I remember jumping out of the taxi somewhere in the West End and doing a flying kick at the window of a random shop. What a mess. What a mess. Gemma said she decided to quit – she'd had enough – when she found herself in a store cupboard under the stage at the Astoria fighting people who were trying to destroy her drum kit.'

XIX
Kate

2005: Meeting Kate Moss. Alan the soul man. The Max
Carlish incident and a short stay in Pentonville. Press
intrusions. Ups and downs with Bobby Gillespie. The strange
world of Kate, a kind of Arcadia. Mullord loses it in Wales.
My first implant. A friendship with Hedi Slimane.

'That first night with Kate Moss at her country mansion in the Cotswolds was carnage. Alan Wass was running about the house acting crazy in his cowboy boots and cowboy hat. He didn't really think I should be with Kate and was screaming, You're not having him, you're not stealing his soul. I was like, Yeah, Alan, man, it's gonna be fine, she's not the devil. He went, She is! She is the devil – you're coming with me to San Jose.

He crashed into Miranda Jones, Mick's wife, and they all went tumbling down the stone staircase. In the end, he had one cowboy boot on and a bloody nose, and they managed to pile him into a taxi to get him back to London, but halfway down the path he got out, and he was last seen running across the fields, screaming, It's for the boys, it's for the boys – you're not having his soul!

Earlier in the night, Alan had taken me to one side and said, Look, it's all good, Peter, but don't get sucked into this world. It's for the boys, isn't it, we'll just have a few drinks, you do the little show for the birth-day – it was Kate's bash for her thirty-first – and we'll get back to London. I was thinking, Well, I don't know, Alan, might just see what happens, do you know what I mean?

There was all kinds going on that night. Bobby Gillespie was playing. Mick Jones built a band up around him, and we did a load of covers. Danny Goffey was on drums, the guy from Spiritualized, lovely fella, Jason Pierce, was playing. Shane MacGowan was knock-ing about. I was there with my little shoebox with all my emergency supplies in it, and all these random celebrities were coming up asking me for a pipe. I had half the party trying to score crack off me and the other half trying to chase me out, saying, What are you doing here?

Jefferson Hack* was really concerned about my presence. It turned into a long weekend, and on the morning of the second day, he was just sat there on the stairs with his head in his hands. He looked up at me and said, How could you do this? I wore a 'What a Waster' badge for your band. What? I wasn't really sure who he was.

It was a mad weekend, but I remember clearly thinking, Wow, this is a bit of me – a big country house with a pool and shitloads of amazing records and fancy carpets and strange artwork and this girl who I sort of fell head over heels in love with. It was a bit like the Dot Allison thing, where I'd met this girl who I thought could be perfect, but whereas Dot wouldn't give me a set of keys to the house, Kate was like, Look, you may as well just move in if we're going to be in love. I was like, Yeah, that's more the vibe.

Apart from that first weekend of debauch in the country, a lot of mine and Kate's early meetings were quite clandestine. We'd meet in

---

* Founder of *Dazed & Confused* magazine and father of Moss's daughter, Lila Grace Moss-Hack.

strange back rooms of restaurants in London. Despite being this multimillionaire, she was saying how she was really just a girl from a council estate in Croydon, so in that first week we were together, I insisted she get on a bus with me. She went everywhere in a limo usually. We got dressed up in disguise, put on wigs, and jumped on the bus around London. We used to have a bit of a laugh, really. We got matching tattoos that first week too. I think I insisted on that. I wanted her to prove her love, so I said, You've got to get a tattoo with my initials on, you've got to get branded – it was more of an insecurity thing on my part. I tried to get her to come to the Pink Tower and to Paul Ro's and places like that, but that was a step too far – she was just horrified by the suggestion.

I met her parents early on and got on quite well with her mum. My mum and dad and Emily came and met Kate at this new little flat I'd moved into on Dove Road in Islington, quite close to James Mullord's. I'd filled it with a load of red plastic furniture and a couple of inflatable chairs. My dad said to Kate, What do you do? She was only small, and he didn't associate her with the supermodel from the papers. She just laughed. My mum and dad were more interested in the Welsh actor Rhys Ifans, who was also there that day. My little sister was really into that: Oh, you're the guy who was in his pants in the film *Notting Hill*, so it was all a bit of a coup, really, for the family.

Bobby Gillespie lived very close to that flat on Dove Road, but his missus, Katy England, was dead against me. She forbade him from visiting, but he turned up one morning with his parka hood up over his eyes making a little pipe sign. It was just me and Alan at the flat, and Bobby was going, You're all lightweights, nothing you could give me could knock me out, so I thought I'd cook him up a special. He completely went down, fell down, and I thought we'd lost him. Then he levitated back up about ten minutes later, saying, Y'see, didn't even touch the sides. Katy England phoning him constantly, You're not at

Doherty's, are you? Me saying, I'll pop round later and we can have a jam and that. Aye, probably not a good idea, Pete.

There's a quite well-known photo of me with one eyeball going up my head looking absolutely shocking. It was taken at a Babyshambles gig we did with Danny Goffey on drums in January at the Garage in London. It was a bit of a celeb-packed gig, and we were really tight, really good. I just sneezed, halfway through the gig, and that was the photo. It ended up in the *Evening Standard* and *The Sun*. Bastards. They wrote I was out of it – 'Kate's junkie boyfriend', looking like 'the living dead'. Gutted. It was really the start of a very strange few years with the tabloids. You can't win with them, really. At first, I thought I'd be able to crack it: I'd give really good interviews, but they'd always make me look like a complete cunt.

The *Sunday Mirror* ran a photograph of me smoking heroin on the front page – same vibe: 'Kate Moss's new lover is a junkie!' Word got round that Max Carlish had sold these photos – they were stills from the video footage he'd shot at the 'Killamangiro' recording session – to the paper. It was quite a good photo, actually. I was wearing a crash helmet with a QPR shirt on. Max admitted it and said he was going to give me a cut. The whole thing was messy.

Alan and I went round to pick up the money at this nice hotel called the Rookery in Farringdon. Lovely place, good little hideaway, expensive though – £400 a night. Max had promised me £30,000 in cash, but when we met him, he threw a crumpled fiver in my face and said, Feed your habit with that, you junkie. So, I knocked him out, and then it just went a bit mad from there. I took his cash card, thinking he had all the money in his account, made him give me the pin number and went down to the cashpoint, but he was overdrawn £250 with no available funds. That was lucky, really, because God knows what would have happened if we'd actually taken cash off him.

Basically, the next thing I know I'm being held underneath the Highbury Magistrates charged with robbery and blackmail. Alan got released, but they set my bail at some stupid amount, £150,000. I just presumed Kate was going to stump up the bail, or if not, Rough Trade were going to do it, but no one did. I was already on a suspended sentence for the flick knife, and they were saying I could get four years if found guilty of the new charges. I then had to spend the next six nights in HMP Pentonville while the bail money was raised. The whole thing was a con, a swindle. I was a rampant addict, but I hadn't really done anything – this blackmail and robbery thing that was eventually thrown out, dropped by the Crown Prosecution Service a couple of months later, was a complete joke, complete persecution. Have you seen the documentary Carlish ended up making? Where's he's singing 'Together in electric dreams. We'll always be together', that horrible song, and he's filming himself to camera going, 'Max on Pete, inside Kate' . . . it was all pretty creepy.

While I was in Pentonville, Will Brown sold a story about me. He said he thought I might 'swing', commit suicide, while I was inside, saying how he'd saved my life in Wandsworth and how I was not a bad boy, really, just a middle-class goody-two-shoes. I was so embarrassed. Pentonville is a Category B prison but a lot more chaotic than Wandsworth, and it's a local jail – so there were people I knew, or half knew, or people who reckoned they knew me. Also, in Wandsworth I was anonymous, now I was with Kate and in the tabloids – it was a different ball game. My head was a bit more mangled too, and I was very paranoid. People kept saying, You want to watch out, this guy says he's gonna knock you out. Even people saying to me, Which one's Doherty? I'm gonna knock him out, not knowing that I was he. This is when I met General Santana, Jamaican fella – his real name was Roy Billings. He seemed to have the walk of the wing, a good person to know. General would communicate with me by singing mostly, and we wrote a song, 'Pentonville', that we recorded together when we got out and I put on *Down in Albion*.

There was uncertainty while I was in Pentonville over the bail money. I didn't really know what was going on. Eventually, they reduced the bail to £50,000, and it was paid for by a deal Mullord set up with *The Sun*. It was the worst story ever, had me in my fatigues, my prison tracksuit, on the steps in Mullord's office saying loads of lame stuff about Kate, which I thought they'd never print but obviously in hindsight that's all they were interested in printing. They also ran texts and pictures of Kate. That sort of thing really wound Kate up. She was fuming. From her point of view, she'd spent years building up this empire – this pristine image – and then I sort of turn up with this complete non-understanding of how her people work with the media. I thought we could just make a go of it as a couple and fuck everything else, that was my approach, but she was more like, No, you've got to get clean and then everything will be fine. That was the running battle for the next two and a half years, really, the drugs and her obsession with the tabloids and her image. Kate's big thing was not taking her for a cunt. It was her favourite expression.

When I got out of Pentonville, I was on 10 p.m. curfew, which was absolute hell, really restrictive. The other part of my bail conditions was I had to go to the Nightingale Clinic for twelve weeks of counselling and therapy. It was quite close to Kate's London home in St John's Wood. She turned up in the middle of the night and I decided I'd done enough, I'd had enough detox, I was getting out. She came in disguised as a Russian peasant with a blanket over her head. They wouldn't let me out, but I kicked the door through. Walking back to her house, we watched this pre-dawn terrorist raid, just plotted up on this wall, four in the morning, as it was getting light, all these cops going into these flats, banging and shouting and dragging people out.

KATE

The court extended my curfew for two hours so Babyshambles could play what was our biggest gig at the time, at Brixton Academy at the end of February. I said to Pat on the way to the gig, Look, let's just throw a couple of punches at each other to make it look like we're having a fight, it'll be fine, and he was like, No, I don't want to do it, I just want to play guitar. It was a bit weird, a bit of the Carl syndrome, but all part of my vision of the ultimate rock-'n'-roll decadence and coolness. Pat wasn't having any of it, and in the end we wound up fighting on stage about him not wanting to fight. There's footage of Alan and Mick Jones running over and dragging us apart.

Recording the *Down in Albion* album was a dark, paranoid time because I couldn't take any gear. I'd just got my first naltrexone implant, used to reduce the effect of heroin. It's a slow-release block. Nowadays, they can do it with an injection, but back then they had to put a plastic tube under the skin that had slow-dissolve pills in it, and that fucked me up royally, just fucked my head right up. I was smoking a lot of white and there was no comedown. My whole balance system, my whole self, was out of whack. I couldn't fly, really, because I had this implant.

Between them Kate, Miranda and Mick had conspired to book this residential studio in Wales, Twin Peaks, that was in the middle of a beautiful valley in the foothills of the Brecon Beacons. I think we were only there seven days in March. From day one there were problems between the people who ran the place and James Mullord. It started when they offered us some vegan stew and James was just sat there with his hood up, fiddling with his crack bottle in his pocket. It created a very strange atmosphere. I loved James, he was my best friend and manager, but he had quite a dark personality in a lot of ways. He had this eternal punk attitude: he was actively hostile in a lot of his attitudes to the world, and he was really anti-music industry. Mullord was public enemy number one at Rough Trade.

I found it strange that this first Babyshambles album was tied to Rough Trade but Carl's album that he did with his new band, Dirty Pretty Things, was nothing to do with them.* I would have thought they'd have preferred to keep working with Carl after all the trouble they'd had from me.

Kate and Miranda came down to the recording, and I've got really dark memories of them doing this weird goose-stepping march round the studio while I was trying to record. Kate sang on the song 'La Belle et la Bête'. It was a song I'd written with Wolfman and Chev, Robert Chevalley, who was an acquaintance of Wolfman's, a streetwise cockney chirpy sparrow who used to drive me around and act as a sort of minder. The odd line was Chev's – 'That girl's out way ahead of the game' was his. The line 'One was a pikey with a knowledge of scriptures' was what Wolfman wrote about Chev. Kate and I had a really good night at the Boogaloo Bar when she came on stage and did that song. I was really impressed with her that night – the only way on stage was along and across the bar. It was the sort of thing that I thought might have put her off, but she was up for it. I was delighted. But I don't think we got a lot done in Wales, maybe the basics of tracks like 'Fuck Forever'.

We tried to relax one day while we were in Wales, just enjoy the local scenery. We all got on a barge and went down this local canal, and Pat dropped a massive rock of crack off the side of the barge and had to go in and get it. It was a disaster. I tried to escape back to London. I nicked the security guys' Land Rover, but I was so fucked I drove off the side of the mountain into a ditch. So, it all fell apart, really, that session.

---

* In February 2005, Barât signed a solo deal with Mercury Records that was negotiated by Alan McGee and worth a reputed £1 million.

The effect of an implant doesn't last for ever. Once they wore off, Kate was always on my back to get another. I must have had about fifteen of them over the time I was with her – sometimes they'd last a month, sometimes for three months. It'd always be the same – they'd run out and she'd say, OK, well, let's see what's so good about this heroin, let's see if you can handle it, and then invariably after a couple of weeks she'd say, Look at the state you're in, you've got to get another implant. But there were those moments of grace where the implants weren't working before I had to get the next one where I was able to do what I wanted – where I just felt like I was king of the world, staying out at her gaff in the country in this big massive four-poster bed.

Ever since I'd left home, I'd never really had a telly, so it was good just to be able to sit in bed watching telly with a big fat remote control. She'd be off somewhere round the other side of the world modelling, and I'd just be pottering around with my guitar in this big old dusty country house, tripping my balls off, really, really happy, actually, alone in the midst of luxury. I can't tell you, man, felt proper – I'd reached Arcadia. Wolfman or Gill would turn up with some bits, and Kate would be on the phone within half an hour, saying, My housekeeper has told me you've got some scumbags round, rah, rah, rah, rah. I'd be, No, no, they were helping me with a project.

I also used to love the weekends when her place in the country was almost like an Evelyn Waugh-type scene, loads of fashion boys talking about their exploits the previous night over Bloody Marys for breakfast. She used to have loads of amazing camp friends who worked really hard and were really talented. There was James Brown, who used to call himself hairdresser to the stars, which was an understatement, because he literally did everyone's hair in fashion. He was always trying to get me to invite Drew over for the weekend. We'd all dress up and do funny accents, go to the country pub, pick magic mushrooms in the fields, boat on a little lake or just go walking.

Hedi Slimane was another of Kate's pals, a lovely camp designer who was creative director at Dior Homme. He was a really caring, sweet, sensitive soul but also uber cool in terms of his profile. With Hedi we proper connected. Even when I split up with Kate and he went to YSL, he still always sent me suits or turned up at gigs. I did loads of fashion shoots with Hedi for a load of international magazines that probably wouldn't have touched me otherwise.[*]

For a long time while I was with Kate, Babyshambles was on full throttle, writing and recording. Occasionally she threw a spanner in the creative works, but on the whole she was really encouraging of me as a songwriter, and I think she was quite proud of my songwriting, so in a lot of ways it was a positive relationship. It was like when I did a version of 'Chim Chim Cher-ee', from *Mary Poppins*, with an orchestra at the Meltdown Festival that Jarvis Cocker curated. It was part of a Walt Disney songbook gig. She came to all the rehearsals and made sure I worked really hard on it. Then she insisted I was involved in the dog song 'Home Sweet Home' from *Lady and the Tramp*, with Shane MacGowan and Nick Cave and Jarvis, so I somehow ended up on that as well. She was pushing my musical career.

I think people often don't think of her as a person, but she was a great kid, really – but definitely a mixed old bag. One time I was supposed to be going to record this song with Dot Allison. There was a big producer and a big studio, Metropolis, booked. Everyone loved the song we were going to do too: it was a twist on the lyrics of 'I Wanna Be Adored', 'I Wanna Be Your Dog', 'I Want to Hold Your Hand' and 'I Wanna Be Your Man'. The chorus went 'I wanna hold your hand, I

---

* Such as Italian *Vogue*, *Arena Homme+* and *Interview*. Slimane also published a book in 2005, *London: Birth of a Cult* (Steidl Verlag), largely made up of photographs of Peter, who he also named as inspiration for his spring 2006 Dior Homme collection.

wanna break your heart, I wanna be your man, I wanna break your heart, I wanna be your dog, I wanna break your heart, I wanna be adored, I wanna break your heart'.

I didn't go to the recording in the end and fell asleep in this little room they called the snug, which was all old sofas and dusty books. Kate woke me up saying, Dinner's ready, and apparently, this is the story Bobby Gillespie told me afterwards, I came round and just pushed her in the face and told her to fuck off – doesn't really sound like me, but he said that's what I did. The next thing I knew Bobby was coming at me with a candelabra, and then at the last minute Katy England's hand appears and pulls the candelabra back and everyone tumbles into a ball on the floor, lots of screaming and shouting, accusations flying. There were a few punch-ups like that at hers.

Quixotic is a word I'd apply to my relationship with Kate. But I always thought I was causing her more trouble than I was worth, really. On the other hand, some of my pals thought the relationship wasn't great for me. That was always Alan's gut feeling – hence his one-man mission to save my soul.'

XX
Down in Albion

2005 (part 2): Witchcraft in the recording studio. Booted off the yacht. A summer of huge gigs. That performance with Elton John. Kate and the missed Babyshambles date with Oasis. Who the Fuck is Pete Doherty? Nutting Johnny Borrell and banging in the winner at the Soccer Sixes.

'There was a strange witchcraft in the air over the summer when we were at the Doghouse in Henley-on-Thames finishing *Down in Albion*. We went down to a swamp in the woods to record sound effects for the start of 'Back from the Dead', and I was thinking, If this album comes together, anything is possible. There was a lot of primal screaming going on, with a lot of lyrics that drained me spiritually, like 'The 32nd of December', which I wrote about the Astoria gig and the end of The Libertines and Carl, especially the line 'You were always a stickler for manners, but you never said goodbye, how come you never said goodbye'. I started getting jittery. I felt like I had to go into such a dark space to convey the songs with real energy. It just used to murder me. I'd put myself in a right state. A lot of the songs were about the situation I was in – my broken heart over The Libertines, jail and the strange upside-down world of Kate Moss celebrity. I was self-mythologising in a way.

That's what I'd always done and probably always will do – trying to make sense of, or describe, everything that's going on in my life.

On that album I capture some of the more ominous undertones. My life was monstrous in some ways at the time, and I was scrabbling around for some direction or some light. I'd been pretty debauched before I met Kate, but this was a whole new thing. There was a guy whose wife and daughter had been killed in the December 2004 tsunami. I came back one time, and he was there saying how the only way for him to recover was for Kate to marry him. Kate was asleep in this silver gown with massive sunglasses on. That was the night 'Uncle Ronnie' came round as well – Ronnie Wood – I ended up having a bit of a set-to with him. I also had a bit of a scrap with Joe Corré, the son of Vivienne Westwood and Malcolm McLaren – he was dancing with Kate a bit too familiarly at some party at the house, and I pushed him away. I didn't mean to knock him down, but he went arse over tit and cracked his head on the floor and got up and started screaming how he'd been trained to kill with his hands by Special Services. People were holding him off me. With Kate, sometimes I'd be like, What the fuck is going on?

There were a lot of aggressive songs on *Down in Albion* too, like 'Pipedown', another song I co-wrote with Pat, and which was just what the band needed – 'Pipedown' and 'Fuck Forever' were always great live. 'À rebours' was a belter too. Jake Fior takes the credit for introducing me to the book by J.-K. Huysmans that the song was named after. He gifted me a copy of it. I was fascinated by the description of the jewel-encrusted tortoise in *À rebours*. I developed a bit of a penchant for tortoises. When I was out at Kate's in the country, I bought a load from *Loot*. I also bought a goat at some point as well.

It was such a sacred thing to be calling the album *Down in Albion* and finally recording 'Albion'. The Libertines really should have done 'Albion' for the second album – I don't know why we didn't. It was a point-blank, slam-dunk, stonker of a Libertines song – we'd done 'Albion' from day one. The Babyshambles version was great, but something happened in the production of the album that made the whole listening experience somehow incomplete for me. I really thought 'La Belle et la Bête' was a strong, well-crafted song, but we sort of did an ad-hoc live version of it that goes round and round in circles. I was really disappointed with it. Mick Jones does these backing vocals that I thought were a bit off, too comic, where he goes, Eeeeeeviiiiiiiill. It didn't hit it. I had trouble listening to that over the years. It was such a strong song. When we used to do it live, we'd smash it.

'Up the Morning' was another one on the album where I really believed in the song, really had my sights set on it, and we never quite captured it. I can't listen to that for more than a few seconds without thinking of how much I failed with that song – it's heartbreaking for me. I've even got 'Up the Morning' tattooed on my arm. Pat had this guitar sound on the demos that we couldn't replicate when we were recording it, we couldn't get it, and it all fell apart. Also, the lyrics were incomplete when we were recording – basically, there are no lyrics, I'm literally mumbling. I'll never know to this day what I was trying to say, but again it was one of those long-lost nights at the Doghouse completely strung out and trying to rely on the music to take me back to a place of harmony.

I was sitting in a jacuzzi on Sadie Frost's boat in Cannes feeling really out of place while Mick Jones and everybody were playing the Nellee Hooper mix of 'Fuck Forever'. I was thinking to myself, This isn't how I wanted the song to be. I wasn't really sure who Nellee Hooper was, to be honest – someone said he'd worked with Madonna. It was just assumed I'd know who he was, and I didn't.* I eventually got

---

* As well as Madonna, Hooper had produced Soul II Soul, Björk, Massive Attack and U2.

thrown off this yacht because they said I was smoking crack in the engine room.

After that week in Cannes, things weren't good with Kate. I holed up at Gill's, and Miranda came round. I heard Miranda saying to Kate on the phone, You've lost him, you've lost him, he's been captured by dark forces. So, Kate came over to Hackney in a limo, and finally I got in the car.

There was psychosis all around me. Mullord would have this thing of keeping things in his sock for me, and he'd just pull them out one by one – they'd always be there if I wanted a pipe. I remember his socks were bulging the day we did the anti-fascism rally, *Unite – May Day Music Against Fascism*, in Trafalgar Square. It was a great day. I played with Alan, and it was really celebratory, and we felt we were doing something positive amidst the melee of my life – felt like we were fighting for something we believed in. Those anti-fascism gigs were normally quite serious, just speeches and you do a few songs, but the tempo really picked up that day – the crowd, there was 40,000 there, basically went mental, and it was a good young mixed-race crowd as well, and they fucking loved us. I was so happy with what I saw as the mainstream kids' response to me.

Another affirmation came when Babyshambles did Glastonbury for the first time, and we played the main stage to what they said was the biggest crowd of the day. I was running really late. Kate's people insisted they had to drive the blacked-out Range Rover Vogue, the 4x4, all the way through the crowd up to the barrier. I was wearing an amazing Vivienne Westwood cardigan that I'd nicked when I'd gone down to see Kate doing a shoot somewhere – turned out to be an £8k cardigan. I thought if I wore it on stage at Glastonbury it'd be good publicity for them, and then they'd let me have it, but they actually sent someone to get it back off me. I was absolutely gutted.

While we were playing, I saw Scarborough Steve in the crowd, shirtless, looking as amazing as ever, right down the front. It was like a proper bolt of joy straight into my soul – not only because he looked fantastic but because he was obviously having a great time, getting off on what we were doing.

There was a lot of attention on us, on Kate, at Glastonbury, but I put on a fake beard, long black wig, sunglasses and a poncho, and she put on a black wig, and we went walking around the site. We were recognised in the end, at about five in the morning. Things like that were really, really good fun.

The Wireless gig in Hyde Park at the end of June was another absolute belter. There was something magic about that gig – it was bonkers, we were all buzzing, the vibe was great afterwards, everyone really together. I met Ian Brown that day. I couldn't wait to tell him how beautiful his lyrics were and what they'd meant to me growing up. In fact, on 'What Katy Did Next', a song on *Down in Albion* I co-wrote with Alan, there was some Stone Roses lyrical tinkering going on, a complete rip-off of 'Good Times' on *Second Coming*. Unfortunately, I think my hands were black from the pipe that day, and Ian kept saying, Have you been gardening, have you been gardening? Then he said, There's something not right about your missus, and, Isn't she a model? Difficult nut to crack, Ian Brown.

We were supposed to support Oasis that summer at the Milton Keynes Bowl in July, after playing the Isle of Wight and Ibiza Rocks festivals, but we missed it. Mullord and the rest of the band were left stranded at the venue. Awful. Kate and me had been in Paris for Hedi's birthday, his thirtieth. At the gig someone had a giant inflatable penis in the crowd, and Liam Gallagher said, Oh, I'm glad to see Pete Doherty did make it after all. Which was not a bad line, not bad at all. Hedi's birthday party was actually one occasion where I really felt like me and Kate were just together in the right environment, dancing to the Pet Shop Boys. When I was a kid, my dad had Hancock in the car, but he used to have a mixtape of the Pet Shop Boys too, and whenever we'd have long journeys in the car, which was half our life, going to see QPR or AmyJo run, it would always be Pet Shops Boys as driving music. Their version of 'Always on My Mind', I heard that a million times before I heard any other versions.

Unfortunately, the gig most people remember from that time is the one with Elton John at Live 8.* It was Kate's idea; she introduced me to Elton. We went on this excursion to Watford football stadium where he was preparing for a gig, and they were like two old friends meeting. He asked if I wanted to do a song for this charity gig, and we ran through it at the stadium, and it was all good. We chose the song, 'Children of the Revolution' by Mark Bolan, together. We were listening to stuff in the Watford football dressing room, and we decided on that.

It was disastrous on the day. I felt that Elton John's band had it in for me – they changed the key of the song. It was so embarrassing. They were sort of smirking. I think I pulled it back from the brink by kissing him on my way off – that's what took away from the poor vocal performance. I was shockingly displeased with my performance that day. The reviews afterwards ranged from 'unprofessional' through 'shambolic' to 'rubbish'. Maybe it looked like a sabotage job on my part, where I just turned up, looked cool – I looked the nuts that day – and did an absolute god-awful performance in true punk style, but I was actually pretty ashamed. I'd like to have nailed it. I had to scuttle back to Kate's country mansion shamefaced, and there was a strange atmosphere. It was another of those long weekends with Mick Jones sitting by the pool, all the kids running round, that would invariably end three or four days later in some sort of drama.

* There were 210,000 present and a multimillion audience watching or listening live on Radio 1 and BBC One for the charity concert at Hyde Park.

It went to number four, but I don't actually remember 'Fuck Forever' doing that well as a single when it came out. It's definitely stood the test of time – it's still a fucking stonker of a song. They did a mini edit of the word 'fuck' so it could be played on the radio. The chorus was a riposte to the line in 'What Became of the Likely Lads' 'What became of the likely lads? What became of forever?' – it perfectly tied into it. That's always what I was thinking when I was singing it, as opposed to what Sylvain Sylvain from the New York Dolls thought. I saw him at Benicàssim a couple of years ago, and he went, Hey man, I know you, you're that guy who wrote that song about banging a chick all night, 'Fuck Forever'. I went, Er, yeah, that's it. He was on his way to the stage, and I didn't want to say to him, Well, actually, it is self-referential, pertaining to The Libertines lyric about not maintaining a friendship for all time. For people who know their onions, the title is also a blatant rip-off of the title of a piece of Sex Pistols-related graphic art designed by Jamie Reid. When Carl first started hanging round with Danny Goffey, there was a massive 'Fuck Forever' print in Danny's house, and something about it blew me away, and I had the title away. I remember filming the video for 'Fuck Forever' on Brick Lane, and the hat they had me wearing was more of a pork pie than a fedora. I'll never forgive myself for that. I really felt like it was mission aborted that day.

There was lots of chaos and melodrama at that time. They were filming that documentary, *Who the Fuck Is Pete Doherty?*, for Channel 4, and they got a lot of it. The director Roger Pomphrey, with his perm mullet, was another one of Mullord's connections. He was someone else who was going to catapult us into the public consciousness; there was an element of Max Carlish to the whole thing. I think I attacked Roger at one point or spat at the camera.

I also nutted Johnny Borrell when Babyshambles and Razorlight both played the Reading Festival in late August 2005. It was actually Alan Wass who had the beef with Johnny – something to do with his girlfriend. Alan was saying he was going to hurt Johnny, and I thought, This is not going to end well, we're going to end up getting chucked out of the festival. So, I went down to stop it, but when I got there Johnny was so arrogant and so weird with me I thought, Oh fuck it, I'm going to have some of this myself.

The next week we were actually up against Razorlight in the Soccer Sixes, the celebrity charity football event, at Upton Park, and Johnny Borrell had two minders with him and sunglasses on. We won again that year – beat Razorlight, the *Sun* and Radio 1. Jai was in the team, great footballer, and because Kate was there, we had David Beckham's agent, Dave Gardner, who'd been a schoolboy international. Kate was mates with his wife, Davinia Taylor. Former West Ham striker Frank McAvennie played for us too. We also had the General, who'd just got out of nick, and Alan playing. I think there were only two actual members of Babyshambles in the team: me and our drummer Adam Ficek. Babyshambles actually won the Soccer Sixes three years in a row. I scored the winner in the final at Upton Park. It was an amazing, beautiful day, and my little boy Astile was there to watch. The press didn't report any of that. Didn't even say we won. They said that I pretended to sniff the chalk line like Robbie Fowler when I hadn't. Typical.'

XXI
High As a Kate

*2005–2006: The Kate Moss cocaine scandal. Phone tapping
and the paranoia. The end of Mullord. Pat falls to pieces.
Failing to impress Terry Hall. Police raid the gig. Gio-Goi
poster boy and abandoned solo album. Rehab in America.
Breaking up and making up with Kate. Arrested three times
in twenty-four hours. A two-week stay in Pentonville.*

'I've always wondered if the big Kate exposé, where she was photographed appearing to snort cocaine in Metropolis in Chiswick during a Babyshambles session, had something to do with Paul Ro. The pictures were supposed to be worth £300,000. They were used on the front page of the *Daily Mirror* on 15 September 2005, under the headline 'High As a Kate'. Paul had everyone's mobile number, and he was always trying to set things up with the papers. He'd say I've been in touch with a guy from *The Mirror* or *The Sun* and they want to do a positive piece, and he'd end up brokering the deal.

The phone tapping was bonkers, but back then the fact the press was accessing my phone did not occur to me, not for a second. I remember saying, though, I thought I was being bugged, and the tabloids lambasted me as a paranoid drug addict. In 2013, following the Leveson Inquiry into phone hacking, I was paid by News International as a victim. I didn't want to get too much into it. I felt like if I really went back through the papers and some of the ridiculous things they were writing, I could take them to the cleaners, but then again sometimes I think it wasn't so bad. I used to get away with quite a lot as well. In the end, I just went for the stock settlement.

Old friendships were destroyed by the phone tapping – everyone was accusing everyone else of selling stories. They even tapped my sister's phone, and we believe my mum was tapped as well. AmyJo got a payout. My mum didn't want to go through with making a claim. There had been times in the past when photos had been taken off my phone and used in the press, so after the 'High As a Kate' thing Kate turned against me. She said, If you didn't sell the photos, how did they get in the papers? And I couldn't say. I just presumed a friend of mine must have done it. At the time, I blamed James Mullord. Nothing else made any sense other than Mullord was involved. He'd told me in the past he'd been offered a hundred grand for pictures of me and Kate together. At the time, it was such a big scandal that Mullord appeared on the front of the *Evening Standard* claiming he was innocent – that was seen as newsworthy.

That was the end of me and Mullord. It was sad, because I don't think Mullord had anything to do with it. I'm fairly certain now those photos of Kate in the studio were actually taken by two Bangladeshi crack dealers. They disappeared soon after. I first met them when they were just kids, thirteen- or fourteen-year-old shotters. The word on the street in Whitechapel was they'd made a shitload of money somehow overnight and disappeared to Bangladesh to buy some land.

The whole thing really fucked up Kate's contracts – she lost loads, including a reputed £4-million-a-year deal with H&M – and all her people were fuming at me. The police even wanted to speak to her, but all charges against her were eventually dropped for lack of evidence. As a sort of mea culpa, she went to treatment at the Meadows in Arizona, a well-known celebrity rehab place. She was also supposed to have dumped me, but we were actually still in touch – the agreement was after she'd gone to rehab, I'd go for a month as well. There were all these stupid things in the papers about us breaking up, but it was all bollocks.

The Kate stuff overshadowed *Down in Albion*. It came out at the same time. I always look forward to having a good read of my album reviews, but they were all about shit that was nothing to do with the record. I was getting so much attention for bollocks or for the relationship but at no point were people saying, This guy can write tunes. I was really disappointed. The album didn't have that bounce when it hit, didn't blow up. It didn't equal what the previous Libertines album had done. I didn't have a manager either. I was in a bit of a free fall. I was asking everyone to manage me – everyone had a turn, I think. The General did his best, but he was an artist first and foremost. Paul Ro had a go, and then my old fantasy literary saucepot Sally Anchassi popped back up, and I gave her a go at managing Babyshambles.

She was going out with Terry Hall from The Specials and had turned up at a few Babyshambles shows with Terry's son, who was a big fan of the band. When Sally came back into the fold, she sorted it for me to meet Terry Hall. I was really into The Specials and wanted to impress him, so I'd been rehearsing 'Do Nothing', a Specials single from 1980, and I planned to play it when he came through the door. I was with Purple, who I was trying to get to join Babyshambles for the tour. He was a Jamaican, from the square by the Pink Tower. When Terry turned up with his son, I was tripping my nuts off – I'd injected ketamine. I thought Purple was this giant hippo, and I thought I was in Aswad, and I tried to sing 'Do Nothing' but at the wrong speed, Blackpool Empress Ballroom speed, temazepam remix. Terry tried to be as friendly as he could, but sort of backed away and ushered his son out.

Pat really started to fall apart on that tour we did to support the album. He'd spent nine days in Pentonville after some sort of argument with his missus, and then while he was inside she came round to see us. We sort of threw her out, her and her friend, this lovely ballerina. It got back to him that she'd been round to see people while he was in prison. That was the beginning of the end for Pat, even though all the charges against him were dropped. There was a gig at Dublin University where he smashed his guitar and left the stage.

A good example of the chaos on that *Down in Albion* tour was when we played Shrewsbury and the police raided the venue, running around with dogs looking for vast amounts of drugs. We were all functioning addicts who just bought drugs and took them almost immediately – there was no large shipments or anything – but they were on this mission to tear up all the amps, the vans and everything. I saw Pat running through an emergency exit, proper Keystone Cops vibe, Benny Hill, and he got away as well. I was on the stage waiting for them to come and get me so I could show them I didn't have anything, but they didn't even search me or offer me any reason for detainment – it was just enough I was Doherty. I got arrested for nothing – they didn't find anything on me. They went through all my journals at the station and found some Valium inside the pages of one of them, a prescription drug. It was all so ridiculous. I was held in the station for a couple of days, and we had to cancel three gigs, and when I was released without charge, there was a paparazzo there – just him and no one else. I was just sitting on the bonnet of his car talking to him for ages.

Once the tour ended, I was homeless again, so I was staying at this cheap hotel on Brick Lane, the International, but I got banned after the police raided it and I ended up in Bath, Somerset. I managed to get this flat that was attached to Bath Moles club, their recording studio. It was a really modern apartment flat. I thought it would really put Chev to the test, because it was like, How are we going to score round here? and actually he scored in about thirty seconds. I went down there to do some demos for a solo acoustic album I had planned. In exchange for letting me record there for free, I was going to lend my name to something they were doing. It was some harebrained scheme, and I ended up getting this apartment to live in.

Kate got out of treatment, and we had this really emotional encounter. So, I set off for my treatment at the Meadows in Arizona with all my drugs hidden in my luggage and fell asleep on the motorway hard shoulder on my way to Heathrow in my Jag. I'd stopped for a pipe. I was woken up, with a crack pipe in mouth, by a policeman banging on the window. He went, All right, Pete, you off to rehab? It was like he knew what was going on, and then I followed the police car all the way to Heathrow. It was so weird.

When I got to the Meadows, they found all the bits in my baggage, plus what I'd hidden inside the lining of my jeans – they really knew their stuff over there. It was a different vibe than UK rehab – a mix of absolutely loaded trust-fund kids and people trying to avoid federal convictions by doing rehab. One guy shared in the group therapy how he was in for looking at child porn on the internet. I couldn't handle that. I refused to be in a group with him. I was horrified. After two weeks, Kate was supposed to come and visit me and take me to the Grand Canyon in a helicopter, and I got the right hump when she didn't show up. So, in the end I did a runner.

Then, as soon I got back to London at the end of November, I got arrested again, charged with coke and heroin possession. That was Wolfman's fault. He wanted me to go look at some art with him, and we found ourselves in Kensal Rise, and I said I'd never seen my paternal grandfather's grave, so we detoured to Kensal Rise Cemetery. It was the middle of the night, and I had no idea where the grave was, and Wolfman got really pissed off, saying, We're not going to walk round and check every name on every grave. Then he was driving a bit dodgy, and we got pulled.

When Kate found out I hadn't finished the treatment, she told me point-blank that that was it, there was no way we could see each other now. I said, Yeah, but you were supposed to come and get me in a helicopter for a day trip to the Grand Canyon. The split was all over the press. Kate was quoted in the *Daily Mirror* saying, 'I wish I'd never met him, he's a user in every sense of the word.' Everything was falling apart. I dyed my hair blonde and sang a strange version of 'Karma Chameleon' on Paul Ro's computer. I also did 'Last Christmas' as well, just crying into the camera. There was a lot of blood too. He got me on film razor-blading a 'K' for Kate into my arm. I'd just started using blood on my artwork – one of these 'blood paintings' had featured on the cover of *Full Moon Empty Sports Bag*. Paul sold the original to a gallery for £1,000. That was the rather inauspicious start to my professional art career, more of which later.

Luckily Kate had me back for Christmas. She called on Christmas Eve and said, I'm sending a car for you to come down to the country. It was all supposed to be secret. It was amazing, actually. One of her security guards, this Maori bloke, had all his family there, and they sang their equivalent of Christmas carols in the big stone reception hall. After that me and Kate would just have these clandestine meetings. James Brown would get in touch with me, call from a certain payphone using some code word, and I'd have to go to this flat in Pimlico, across the river from Battersea. It was like a strange tenement flat that was used for that purpose — we'd meet for the night, or meet for a couple of hours sometimes, but I wouldn't be allowed to tell anyone.

We were attracted to each other. I really loved her, and I knew she loved me – there was just all this messiness in between us, with all her chaos and my chaos. Sometimes we just needed to see each other.

Basically, she'd click her fingers and I'd come running. Then it would all go sour again. There was a great photographer called Nuha Rahik who I'd met in Nottingham at a Babyshambles gig, and she came to London with me on the bus. We were firm friends – she was taking photos – but the papers ran a story about her that was complete bollocks, saying I was shagging her. Obviously, Kate was not happy about that. That was a typical example of the tabloids creating problems between us.

It was a period of non-stop using and arrests and just trying to keep my head above water. I don't know if the press was tapping my phone and tipping them off, but I was getting nicked every other day. The police used to have a little league table – if one of them nicked me, they got a point, and if I got charged, it was three points. It was a competition among themselves, and they had a little award ceremony at the end of the month, like a fantasy-football thing. It was the same policemen nicking me all the time, and they used to have badges on, saying Free Pete Doherty. I look back and find that quite funny, but at the time it was awful. It was like the start of *Watership Down* when he says that thing about, You must move fast, because they'll try to catch you, and when they catch you, they will kill you.

A car I was in got stopped at the start of December and searched. They knew they would find something, and they did – heroin and crack. When they'd booked me in at Bethnal Green station, I saw Paul Ro getting escorted into a back office. Around the time of the 'High As a Kate' photo he was convicted of possession of Class As and handed a twelve-month conditional discharge. Paul knew everyone, from the Bangla boys to the Yardies over towards Hackney, where we used to go whenever we were flush and could afford some quality stuff.

I was never insured, never taxed, when I was getting nicked all the time. I regret that now. I think the police presumed that I wouldn't be stupid enough to drive without insurance, tax or an MOT. I was pulled four times in January 2006 – often just stopped under the pretence we were driving erratically, and then they'd search the car. All they ever found were these small amounts of drugs, so it was just possession charges.

One day I got nicked three times in twenty-four hours. The first time was really unfortunate, because I met this girl who looked just like Nefertiti, bumped into her on the street, and really hit it off. I must have been having a bad patch with Kate. I was going over to meet this girl for our first date, feeing really positive about it, and I got nicked that night driving over there and was held on remand. This girl was probably the one person in the country who didn't know who I was – she was properly in her own space. She'd cooked dinner, and it was waiting on the table, and I couldn't get in touch with her because the police had my phone. When I did eventually get out, she wasn't having any of it. She basically said, I don't believe you couldn't have called and told me you weren't going to make it. I was gutted. I got put into court in the morning, and then when I got out of court, I went to score, and they got me coming out. It wasn't even as if I was carrying big amounts. I never was. It was actually lucky the police did stop me that time, because I had this mad scheme on the boil of going to Europe with some New Age-type people, circus performers. They were going on a boat to do a show in Spain or Bulgaria, and I thought, Fuck it, I'll come with you, and I was just getting myself together to go meet them and do three months on the road, literally run away with the circus.

Then I got nicked that night as well. I went up to Birmingham in my Jag with a couple of lads from The View, who were just starting out, to watch Dirty Pretty Things in an attempt to try and clear the air with Carl. Wolfman and I had gone to see Dirty Pretty Things in Paris at one of their first shows in late 2005 and left after a couple of songs. Wolfman hated it. It turned out Carl had found out I was there, and he'd invited me on stage to do some songs, but Wolfman and I had already left. Shame. I thought the debut Dirty Pretty Things single 'Bang, Bang You're Dead' was quite a good tune, but it was definitely built on an old chord progression. I was actually quite impressed, secretly, when I heard it, because it was, Oh, it's about time he did something with that idea. The lyric was really upsetting, completely about me: 'I knew all long I was right from the start, about the seeds of the weeds that grow in your heart ...' Something like that. 'Bang, bang you're dead, always so easily led'. It doesn't really pull any punches – it's quite detailed in its bleak analysis.

Anyway, we got pulled over in Birmingham. I'd bought the Jag that day, and it hadn't been transferred into my name yet. Also, it turned out the Dirty Pretty Things weren't playing in Birmingham that night, they were playing in Norwich, so my whole alibi was to cock, which was a bit unfortunate. The cops charged me with theft and confiscated the car. I was held on remand for two weeks, and when I went up to get the car after I got out of Pentonville, it had been squashed into a little box . . . the bastards. It was a lovely car as well, that XJ6.

That second time in Pentonville at the end of January 2006 was really depressing. As well as car theft, there were all these other charges stacked up, for drug possession plus some minor driving infringements. We had to cancel a load of Babyshambles concerts. I got these pills pushed under the door of my cell, and I overdosed on whatever they were. I didn't know what they were. Someone said, Here you are, have a day out, Pete. I just took these pills, and they found me face down in my Rice Krispies, took me to the hospital wing. I spent ten days of the fourteen in the hospital wing, three or four of those days completely fucked in bed on a drip.

When I got out, I pleaded guilty to all charges and was banned from driving for six months and handed a twelve-month community order that stipulated I must undertake non-residential drug rehabilitation, including regular drug tests. Those old drug community orders, DOs or DTOs, drug orders or drug testing orders, meant they had complete tabs on me, because I had to go down there once a week and have my piss tested. They were the same as probation orders – there's no way you want to break them or you'd get a serious stretch inside. It meant that they would not only know when I was using, but every time they nicked me they'd be in with a chance of putting me away if they found any drugs. They had me by the balls, really.'

XXII
Mick

2006 (part one): Enter Mick Whitnall – new songs, sound and look. Ketamine times. Johnny Headlock loses it. A scandal over stolen photographs – 'You Sick Idiot!' Avoiding jail – 'One Lucky Crackhead!' New management and a big-money record deal. The Blinding EP and brushes with Alex Turner, Lily Allen and Mike Skinner.

'Mick Whitnall stepped in for Pat on guitar. I'd known him since the early days of The Libertines, and he'd been around Babyshambles, as a roadie and confidant, since the start. Mick brought a new musical influence to what I was doing. He was an old left-wing skinhead, into the Oi! scene, been a roadie for Bad Manners and The Exploited, and was really into ska and reggae. Jimmy Cliff was someone I started to listen to a lot.

My look changed too, because Mick and Hannah, his missus, who was a lecturer in art at Goldsmiths University, always had loads of clothes. I adopted a bit of a skinhead look: a Fred Perry T-shirt and jeans with braces – it was a look I'd always been interested in. You couldn't leave Mick's place in Lewisham without him giving you a shirt, or he'd say, These sunglasses will suit you, Peter, or, You wanna try these red socks? Wherever we went in the world, the first thing he'd do – well, apart from the obvious: Mick was another heavy heroin user – was hunt down a reasonably priced shoe shop. He definitely became the band's inbuilt stylist, style radar – all bands have them. I acted as one at certain times, but definitely Mick and Scarborough Steve were strong style icons – it was difficult to be in a band with them without that rubbing off or without wanting to nick some of their clothes.

But after Pat left I wasn't really sure whether to continue with Babyshambles. I thought about going solo or even starting something new with Mick – I told the *NME* we were working on an album together called *Whitnall and I*, which I thought was a clever title at the time. I suppose in a similar way to Pat, Mick and I were enabling each other's heroin addiction, but I was being regularly tested as part of my drug community order, so we were banging up ketamine instead and getting out there on some strange plane. Something I learned quite early on was ketamine and LSD don't show up on any tests.

The first gig Mick did with Babyshambles was at the *NME* awards in February 2006. We did 'Albion', and in the footage Mick's eyes are kind of inside out he's so fucked – you can just see the whites of his eyes as he's playing harmonica. We weren't allowed a table that night – we weren't allowed to party or anything, *and* I'd won an award, for Sexiest Man. It really pissed me off that they escorted us in and out because they expected us to cause trouble. So we did: we were swinging at any band we could find and then fighting with security when they threw us out. Halcyon days.

We had one or two gigs in Europe and the UK already booked, so Mick did those, and they seemed to go well. After a gig in Paris, I stayed on in the hotel while the bus went back to London. Gill had been following us in her old Vauxhall Cavalier, and she stayed behind in Paris and offered to drive me back to London. Johnny Headlock was knocking about too. When the three of us finally got to the ferry, customs ripped the car apart and found that *NME* Sexiest Male award in my chest of trinkets. They were all laughing at the award.

I'd got a new place to live on Laburnum Street in Shoreditch in a block of flats, and there was a lot of ketamine going around, and Johnny Headlock shouldn't have dabbled in that. I caught him trying to swim out of the flat, trying to swim down the steps on the stairwell. He was really confused and upset that he wasn't getting anywhere. He was like that for hours and hours. We were supposed to be going off to do a gig, and he was supposed to be loading up the van. Instead, he started going on about how he was trapped inside an episode of *Futurama*. He kept doing the character's voices to the point where he couldn't remember his own voice, and he ended up just sat crying on the floor because he'd forgotten who he was.

I went to do a couple of solo gigs in Austria for this mad woman, Bettina Aichbauer, who had booked us to appear at a porno cinema. I was supposed to have this big important meeting with Rough Trade when I got back. I can't remember what the meeting was about specifically, but it began to dawn on me I was going to need to find someone to replace Mullord. I needed someone proper so I could, sounds a bit trite, get back in the game, someone who could hold a functioning band together. I needed some help. I couldn't go round touring in a Jag for ever.

There was this very small gated-off area in front of the flats at Laburnum Street, and I had an old taxi that got squatted by a couple of ketamine brewers, and three Jags – an XJS and two old Jags – parked up. I got the Jags off Tony 'Big Vern' Smith at the Jag garage by Odessa. I had about ten Jags off him in total. If they broke down, we'd just leave them where they were. I was doing lots of gigs for cash in hand at the time. The next day I'd buy gear, a new hat and a Jag. That was my life for a long time, and I loved every minute of it.

Alize Meurisse and her mate Stephanie ended up moving into Laburnum Street, and it became like the new Albion Rooms. Alize was only twenty, but she was a photographer, artist and author. Her debut novel, which came out in 2007, was well received in France. She really tickled my literary ambitions. Initially, Alize documented everything with her little camera, took some great photos – really candid on-the-road stuff, or at the flat with dealers visiting, or pictures out of the flat window of me scoring in the street. She also ended up doing quite a bit of artwork for me. The *Grace/Wastelands* front cover is hers – I let people assume it was mine – and she did the cover of the next Babyshambles album too, *Shotter's Nation*. It was my idea to do the sketch of Thomas Chatterton on his back, but it's her artwork. Kate got really funny about Alize staying with me.

She was around when the flat was broken into and photos were stolen that ended up on the front page of *The Sun* under the headline 'You Sick Idiot'. That referred to one photo they took where it looks like I'm injecting an unconscious girl. Alize said she was asleep, and some-one came in through the window, and she was too scared to confront them. The place was ransacked – all of Alize's stuff was strewn every-where. They also took a photo I had of Kate in bed, and *The Sun* published that too.

The day that 'You Sick Idiot' paper came out, I went to buy a pint of milk from the paper shop on the corner, and the police nicked me. One of them had *The Sun* in their hand, and that was their exhibit A. The week before I'd been nicked and charged with possession, so I was now on twice-weekly drugs tests, and I got the impression the police thought they were finally going to be able to send me down with this new scan-dal. They raided the flat while I was being held for questioning and found a needle that contained the blood of this girl in the photo. She was a mate, came to loads of guerrilla gigs, and we were just doing stupid photos, an art project. I'd never slept with her, but when she spoke to the press, she was saying she was in love with me! I just needed for her to say I hadn't injected her with heroin, which was what the papers were saying but which wasn't the case.

I was shocked by that whole incident, how horrendous the accusations were. It makes me sick to my stomach that someone could actually think I could inject an unconscious kid like that, as opposed to thinking it was a stupid thing to take a photo of – which maybe it was. The point is the police and the papers brought my name into disrepute. It was libel. Something like that can taint a reputation. As soon as the police got round to interviewing the girl, it was obvious nothing had happened, otherwise I'd have been charged.

After that *Sun* article, it became a proper raging war with the tabloids. Those lads who were dealing on the 'Murder Mile' who I was knocking about with would have the paparazzi photographers' cars destroyed, their cameras smashed. I'd give the little urchins around Laburnum Street a tenner, and they'd set about them en masse, throwing bricks and stuff. There'd be swarms of paparazzi. I got done for assault for fly-kicking what turned out to be a BBC reporter in this scrum of them when I came out of court following a review of my community order – the judge actually said that I was making progress with my addiction and praised me for my determination. Obviously that news was buried beneath the assault headlines.

This is when Adrian Hunter and Andy Boyd came on board. They'd be my managers for the next ten years almost. I'd crossed paths with Adrian over the years. He was one of the cooler older crowd, a bit like Mick Whitnall. I used to see him dance to Northern Soul at this club he ran in Camden, Solo. I always liked a man who could dance. During the day, he was this grumpy Scots bloke, always in cool denim, doing the *Standard* crossword at the bar of the Good Mixer with a pint of Guinness. I'd tried to get a gig at Solo when I'd been booted out of The

Libertines, but he'd taken one look at Owen, who I was with, in his black Adidas tracksuit, and turned back to me and said, I'm not going to give you a gig, I know where the money's going. I actually felt like I could trust him because of that.

Adrian said he would consider managing Babyshambles, but first of all I'd have to give up drugs. I'd been fighting tooth and nail, letting everything be destroyed in my wake, just to keep hold of my pipe. He stood his ground for quite a while with the drugs, but it basically went from him saying I had to give them up to him not being able to be in the room when I was using to him basically refusing to facilitate.

Andy Boyd was his partner, and I was quite put off by Andy the first time I met him. I don't really know what vision I had of commercial success, but it wasn't Andy Boyd. I think I was waiting for more of a Colonel Tom Parker figure to emerge. Initially, I actually said I didn't want anything to do with Andy. I didn't think he was right for me or the band, but Adrian explained there was no way he was going to do it without him. Andy was quite arrogant and reminded me of a typical smug industry character. He'd been managing and in a relationship and songwriting partnership with Sophie Ellis-Bextor when she had that big hit 'Murder on the Dancefloor'. She ended up getting pregnant by someone else. Andy never really talked about it, but Mick knew all the gossip. He'd also been in a Britpop band called The Shave that almost made it. He was always singing, a karaoke king. The only way he could win my trust and confidence was to become this strange lynch-pin in the underworld. He changed from this BMW-driving Alan Partridge-like figure to the man who'd drive us about and pick things up. Andy got quite into the swing of it in the end. I insisted he started driving a Jag, and he went through a series of nice old Jags – he underwent a metamorphosis.

Sounds a bit mean on my part to say there was something at the beginning I didn't like about Andy, but I think it was mutual. He and

Adrian had visions of managing a big band, and they felt they could do it, but what they actually inherited was basically me in some kind of spiritual and creative cocoon, literally surrounded by blood and syringes. Mick and I started to have these long sessions, plotted up writing, and it became a very creative, fertile time. We went in and recorded a load of songs, and that was the genesis of *The Blinding EP* that came out towards the end of 2006. We recorded it in this studio under Fabric in Farringdon. This young northern lad, seemed about fourteen, popped down to say hello. I thought he was just some fan who wanted something signed. He was just getting in the way, so I was sort of a bit brusque with him, saying, Look, we're recording here, unless you've got any crack for me, you best toddle off, and he seemed a bit miffed. It was Alex Turner. Arctic Monkeys were at the peak of their first wave of fame, but I genuinely didn't know who he was. He obviously didn't have the heart to say, Look, I'm in Arctic Monkeys, I'd like to come and hang out in the studio. He just turned on his heels and tottered off. He must have thought I'd fobbed him off, because I tried to get backstage at an Arctic Monkeys gig later with Kate, because she really liked them, and he put out a request that we weren't to be allowed to watch from the side of the stage. I remember running up the ramp at this festival trying to avoid getting rugby-tackled by the Arctic Monkeys' security.

The actual recording session was ace though – they just let us have the run of the downstairs studio, and we produced this wicked EP ourselves with the engineer. Drew and Mick and Adam were really at the helm in the studio – it was our best collection of songs at the time. 'Sedative' was a top song, beautiful, pure Doherty/Whitnall. We also did old songs of mine, like 'The Blinding' and 'Love You but You're Green', complete tunes, or tunes I had a complete vision of, that I just needed the band to learn the parts to, didn't need anything added structurally. I think people presumed 'The Blinding' was about drugs, but that song goes way back, pre-dates drugs. It's more a biblical reference, medieval, someone getting their eyes gouged out to be able to see more clearly with their soul – a play on words, 'come and see the blinding', a really bad pun. 'Beg, Steal or Borrow' was another song on that EP, one I really believed in, and I'm so proud of the recording of it. I did this mad solo in one go, completely spangled, and I've never been able to do it again. That moment was actually captured for the *Arena* documentary that was shown on BBC Four at the end of the year.

Ashtar Al Khirsan followed us for a few months to make that documentary. She was an elderly woman, quite small, dressed in blouses and Second World War skirts and flat shoes. She struck me as quite earnest, interesting, not the usual sort of person that we'd have hanging round. And I was sort of wooed by those three little letters, BBC. I first met her when I was interviewed for a piece she did on Ray Galton and Alan Simpson, the comedy scriptwriters who wrote for Tony Hancock and who did *Steptoe and Son*. I just implicitly trusted her and admired her because she was involved in that.

She popped up on a Babyshambles German tour and interviewed me in this weird B&B, really broke me when she started asking about my dad. You can see me in tears on the documentary. I don't think I realised how affected I was by the things to do with my dad. She got it on film how upset I was. The relationship with my dad was lost completely during this period. I think he was unable to deal with his son being a drug addict, like a lot of parents. I was a little bit annoyed he was taking that attitude. It didn't really occur to me that at that time he was still very much working with the army, and for him to see me in the tabloids all the time, and not for positive things, especially because it's his name as well . . . it was a bit of that old-fashioned sense of disgracing the family name.

My mum's book *A Prodigal Son* came out during this period. In fact, a load of books came out about me at the same time. They were all kind of unreadable. A *Daily Mirror* guy did one: loads of misquotes, strange book. I remember looking online at some of these books, and it seemed like they weren't really proper books, just covers, or collections of photos and strange quotes. My mum's book was obviously different. I found it emotional and quite interesting to hear her side of things, but maybe some of the things that were being presented as quite tragic and upsetting I thought were, not exactly amusing, but just not as serious as interpreted, like when she had me lying on my back in the cemetery. She did a lot of prison readings with that book, and it became the book that was most taken out of prison libraries that year. This was when she was invited by a prison padre to do talks in prison and started doing stuff with drug-related counselling with families affected by addiction. That and the book were all tied in to my mum's quest to find some sort of healing or understanding of my addiction.

Adrian and Andy got all the apparatus in place for mainstream success. They squared off Rough Trade and sorted Babyshambles a new deal with the EMI label Parlophone, the same label The Beatles had been on, so that was quite cool – great for the band. It was quite a lucrative deal, and we were all really excited by it. It was what led to me having quite a lot of faith in Andy and Adrian, because they kept putting their plans on the table in terms of who they wanted to sign to and for how much, and it all materialised. Andy Boyd was always the negotiator in chief in these affairs. It was where he came into his own. He and I developed this comic character for him, which was like a twisted extension of Andy Boyd's alter ego called The Boydster, an ultra-Alan Partridge-type record executive. He'd say things like, We're going to line up the ducks on the wall and shoot them down, and he'd always be in a hurry, and when he left he'd say, Got to go. Andy played up to this character quite well.

I went to see Suede play at the Astoria, rumoured to be their last ever gig, in December 2003, and I took a Christmas tree in with me. It was a pine tree, not huge, about 5ft 3in. I gave whoever was on the door a tenner to let me take it in. I told them it'd been a Suede fan since it was sapling.

Peter sleeping, 2003. *(Courtesy Peter Doherty)*

I was writing things down and that was an anathema to Wolfman – half the time he could hardly hold a pen. When he did write stuff down it was incredible.

Peter and Wolfman, 2002. *(Andrew Kendall)*

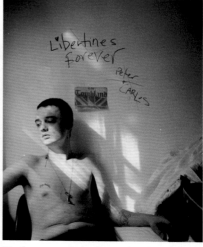

I built up a very high tolerance by taking repeated, small amounts over a long, long time. I didn't just suddenly jump into being a manic crackhead.

(left) Performing in skirt, HMV London, 2002.
(Courtesy Jackie Doherty)

(above) At home, 2003. *(Andy Willsher/Redferns/Getty)*

Pat Walden was creating a bit of a legend around himself. His guitar playing was wild: lots of crazy antics, it really got me going. But Gemma and Drew weren't into hard drugs – it wasn't like Babyshambles were just all-out junkies.

Babyshambles, Walden far left, 2004. *(Roger Sargent)*

Quite fancied myself as a country squire at the time, falcon perched on my head and a walking stick. I thought this could be a bit of me.

Peter and Kate Moss, Primrose Hill, 2005. *(Shutterstock)*

Carl said he was really shocked when he saw me with my skinhead. Wolfman shaved his head as well. I had this impending sense of doom but felt like I was embracing the doom somehow.

Skinhead look, 2005. *(Peter Macdiarmid/Getty)*

I was in a general state of mental flux but, creatively speaking, I was still a very determined young man, wanting to find a way to break through to the mainstream with my own particular brand of melodic rock 'n' roll.

Babyshambles, with Mick Whitnall (far left) and Adam Ficek (far right) replacing Pat and Gemma, 2006. *(Dave Hogan/Getty)*

I wouldn't say I consciously made myself seedy – that's a terrible word – but I always felt I was existing in some sort of defiance of my own personal health.

Leaving Thames Magistrates Court with Alan Wass and Peter Wolfe, 2010.
(Mark Large/ANL/Shutterstock)

The open sores was never a good look. My arm is weird even now. The track mark is never going to go away and there's still a shitload of scars from what look like fag hole burns. I think they're just old infections.

Peter and Carl, backstage at Reading Festival, 2010.
(Courtesy Katia deVidas Doherty)

I don't look at how I stack up against my contemporaries over the past twenty years. I look at it over a two hundred-year period starting with Arthur Rimbaud and going from there.

Glastonbury festival, 2015.
(Richard Isaac/Lnp/Shutterstock)

Some of the songs on the Puta Madres album are as much hers as they are mine musically.
Katia (left) and Peter (right), Thailand, 2015. *(Adrian Hunter)*

Thailand, 2015. *(Courtesy of Katia deVidas Doherty)*

As long as I had new songs and a place to play, I felt justified in creating moments of peace and oblivion.

Thailand, 2015.
(Courtesy Katia deVidas Doherty)

I'm not the perennial outsider. I've always felt comfortable in mobs and crowds. I'm fascinated by the mob.

With Narco and Zeus, Margate, 2019. *(Geoff Bell)*

Just tell the story as it comes out; Carl won't begrudge me. I'm sure he'll take a few hits but I'm also sure he'll be pleased with quite a lot of what I said.

The Libertines, Glastonbury, 2015.
(Roger Sargent)

There was always something magical for me about being on tour – exploring new towns, meeting new people and inviting them to the gig, finding little trinket shops …

Mick Whitnall, Alan Wass, Peter and the Bouboumobile, with The Libertines tour bus behind, 2014.
(Courtesy Katia deVidas Doherty)

Chas & Dave used to do seaside tours a couple of times a year and I'd always go, whether Morecambe or Margate or Southend. I'd never introduce myself. I'd stand at the bar and revel in it. I'd notice at the end of the gig they'd sit on the stage and sell their albums out of a box which, for me, is still the ultimate way to do it – to go around touring and sell your records out of a box.

Puta Madres, 2018.
(Thibault Leveque)

One of Katia's uncles made this comment about how he thought I was this Irish soul in pain. He also said, I like you, Doherty, you sing from the gut.

Wedding, 2021. *(Alexandra Fleurantin)*

I'll get my little farm house in the country someday. I feel really detached now from drugs.

The Libertines, Coventry, 2021. *(Sarah Thompson [GigJunkie])*

They also booked the longest Babyshambles tour we'd ever done: six weeks across Europe and the UK, and a load of festival gigs. Wolfman, Mick and I went to Portugal in the middle of that tour to get naltrexone implants. I also did a big trip to the Priory hospital in north London that summer. That was to do with the court case. I'd got arrested again in London. It must have been quite a bit they found that time, because they were also trying to get me with intent to supply, and I was ordered to remain in rehab until sentencing. The police were saying I was going to go to prison, and as I was being taken from the station to the court this detective inspector made these suggestions, saying it'd be in my interest if I could start giving them bigger dealers' names, how they'd take the screws off me. I said, A, I don't really know any big dealers, and B, I couldn't possibly tell you anyway, surely you know that. Going to rehab was a pain in the arse but not enough for me to become an informer. In the end I managed to stay out of nick, but I had to do thirty-one days in rehab. The headline on the front page of *The Times* or *Telegraph* was 'One Lucky Crackhead!'

Kate came to visit me at the Priory, which was quite nice. I smuggled in drugs too. Sometimes the staff would have a hunch something was going on with me and drugs, but they couldn't really put their finger on what it was. It was in a Grade 1 listed building in quite luxurious settings in Southgate, Enfield. I built up quite a big gang of mates in the Priory, young addicts who were also music fans. It was almost like a summer camp in some ways – we were all doing ketamine and having a laugh in group sessions.

Babyshambles actually headlined Loaded in the Park on Clapham Common while I was in the Priory. I turned up to the gig in my dressing gown straight from rehab, did the show and had to go back straight after, curfewed to the Priory. Lily Allen was on the same bill, and she came running backstage and said something really strange to me, she went, You're like me, Pete, you're middle class. My grandad was a tax inspector, and I said, No, my grandad was a taxi driver. I was sick on Goldie's shoes that night as well.

I was always concerned I wasn't doing enough collaborations with famous people, so I was really excited to be asked to do something with Mike Skinner from The Streets on the single 'Prangin' Out'. He was massive at the time, but I'd had my eye on him for a while, liked his lyrics and his whole poetic geezer persona. When I got out of the Priory, I went out to his studio somewhere in west London to do the vocals, but he wasn't actually there. I think he was getting clean at the time, or he was clean, so I did it with his engineer or producer. When I finally met up with him face to face, I think I might have vomited. No wonder no one wanted to work with me! But we did a joint *NME* front cover, and we always had mutual respect – he said some very nice things about my lyrics. Really, though, in terms of my contemporaries, or contemporary artists, people like Lily or Mike Skinner or Noel Gallagher, we were like ships that passed in the night – there wasn't really a lot of close contact.'

XXIII
Mark Blanco

2006 (part two): Engaged to be married to Kate – a
visit to Florence. 'The battle of Rome'. Shooting videos
with Julien Temple. The death of Mark Blanco – the
night and the investigations that followed.

'Kate announced our engagement in October 2006. We were going to get married in the little church near her country mansion. She put her feelers out to the vicar, and he came to meet us and bless us and talk about arrangements. That was embarrassing. I was so offended that I had him thrown out. He was like, Now, you've considered this, Kate? He's a little young, and he's a little unsettled. I was like, Get the fuck out. I remember sitting at the kitchen table listening, thinking he must think I'm deaf.

We played charades quite a lot, and when I met Kate's brother for the first time, when there was talk we were going to get married, he said, You can marry my sister if you can beat me and my missus at charades. He wasn't a camp fashionista, by the way, he was a proper Croydon lad, and we beat them at charades.

I was really happy at the time because Kate had made an effort with some of my friends. I woke up in the middle of the night after a London show in her place in St John's Wood, and she was with Sally Anchassi at the kitchen table chatting. They were very different people. It's difficult to get people to trust each other when there are different worlds colliding and different dynamics, but I like people working together. Sally was still road-managing Babyshambles, and Kate actually came with us when we toured Italy, came on stage to sing on 'La Belle et la Bête' in Milan and Florence.

The main reason she'd come was not to perform. There was supposed to be some jewellers in Florence where I was going to spend my whole fee from the tour on this particular ring, a renaissance Venetian ring. It cost me about £14k. It was awful – I mean it was a magnificent ring but gobsmackingly expensive. Kate was back home by the time we played in Rome, which turned into what *The Sun* called 'the Battle of Rome'. That was carnage – got very feisty. Adam got assaulted on stage, and Adrian was stood on a monitor wielding a microphone stand to keep the crowd away. There was a picture of me with blood coming out my head when we got into a mass brawl with some Italian paparazzi afterwards. That was my one *Sun* thing where it was actually, Yeah, that's a fucking good article, as opposed to that's really embarrassing. That whole Italian Babyshambles tour was spectacular, actually. Rimini was the one really – the legendary episode of the Rimini slasher, this girl who just insisted on cutting up Mick and putting fags out on him. I was in my room with two girls, and he came to the door with this girl slashing him, cut to ribbons, and she's saying, Let's all get Roman, have an orgy.

Although things were going quite well with Kate, it was still very up and down. It was an on-off relationship all the way through, really. I wasn't exactly an angel, but the tabloids were running loads of made-up stories. One time they said I'd had a fling with this South African model Lindi Hingston on tour – I did have a thing with her but not until I broke up with Kate. By now Kate's career had recovered from the cocaine scandal, and she was signing new contracts left, right and centre.

She said we could shoot the video for 'Love You but You're Green' at her place in the Cotswolds. Julien Temple was directing. It was a right disaster. At the last minute there was a change of plan and we couldn't do it at her place any more. Julien filmed in country lanes, our tour bus parked up round the back of the house. He'd already shot a video for 'The Blinding', and we felt honoured and excited to be working with Julien, because of all the stuff he'd done with the Sex Pistols. It was all part of the new promotional push from Parlophone. *The Blinding EP* did really well for us, but 'The Blinding' video was particularly strange. We always had trouble with videos, took me years to make a good one. It was through Julien, though, that we got involved in Strummerville, the Joe Strummer Foundation. Babyshambles did a cover of 'Janie Jones', the Clash song, for that, and it was released as a single. That was Drew in charge: he produced it and got loads and loads of other bands involved. Carl sang on it. Drew always seemed to have his fingers on the pulse of the record-industry crowd or music-people crowd. He was always out and about. Social Drew, Mick and I used to call him – he was always in some trendy charitable line-up doing London gigs, on the scene.

Babyshambles were constantly on tour in this period – Adrian and Andy had us doing gigs non-stop from the end of September all through October and December right into 2007, all over Europe and the UK. We were recording too, at the Doghouse again: we did 'Terrible Pain' with the General and a song of Alan's called 'Hired Gun'. It was right in the middle of this really hectic time that the Mark Blanco death happened, early in December.

It was strange because I didn't really know the bloke, but after he died quite a lot of his friends came out of the woodwork. Martin Tomlinson, from the band Selfish Cunt, was determined to get to the bottom of what he saw as this mystery. I met up with him at Kate's house in St John's Wood – a rare period where I had the house to myself for a week. He was basically saying to me, You ran off and left my friend to die on the street. Erm, well, yeah, I did. What can I say? You're right. It was like shoot on sight with me at the time, I didn't want to be within five hundred yards of the Old Bill, especially not with an unconscious body on the street. In fact, at the end of November I'd violated my community order again, been arrested and charged with possession of crack and heroin. I was due to appear in court on the Monday for sentencing.* But how do I explain his death? Can't really. No one really knows what happened.

That was a messy Saturday night. I was at the Malmaison hotel in Farringdon having a knees-up. I needed some respite, so I went with Kate Russell-Pavier, who I'd just met that evening, to Paul Ro's to relax for a bit. I just needed to score, have a quiet smoke before getting back to the hotel. When we got to Paul's, there was an incident, a fracas, where this fella was in my face and drunk. Basically, I put it on Paul, saying, Look, either he goes or I do, and I was relieved Paul chose me over him. I knew they were mates. That must have really wound Mark up – that this so-called rock-'n'-roll star he was always hearing about from Paul had been chosen over him when he probably felt like he should be the one getting acclaim or a bit of fame, because evidently, from what his friends say, he had something about him, and he was a bit of a character and destined for some sort of recognition.

I didn't see any of that side of his character – there was no cordiality or extension of a hand to me. He was just giving me grief and being a pain in the arse. Maybe he'd heard I could be a bit of a live wire and a

* Peter was fined £770, banned from driving for four months and warned that he must comply with his drugs order or he'd go to jail.

bit lairy, but I wasn't that night. I was really mellow and just basically worn out, and he was just fucking prodding and prodding. I thought he was very disturbed, agitated more than anything, and he kept going on about this play he was doing, *Accidental Death of an Anarchist*, round the corner at the George Tavern pub. He was thrusting these posters for it under my nose. Normally I'd have been really happy to discuss an interesting bit of local theatre, but he was really out of it, being really in my face and a bit out of control. If I could go back in time, I think I'd just embrace him, give him a big hug and ask him to tell me all about the forthcoming play, that sounds really interesting.

He was huge as well. And because he was so out of it, when I went to stand up to him, he was actually quite intimidating. He had me pinned up in a corner. It was a great surprise to me to hear there were no drugs on the coroner's toxicology report. He kept banging on about crack. He was right in my face. Do you want some crack? You like crack don't you, Pete? You want some crack? The way he was saying it was really weird – he was really enunciating the word crack, with kind of a lisp. Obviously, if he wasn't on crack, which I thought he was, he was saying it in a derogatory way to me . . . taking the piss. Either way, it was like, Paul, get him out of here. We got him out, and Mark was banging on the other side of the locked door, and the bolt went across on the inside. I was content then. That was enough for me – he was out and locked out.

The banging on the door stopped and I started to relax. Then, a little later, there were shouts from the street. I went down, and he lay there, blood coming out of his head. I was utterly horrified. Someone called the ambulance from the flat, and I legged it away. I didn't know he'd gone over the balcony until two days later when it was in the papers. That night, my first thought was he'd just fallen and cracked his skull, and even then it didn't occur to me he was dead.

I don't feel bad about leaving. I just know that it looks bad. I think I did the right thing. I had to protect myself, and I also wanted to protect that kid I was with who I'd dragged along to that place. She was only nineteen. I don't remember Johnny Headlock really having any part in any of it.* I don't know how he got to Paul's or when he got there. The guy from the Limehouse Murder Squad who interviewed me was very reassuring. He let me know from the word go he knew I hadn't done it. I can't tell you how grateful I was to hear that. I'd got involved with the big boys, as opposed to the cops who handled the petty drug charges, who always threatened me with how they were going to throw away the key.

The investigation got reopened a few times, so I now have a clearer idea of who was at Paul's that night. Annabel was there.† I liked Annabel. She was one of Paul Ro's secret squirrels, quite a civilised person who'd have a little nibble. A girl called Naomi was also there. There was a lot of mystery around her. She was a bit of a lone wolf, and people were always saying she was a compulsive liar, sociopathic almost. For years I thought she was a stockbroker who did a bit of gear in her spare time. Naomi would come to Babyshambles gigs, but we'd mainly see her knocking about in crack dens after gigs.

After we left Paul's that night, we went back to the Malmaison, and Johnny must have been there because he stabbed Mick with a steak knife. There was so much damage being done to the place when we got back. Someone had taken a door off its hinges. I needed to get people out – I was part of getting that thing broken up. The police came in the early hours to throw everyone out. I wanted somewhere to get my head down, and I had a pricey hotel that had just turned into carnage – all on my room-service tab. I was on ketamine at this point, having vowed

* CCTV street footage later surfaced showing Headlock departing the scene shortly after Peter.
† Annabel Heald Smith, born 1957, the daughter of a top QC and granddaughter of an MP and one-time attorney general. It was likely her who found Blanco on the pavement after leaving the flat to buy cigarettes.

to get more out of my head than ever before after the stress of what had happened at Paul's.

I think in the past I've always been so affronted and offended by someone thinking I was complicit in some plot to murder Mark Blanco that I've never really felt so desperately sad about the whole thing as I do today. I don't think in the past I ever felt this way about it because I was always more angered. Looking at it now, a little more detached, the whole story is just awful, especially the running away from the body.

Someone told me he'd gone away and then come back into the tenement off the street.* When I realised he didn't go over the balcony the first time he got shoved out the door, I found some comfort in that – it was always my worry in the very short term. Paul had this theory he was trying to get onto the lamppost. Paul said Mark had talked about it before, jumping onto the lamppost from the balcony. Paul reckons he might also have been trying to make some sort of artistic statement to do with the play.†

Headlock confessing to it was a shocker. He was totally pissed and homeless. He later said he did it so he could have a place to stay that night. The police wouldn't accept his confession, and I heard some story about him being sectioned. Everyone knew the confession was

---

* Grainy, poor-quality CCTV street footage showed Blanco leaving the block of flats after being ejected from Paul Roundhill's second-floor flat at 12.27am, appearing to stumble by a parked car, walk uncertainly a few yards down the road before turning and reapproaching the entrance to the flats, pausing for a moment and then re-entering the tenement block. Approximately fifty-seven seconds later, the CCTV footage shows him apparently falling from the first-floor balcony. Peter emerges from the flats and approaches Blanco on the floor at 12.39am. After an ambulance is called, Peter leaves the scene at 12.50am.

† *Accidental Death of an Anarchist* is centred on exposing the police as murderers after they claim the anarchist of the title either fell accidentally from an open police-station window or committed suicide.

just Johnny's wannabe gangster psychosis. Maybe he'd been going around saying, Yeah, I judo threw him over the balcony, like, This is how I deal with some bloke being aggressive or annoying, a sort of drunken bravado thing, saying that's how tough he was, but in hindsight it's a bit silly to talk like that when people are grieving.*

The truth is I didn't have a hand in throwing Mark Blanco off a balcony, and I don't believe Mark Blanco was murdered, but I understand there is a gap in the market for a conspiracy, because no one knows what happened in that minute when he came back into the block of flats. What they want and what they're pushing for is foul play. I accept Johnny Headlock is a bone-fide headcase with a tendency for extreme violence, but it just doesn't sit right with me that people are pointing fingers and calling people murderers – as much as I understand their heartache over losing someone they love. It just breaks my heart his mum is not satisfied and thinks that I had anything to do with her son's death. It hits home that his mother is still unable to reconcile with this terrible tragedy.'

---

* The Metropolitan Police's Homicide and Serious Crime Command did not treat Headlock's confession seriously, and they referred to Doherty, Roundhill and Headlock as 'unfairly maligned' in the media, commenting that they were '98 per cent sure Blanco jumped' with the intention of committing suicide. Ten months later, after significant intervention from a QC hired by Mark Blanco's mother Sheila, the coroner ruled out suicide, recording an open verdict, suggesting Blanco either jumped without intending harm or was the victim of a criminal act. He advised the case be reopened. It was, in December 2007, but after what police described as a 'thorough investigation', lasting approximately twelve months, the Crown Prosecution Service again stated there was no clear evidence to indicate an assault or the involvement of a third party in the death of Blanco. Sheila Blanco would not accept the police findings, continuing her own private investigation, using Peter's high profile to interest the media in claims she had uncovered new evidence that proved foul play, pressuring the police to reopen the investigation. Peter was interviewed under caution as part of the new 2010 police inquiry that concluded, in 2011, there was insufficient evidence to bring charges.

XIV
Shotter's Nation

2007: A ceremony on the beach with Kate. A life-saving operation. The cover of Vogue *and a car crash in Ibiza. Meeting Shane MacGowan. First art exhibition of blood paintings. Recording* Shotter's Nation. *Meeting Keith Richards and Paul McCartney. Breaking up with Kate.*

'I found a photo recently, a Polaroid of me and Kate, from when we had a ceremony on a beach in Thailand in January 2007. It was not a proper wedding but this ceremony they do where they wrap a snake around both your necks and give you some flowers and you swear eternal allegiance to each other's hearts. It's a Thai tradition. That became a right mess that holiday. We were there with Sir David Tang, the multimillionaire Hong Kong entrepreneur. He and Kate used to have these regular holidays, with loads of people all together in places like Thailand, on boats and that. Sarah Ferguson was on that holiday too.

I went AWOL at some point and met these backpackers, ended up getting arrested. I was running around like a maniac. These backpackers filmed me banging up in this hostel in Phuket and sold the footage. Kate and David Tang came to bail me out of the police station, and I was so out of my head I called Kate a prick and did a flying kick at her and then ran off down the motorway. The next thing I woke up at Heathrow in a pair of Thai policeman's shorts, didn't even have my passport. David Tang thought it was really funny, apparently, because initially I'd gone off to get measured for a suit, a cheap Thai suit, and somehow that caused an argument. That's when I ran off and met the backpackers. To David's great amusement, the suit eventually turned up like three days later after I'd been deported.

When I got back, I was doing stuff with Anthony Donnelly for his streetwear label Gio-Goi. I'd taken some money from Anthony to be the face of the brand. They also said I designed a range for them, like Kate was designing a range for Top Shop. It was a bit of an exaggeration, but I did have some strong ideas. Turns out a lot of the stuff had been made up already, and it was just a question of saying, Go on, I'll have that bit. I'd done a little gig for the launch of the range at Selfridges, and then we did a photo shoot for the *Sunday Times*, which is when Anthony saved my life. I had an implant that got really badly infected. I was on my back in Anthony's Range Rover with the pus and pills coming out of my stomach. It was not good, and he took me to a Bupa hospital and paid for an operation. Oh God, I was grateful.

When Kate got back from Thailand, we patched things up and went to Dublin with Gio-Goi. While we were there, we went to see Shane MacGowan in some fancy restaurant. I was giving him a pipe under the table. He said, I really like that Johnny Depp. Yeah, I really liked it when she was going out with him. You know he was half Native American, half German, half Irish. I went, Well, first of all, it's very offensive what you're saying, talking about an ex-boyfriend of Kate's to me, and he can't be half of all those things. He went, He was, and he knew a fucking lot about the Bay of Pigs as well. What do you know about the Bay of Pigs? I must admit at the time my knowledge on the subject was a bit lapse.

Kate worshipped Anthony and his brother Chris. We were actually staying in their villa in Ibiza when we had this near fatal accident. It was the time I was doing the Mario Testino shoot for the cover of *Vogue*. Shane MacGowan's wife Victoria Mary Clarke was involved somehow, and Shane turned up at that shoot. He took all his clothes off and insisted I take all my clothes off as well: C'mon, get your clothes off, it'll be a great photo. I ended up falling naked through the giant paper background.

In Ibiza, I drove off the side of a mountain. I've never really told anyone this story, but we lost a car over a dusty mountain road. Kate and me were supposed to be going to some fashion party, and we ended up walking through the hills, completely lost in the dark.

I was now living in a very strange place in Shepherd's Bush, my dad's old territory, right under the Westway. The Shelf is what I called it, this prefabricated shelf of planks and steel girders above a mechanic's yards. A local community pirate radio station was operated from there by a guy called Satan. He was a crack dealer, but he used to work on pirate radio. It was all techno, garage, house and hip-hop stuff, and then I'd occasionally appear with my acoustic guitar slung on my back to everyone's amusement. Lindi, the South African model who a few years later would become the mother of my daughter, texted me once at random and said she was having lunch with Satan's mother.

It was just somewhere I could go to plot up. Andy Boyd struck some deal for the rent with the mechanic guy. It was basically a shithole, but it had running water and makeshift toilet facilities. During the day they'd be tinkering with cars, and I'd have to wait until six o'clock to show my face and use the toilet. The song 'Broken Love Song' on *Grace/*

Wastelands was written there – 'Under the Westway, down by the Scrubs, how long must we wait for them, killing us . . . killing us, they are the loneliest'. It was very close to Wormwood Scrubs and the QPR ground, adjacent to an Irish travellers' community. I had a run-in with these two eleven year olds from there – eleven year olds with the faces of sixty-year-old men. They were like, Peter, our brother's got a present for you, and they pulled out this gun wrapped up in a handkerchief. As soon as I put my fingers on it, round the handle, they were like, Ah, your fingerprints are on it now, we want thirty grand or we're gonna have you done for armed robbery.

I had all my canvases in there, trying to do some artwork and some songwriting. The problem was it was really hard to get people to visit because it was such an unwelcoming place. People probably thought I could afford something better, but don't forget that advance from Parlophone went four ways, plus the management, Adrian and Andy, had an equal share. There was also a daily outflow on drugs, so the money would sieve through constantly.

Andy Boyd had put it together for me to have this art exhibition, *Bloodworks* at the Bankrobber Gallery in Notting Hill. He had this knack of conjuring up money. When I did my first blood painting, the one that was used on the cover of *Full Moon Empty Sports Bag*, I'd said something about using my own blood as being some comment on the 'self-destructiveness of fame', but actually the blood paintings were never a straightforward, intentional comment about anything. It was always about using the material to hand. It's interesting to reflect on me fetishising people, like Owen for instance, because I do that quite a lot – I do fetishise people and things. I think for a long time when I was immersed in drug paraphernalia, the paintings were just a fetishisation of that – of needles, of blood, of cooking pots and spoons. A lot of my work from that time is just me drawing round a spoon, using my finger from the blackened bottom, from the dark side of the spoon if you like, and using my blood. It was a grimy immersion in that world – just capturing moments. It seemed to be a good expression at the time, of salvaging something from the night. Just a few strange lyrics on the canvas and a silhouette of an arm or foot in a tourniquet, a lot of blood.

I love Jean-Michel Basquiat, the New York collagist and painter. My stuff had echoes of that with the collage effect and with text and silhouettes. He wasn't an influence at the time, but over the years I've been really drawn to him. I've ended up having quite a few art exhibitions since that first one; there was one in Paris quite recently, in January 2021, *The Fantasy Life of Poetry and Crime* at the Galerie Chappe. I've had two or three exhibitions there over the years, a really cool place, just by the Sacré-Cœur, on a really narrow, steep cobbled street in the mythical area at the centre of Montmartre, very atmospheric – the same area Carl and I stayed when we wrote 'Don't Look Back into the Sun'.

My painting style has always remained pretty much the same. You can spot one of my works a mile off. At that first *Bloodworks* exhibition, I was absolutely flabbergasted when all the works sold. There were fourteen. I was completely delighted and amazed to see this was possible – people were willing to put their hands in their pockets. Bankrobber was a bona-fide gallery, and the paintings weren't cheap. Robin Barton, who curated the show, was a well-known photographer who became an art dealer. After he did my show, he curated the first Banksy exhibition, in New York. After that first show of mine, the cycle started with collectors, and once you've got people collecting your stuff, that's it, really – that's what it's all about. Still today, from that first exhibition, I've got the same people collecting my work. There are some incredible collections out there belonging to people who've been buying my stuff for years.

I'm quite envious, really, that I didn't hold on to more stuff myself. They've got some great bits, some huge old canvases that I really put a lot into.

The Bankrobber exhibition was tied in with a book I did called *The Books of Albion*, extracts from the journals I'd kept over the years with sketches using blood in there too. I didn't really feel that comfortable with the book – it was edited really weirdly. I was also conscious of upsetting certain people so, for me, it was a little bit of a cop-out; something about that book doesn't sit right.

I was spending a lot of time with an acoustic guitar, and a lot of the gentler songs from *Shotter's Nation* were written alone at Kate's place in the country. There was a pastoral quality to the songs. When I had the house to myself, I'd put on *Harvest* by Neil Young really loud. I was listening to a bit of Bert Jansch as well. I was conscious of having made three quite raucous albums with The Libertines and Babyshambles. I wanted to do some gentler stuff. I was writing lyrics that were ruminations on myself and Kate and having to shift between the desolation and hand-to-mouthness of the Shelf and the absolute luxury of the St John's Wood address. A lot of journals that survived those times are full of variations on lyrics of songs from that period, such as 'Unstookie Titled' and 'Deft Left Hand'.

This was when I started to do more solo shows – just me and my acoustic. The first big one was at the Hackney Empire. It was my decision to do it. I was connecting with something just with the acoustic guitar. At that Hackney Empire gig, Carl came on and we did a few Libertines songs acoustically. It was the first time I'd played with Carl in a long, long time, and it was really emotional. I also did something with Bert Jansch that night, and it went really well. It was a beautiful moment, one of the highlights of my musical career thus far, doing 'Needle of Death' with him. He was this legendary Scottish folk musician who'd influenced people like Jimmy Page and Neil Young. 'Needle of Death' was on his first album, released in 1965, a song about heroin. I was really happy with the version we did together, but listening back to the live recording I genuinely think my fans didn't know who Bert was because you can hear people talking, muttering while we're trying to do this amazing song. And we did a new song of mine together that night, 'Lost Art of Murder'. I have such happy memories of working with Bert. Kate was away somewhere, and he and his wife came over to St John's Wood, and for hours and hours we went through these songs, 'Lost Art of Murder' and 'Needle of Death'.

I've no idea how the introduction to Bert came about, but I thank whoever was involved so much for that. He played on *Shotter's Nation* too. I went round to his townhouse in Kilburn with Alan. He had shitloads of guitars on his walls. I'd told Alan I needed to go there on my own, to get to know him. Alan was, Na, na, it's more about the boys, Pete. We were sat really humble in his long garden, and his wife made us tea. They'd lived there since he came to London in 1969, and it was where he died not that long after – he and his wife died within a year of one another. We were just strumming the guitars in the garden, and I felt a heavy sense of history, really, British guitar history and depth. There was something magical about him. He was a bit of a grumpy old codger as well. His wife was telling him off, C'mon stop being such a grumpy old git, go through it again. He kept asking me specifically what I wanted him to do on 'Lost Art of Murder', and I said, I just want you to do what you enjoy. He was doing lots of really simple things, and I kind of wanted to get something a bit more complicated out of him, a bit more finger-picky, but it turned out to be kind of deceptively simple the stuff that he did in the end.

I didn't think at the time how that song might have come across in the light of Mark Blanco's death, especially the chorus where it goes 'What a nice day for a murder', and how strange that might have sounded. I can see it now, but it wasn't connected with Mark in any way – there was no murder. That was actually a bit of a cock-up, the title of that song. I knew there was a George Orwell essay, and I thought it was the 'Lost Art of Murder', but it's not, it's called the 'Decline of the English Murder' – my balls-up. I was gutted after the *Shotter's Nation* album came out with it on and I realised I'd misquoted old Eric Blair there.

We recorded *Shotter's Nation* in London, at Olympic Studios with Stephen Street producing. He'd produced Blur and Morrissey – they were his main glory, really. From day one until the final day of mixing, he knew exactly what he was going for. He was a man on a mission – he was filling in all over the place, sticking in string arrangements, putting guitar parts in. I don't think there were that many pure live takes, and he'd push and push me on the vocal takes as well. He was similar to Bernard Butler in a way – very domesticated, with his wife and his kids, had quite a stable home life. The stories he told from the early days of working with Morrissey kept me interested in him, kept the embers burning. I was constantly grilling him about it.

I don't think I actually knew I wanted to work with Stephen Street until after the album was finished.* Andy Boyd picked me up from Clouds House rehab around the time it was released when the first reviews came out. He played me *Shotter's Nation* in the car, and I remember being pleasantly surprised and proud. In the past, I'd often listen to the records once they were finished and feel a bit of detachment or disappointment, but with *Shotter's Nation*, notwithstanding Andy

---

* In a December 2020 interview in the *Telegraph*, Street said of the recording: 'He had the Kate Moss circle around him, and I didn't want anything to do with that. When those people turned up, I'd call it a night. I did not want to sit there while they did God knows what. I had to read him the riot act a few times – but I'm very proud of what I've done with him. I love him and I worry about him, and I know he'd hate to hear me say that, but he's up there with Morrissey as one of the greatest poets I've worked with.'

Boyd's enthusiasm, I thought, Fucking hell, yeah, we've made a cracking album here.

Not since the days of The Libertines, after we first got signed, was I ever in a band that was as tight, as focused as that *Shotter's Nation* band with Adam Ficek and Drew as the rhythm section. They were just really hard-working and talented musicians, and Mick and I had written a shitload of great songs together and really believed in them. The album ended up being quite tight and together, but actually the process was really fragmented and messy. I remember being quite impressed by Stephen when he carried a ketamine-disabled Mick from the bathroom stall into the live room, thinking, Oh, he's got a bit more to him than I thought.

He'd scream and shout at us too to get the job done. He'd lost his brother, a crack and heroin addict who threw himself off a motorway bridge into oncoming traffic. So, Stephen was very tense when it came to drug use, which was an unfortunate combination, because we were well into it, Mick and me. Stephen had concerns about a few songs, particularly 'Deft Left Hand', where I kept rewriting the lyrics. I was putting myself under the magnifying glass. I wanted to get it bang on. Wanted it all to be perfect. I felt the music was there. I just wanted to get the lyrics right.

Whenever Kate turned up at the studio, it always got a bit dramatic. She'd be lamenting the state of my narcotic health. There were actually quite a few songs on the album that were co-writes with Kate. At her place, down by the side of the bed, she had these bits of writing in her idiosyncratic scrawl in these golden frames. There was one line about Stevie Wonder, can't remember much else, but I always said, Wow, your lyrics are amazing. So, I took bits of some of the words from some of the frames and used them in the songs. She always used to say, If you're going to use my lyrics, you have to credit me. Also, when I'd be sitting around trying to work on lyrics, I'd take stuff from things she'd say

– she had interesting turns of phrase – so where the lyrics are her words rather than mine, I felt I had to credit her. 'You Talk' was one – 'you talk a good game'. Strange song that, ended up being a single. It's got the line about 'Bevan, he drops stones from heaven, L-O-R-D forever'. That was my line. Bevan was one of our main suppliers at the time, and L-O-R-D was for his Lordship Lane gang up in Tottenham. They were drug dealers and rappers. They actually did a lot of their demos at Odessa, Gwyn's studio. Turned out they knew him, and they all said the same thing as we had when The Libertines recorded there: Him too slow, man, him too slow. I did some recording there with them, twenty-two of them in the studio.

There was never ever any appreciation of Kate as a co-writer. She probably only ever got tuppence from it, but I like to think she still listens to some of them songs and feels something. 'UnBilo Titled' is a cracking tune, a favourite from that album. That was a pure Wolfman/Doherty construction. The line 'The more that you follow me the more I get lost' was Wolfman's – he's a fine lyricist. On 'French Dog Blues' there's a blatant cop from Ian Brown's 'Deep Pile Dreams' in the lyrics. I always loved that song from being a teenager in Nuneaton, in Coventry, listening to the album *Unfinished Monkey Business*. In fact, there's three or four Babyshambles/Libertines/Puta Madres songs that borrow blatantly from Stone Roses or Ian Brown lyrics, and they've never stood in the way – they've always just let us acknowledge them and give them their tuppence. 'There She Goes (a Little Heartache)' was one of my proudest moments as a songwriter. The formation of that song goes way back. I always wanted to write a song like that, a jazzy vocal crooner number. There was a lot of fulfilment for me in that.

There was also some pure melodic rock-'n'-roll songs on the album that I'd written with Mick – 'Carry On Up the Morning' and 'Delivery' – that set us up nicely for the *Shotter's Nation* tours. They were so structured and catchy. 'Carry On Up the Morning' has the breakdown bit, 'I know where to find you, where to find you my love, in that same old place by the river' – that was that secret flat in Pimlico where I'd meet Kate and have to get in through the window.

'Delivery' was supposed to be about a guy working at a brewery, a guy in a Fred Perry and braces leaning up against a wall waiting for a delivery of beer – that was the original meaning. Mick and I were downstairs at the Pink Tower writing those lyrics, and I said, It's about a skinhead who's got an apprenticeship at the brewery, but obviously 'delivery' came to mean something else entirely when you sang it as a drug addict. The birth of that song – it was the first single off the album – came about when we decided we were going to rewrite 'All Day and All of the Night', but we were going to do it in a minor key, and it does go into a minor key in the chorus, but the verse is very much based on 'All Day and All of the Night'.

When that came out, we got together with Ray Davies at his Konk Studios in northwest London with the *NME* who were going to have a Babyshambles/Ray Davies duo performance. He pulled out at the last minute – didn't want to do it. It was going really well at first. He was on this piano, and we were going from the chorus of 'Delivery' into the chorus of 'All Day and All of the Night' – we recorded it, it's knocking about somewhere, never got released. Then Mick turned up, and he terrified Ray Davies. Mick with his eyes inside out, bent over an amp, and Ray Davies was like, I'm calling it a day, lads. I gave him a flag, an old British navy flag with the Union flag in the corner, and he gave me a big hug and the session was called off . . . that was a shame.

Kate took me with her when she went to see The Rolling Stones at the Isle of Wight Festival at the beginning of June. Keith Richards took me aside and had a couple of bits of advice for me. He said, Roll up your sleeve, and he laughed, a throaty old salty laugh like a sea dog. He said there was this particular detective in the '70s in London who, when he saw him in the street, would say, Roll up your sleeves, Richards. Keith was saying to me, Try not to go in the vein. You need to get hold of some good-quality stuff, pharmaceutical stuff, and skin-pop it, and then you're cutting down the risk, and then he gave me another bit of advice: Don't let women tell you what to do!

I was saying to Kate we've got to get in the mosh pit – if there was going to be a mosh pit at a Rolling Stones gig – and Kate wanted to be where all the Richards family were in this private section. I tried two songs in there, and it didn't work, so I went back to Ronnie Wood's dressing room – they had a dressing room each – and banged up, and I went over. When I woke up, I was on the Isle of Wight ferry with Kate, saying they'd carried me out the dressing room and had to sneak me onto the ferry.

I was quite taken with Keith Richards, though. I was never into The Rolling Stones before, and I'm not really a big Stones fan, but Alan was always banging on about them, and so was Kate. When I actually met him, I was almost a bit disappointed I liked him, because I had this thing about them being a wedding covers band or something. Lisa Moorish used to put on that 'Rape, murder, it's just a shot away, it's just a shot away,' really loud and would always want to cover that with me, and I was like, No fucking way. Over the years it creeps up on you, the beauty of some of those songs, but definitely not before I was thirty – it's an old man's game, the Stones. Alan, though, had a mystical vision of anything electric blues. He was into Zeppelin and stuff like that, and I couldn't be doing with it. Johnny Thunders was always more my thing.

Kate was with me the day I met Paul McCartney too. It was for some *Observer* piece. We met at the London Victoria Palace Theatre. He said something very specific to me: he'd seen me on *Friday Night with Jonathan Ross* doing the 'Lost Art of Murder', and he said, I thought,

Oh no, he's not going to make it, and then in the end you made it. He was talking about me fumbling for the notes further down the guitar. I was immensely proud he'd watched me and paid enough attention to debate whether or not I was going to make the right chords. Over the years coming up, I bumped into his son James quite a lot – interesting fella. He'd always tell me his dad was praying for me, praying for an angel to keep watch over me in my darkest hours.

I think Glastonbury that year was the last time Kate and I stepped out together. Something of a fine memory, set in stone. Just wandering about, enjoying a stress-free Glastonbury. I played the Green Field acoustic stage. Gio-Goi were there. They took shots of me and Kate on this low-rider bike they had. I remember giving Stella McCartney's husband the heave-ho from the caravan we stayed in after he made some strange comments about the state of my health. I had them all chucked out of the caravan. I had a massive shoebox full of drugs – really happy times. We got dressed up in disguise one of the mornings, and I think Lily Allen had said something about me on stage, so I went out at five in the morning and wrote 'Lily Allen is a slag' in massive letters on some white tarpaulin in mud.

There was not really one specific incident that finished the relationship. Our worlds were not really compatible in the end. There were all sorts of incidents. She had this panic button by her bed and a panic button in the kitchen. One day, when she was away somewhere, and I was scrabbling down by the side of the bed, for a dropped rock probably, I accidentally pressed the panic button and twelve armed police ended up at the cottage in St John's Wood. She was really unhappy about things like that. It became a running battle, really, that relationship. It was always the same – for all those years: highs and then crushing, violent lows. It was not sustainable. I'm quite fragile, really, within myself. That kind of destructive relationship, there's nothing glamorous about it – it wears you down in the end and turns you nasty.

There was one final big old kick-off. She desecrated this 1930s Gibson, smashed it up. Kate then had Pandy covered in petrol and set alight – it's not funny. I used to carry him round London with me. Deep down in my heart I like to think it's just a lie and Kate didn't really destroy him, that she's still got him, but no, as far as I know, he's dead, ashes. It still rankles – it was the one thing I'd held on to. The only time I've spoken to her since was eight or nine years ago in Paris. She called me up out of the blue. I just said, Have you still got the tattoo? That was the only thing I could think of to say.'

XXV
Sturmy

2007–2008: A long stay at rehab. Moving out to the country.
A hit single and album – and an arena tour. Hanging out
with Amy Winehouse. A most unfortunate photo. A stretch in
Wormwood Scrubs. Recording a proposed For Lovers *album.*

'Towards the end of the summer of 2007 I went to Clouds House rehabilitation centre in Salisbury, Wiltshire, for a long six-week stay, and that went quite well. I had a fresh implant too. My dad visited me there and Astile as well. There was a lot of family healing at that time, and I got myself genuinely clean. In May I'd been arrested in Kensington for driving while uninsured with no MOT, and they'd found crack, heroin, ketamine and cannabis in the car. I was on my own that night. The case had been adjourned until October, so I had to pull my socks up before sentencing. I thought I'd fucked it the day Babyshambles played the V Festival, and I was arrested again for drug possession, spent the night in Bethnal Green Police Station. But I managed to get away without charges – they said it was something to do with them not getting me to court within twenty-four hours of the arrest. That was a lucky one. Andy Boyd had been driving, and Rini was with me in the car. I had a huge amount of gear on me when the police stopped us, and somehow

I managed to hide everything down the side of an electricity pylon. I went back later and retrieved everything.

While I was attending Clouds, I moved to a little cottage nearby in Marlborough. Rini came to stay. Mick was there too. We did the 'You Talk' video at the cottage. Alan's in that video – he was around a lot as well. When I got out of rehab in October, the papers were saying I was engaged to Rini, which wasn't true – it was more a long-term understanding we had. We definitely gave each other lots of gifts, rings among them, but it was one of those spiritual engagements – it wasn't really overly sexual. It was very rare we ever made love, and eventually it become more of a brother–sister thing. I got done for criminal damage around then, for booting a photographer trying to take pictures of me and Rini.

I was actually in Clouds when 'Delivery' was released as a single. If it didn't hit massively, it hit in a way that was acceptable. It was kind of irresistible, really, that song. The video was actually halfway decent too – it had been filmed in and around the Shelf. I had a great hat on. It started to feel like something really good was happening to Babyshambles in this period, when *Shotter's Nation* kind of blew up a little bit. I got a gold disc for that album, and the success we were having must have helped push the sales of *Down in Albion*, because I got a gold disc for that too. It's a shame that after getting out of Clouds my using reached unimaginable heights. I'd probably be a millionaire now if I'd kept it together for a couple of years. At the same time *Shotter's Nation* was released, there were posters up for a Libertines greatest-hits album – something that we hadn't even approved or knew about – and also this Roberto Cavalli ad campaign I'd done came out.

Adrian and Andy had us booked for a big arena tour to support the album, and the Parlophone push was definitely noticeable too, because *Shotter's Nation* also went quite high in the charts in France and Germany. Incidentally, the title of that album came from a bit of graffiti on Paul Ro's front-room wall. It had been there for years, and I'd always liked it. Adrian and Andy were also hoping we might sell some records in America. It was a non-starter, really, because I was not allowed into the country due to all the convictions, but Adrian and Andy used to present a lot of things in court, to do with the economic impact of not being allowed a work permit to tour there or do any promotion – we're still trying to get that permit.

We tried to get Pat back to do 'Pipedown' and 'Fuck Forever' as part of a five-piece for the arena tour, but at the first gig, Manchester Arena, he met some drug dealer with a spider tattoo on his face in the hotel lobby and was never seen again . . . didn't turn up to the show. With massive gigs like that, part of me didn't really understand or accept we could play to such big crowds, so I was sort of defeated before I started – are they Babyshambles fans or just people who've ended up with tickets? I've got a memory of walking up the steps to the side of the stage at Wembley Arena feeling a little bit as if I was walking up to the scaffold. It wasn't, for me, a massive moment of celebration. If I could relive it now, I'd probably enjoy it a lot more. But, actually, looking back at some of the footage, a lot of those arena dates are quite triumphant.

I have very clear memories of an overwhelming sense of everything working for the Glasgow date, which was recorded for the live album we released in 2008, *Oh! What a Lovely Tour*. Wembley seemed to be a push and pull of tensions of some kind, but Glasgow really worked – the crowd were really up for it, and I was just feeling really good on stage, really feeling the energy of the crowd in a positive way and feeling that the band were all on the same page.

The cottage in Marlborough got a bit crowded in the end. I think about seven people moved in. Amy Winehouse had just married Blake and they would come down a lot, and we'd have nights at the Sun pub in Marlborough with them. Blake had just got himself arrested for assault, beaten up the landlord at the Macbeth club.

I'd bumped into Amy a few times over the years at TV shows or festivals, but I didn't really know her. Her *Back to Black* album had just come out, and it had really blown up. She was massive. I loved 'Rehab'. She seemed like a spectacular superhero to me – she had it all. The first proper conversation we had she said, Do you say I ain't got a Scooby or I aint got a Danny, Pete? Well, I ain't got a Danny. She went, You're all right. She hated people who said I ain't got a Scooby, as in Scooby Doo, as opposed to people who said I ain't got a Danny La Rue. Her dad was a black-cab driver, so we had that connection. I'd tell her about riding around with grandad in his black cab in Liverpool. I was always saying, Let's do a Billie Holiday song together. She'd sing at the cottage and have me in tears. I was still very raw over Kate.

She'd also said the same thing to Blake as I'd said to Kate when we'd first met: Yeah, I made him get a tattoo of my name. Her and Blake were very much an item, very much together. To be honest, they were more interested in Mick than they were me – our friendship was sort of cemented around their complete adoration of Mick Whitnall. Amy always had a thing for him – she tried to pinch him as a musician. He was a great guitarist and songwriter, and I think she had a bit of an eye for him. He was always telling us how she'd turn up in the middle of the night with her security at his and Hannah's place in Lewisham, just tottering on her heels and sitting at the kitchen table saying, Oh, you've got to leave him, Hannah. She took him to the Doghouse for some sessions. Mick was playing with her band informally. It was through Mick she met Julie, who we knew from her hanging out with Babyshambles. Julie was the mother of Dionne Bromfield, who ended up singing with Amy, and Amy launched her solo career on her label Lioness. Amy sort of adopted Dionne as a goddaughter, but I was supposed to be her godfather years before when she was living in her mum's council flat. Amy looked after Julie a lot.

At the end of October, I was up in court for sentencing. I'd come out of Clouds clean, and they could see I was making progress, so I managed to avoid jail. That was a touch. But I still got handed quite an onerous sentence of four months in jail suspended for two years, an eighteen-month supervision order and a twelve-month drug rehabilitation order. I had to do twice-weekly drugs tests. I'd often test negative, especially when I could find someone who had clean piss for me to take in. I started to work with Dr Vanessa Crawford, who is a bit of a legend in the drugs rehabilitation world – my mum's still in touch with her. She ended up coming to Portugal to oversee implants and played quite a hands-on role in my treatment, although in those days I never used to be that into methadone or anything – it was all or nothing, really, implant or nothing. She worked with me and Wolfman a lot, hands-on stuff.

I decided to stay out in the country, but I needed a bit more peace and quiet, so Andy found me Sturmy House just outside Marlborough. It was part of the Savernake Estate that incorporated Savernake Forest, where Henry VIII used to do some hunting. I was aware of the history of the place and enthralled with it. The main house, Tottenham House, was this massive Grade 1 listed mansion where they'd done the Hammer horror films. I used to enjoy charging the Jag across the field at night towards the Hammer horror house. Sturmy House was the old stables and servants' quarters. I think it had been a B&B for a while, owned by Hollywood actress Jodie Foster, but it was now completely dilapidated.

There were nine bedrooms and so many lounges. I set up a properly little Arcadian trinket pavilion, all my flags and statues and old metal cigarette advertisements everywhere . . . it was pretty ostentatious, in a down-at-heel way. Within a couple of months of being there, Lisa moved to a neighbouring village with Astile and Mollie, and Astile started going to a local primary school, so I started to see him properly, for the first time, really. They were happy times. There was a whole host of local characters around, hunters and fishermen, one old guy with a metal detector always knocking about.

What first threw a spanner in the works of this upward trajectory was a photo *The Sun* printed of me injecting heroin. It was taken at the start of November at the MTV awards in Munich – a big Shambles celebration of Amy Winehouse's success, where we did 'Delivery' introduced by Snoop Dogg. Amy completely cleaned up – she won all the MTV Europe Awards – and I was drinking White Russians with her and Blake. At that point I owed this dealer eleven grand, and we had an understanding he was going to take a photo of me banging up and sell it to write off this drug debt. I think he got six grand in the end for the photo. I'd known this dealer from when he was a kid. Maybe once a week, he would come out to Sturmy with a shitload of gear. I basically still had a half-working implant, so it was a pointless injection anyway. The BBC refused to play 'You Talk' after that photo appeared. We were fighting this ongoing PR battle from then on. I was being demonised in the tabloids constantly. My attitude was: They should mind their own fucking business – they've got no right to comment on cultural things. Why they were so interested in my drug use is beyond me.

Once the *Shotter's Nation* tour ended, I was jailed for fourteen weeks for violating my probation. I'd missed two appointments with my probation officer – that was what did it. I'd been in Glasgow and travelled all the way to London for this meeting but turned up late. When I protested, it went down as being abusive to staff. I was immensely disappointed at that sentence. There's something about that magistrate at West London Magistrates. I met so many people inside who were like, Who sent you down? I'd tell them, and they'd say, Oh yeah – we all suffered the same fate at her hands. The thing is, all my charges were all really minor offences – they do look bad on paper when you add them up, but at the end of the day they were all for very small amounts of gear. It was a tough one to take.

The Scrubs was another Category B prison, but it had a terrible reputation. It was old, Victorian, dirty, rat-infested and rundown, full of murderers, rapists and terrorists. While I was inside, *The Sun* ran a picture on their front page with a headline about me smoking heroin in my cell. That was a load of bollocks. There was no way of smoking heroin in the cell on the detox wing where they put me after induction. Someone took a picture of me – they must have hidden a phone up their arse – brushing my teeth, which was the photo on the front page of *The Sun*. I remember distinctly someone saying, Smile, and I turned round to the cell door brushing my teeth, and this other prisoner had a camera phone. He said, So, if we get the money for this, how do you want to split it? No, you do what you like, I'm not getting involved, I don't want their money. Then the next day they got the photo out and it was in the papers.

There were all sorts of threats while I was in Scrubs, people saying they're going to knock me out just because I'd got a name in the papers. I was always intrigued to meet the people supposed to be doing the knocking out – they normally turned out to be all right, if slightly warped. Ray, an old bare-knuckle fighter, made himself busy on my behalf – there was all kinds going on in that place. Vanessa Frake, the prison governor, recently brought out a book* about her time at Scrubs where she named all these high-profile prisoners she handled – Myra Hindley, Rose and Fred West – and she said the person she hated most, above them all, was me! Hardly as bad as fucking Rose West! She actually had me sent to the segregation unit after that *Sun* story, thought I was undermining all her good work.

* *The Governor* (Harper Element, 2021).

In the end, my sentence was cut in half and a couple of weeks were knocked off to do with a government plan to reduce overcrowding. I did just over four weeks. The terms of my release dictated that I wasn't allowed to be in London between midnight and 9 a.m. That's when my favourite tabloid headline popped up – it was a free London paper, and the front page had a picture of me coming out, and it was just one word: 'Exiled!' It was great. Exiled from London!

After I got out of Scrubs, I was just trying to create a life for myself in the country the best I could. I spent a lot of time in the woods and on the hillocks of Wiltshire, lost in Arcadia. I threw myself headlong into trying to be an addict but also trying to balance all these rehabilitation orders and trying to enjoy time in the country, creating this strange psychedelic bubble at Sturmy. Lots of people came to stay. I've got fond memories of Alize plotting up there for months on end – when I wasn't there, she'd keep an eye on the place.

There were some lost months in Sturmy. Adrian and Andy would turn up to get me to do something, and I'd tell them, I just want to treasure these days. Babyshambles were supposed to do Glastonbury in 2008, and I refused to go. In the end, Jake Fior turned up and dragged me into his car and drove me there and made me do it. I did my biggest solo show yet in July at the Royal Albert Hall. I was extremely nervous before that show. It's all-seated, but there was a big stage invasion. It was a proper Bill Haley moment, 'Rock Around the Clock' at the Albert Hall with Wolfman in support. It was a full-on stage invasion. There were some right nutters there – it was all pretty good-natured, though. At one point I had a fireman's helmet on – there were some fire safety people wrestling with stage invaders – and I came on to gloriously reclaim the stage, to receive the adulation of the crowd, and they didn't recognise me in the fire helmet, and they were just throwing stuff, saying get off the stage. I have memories of that being a good gig, a successful gig. It was the opportunity I never really got during the

Libertines days, to be able to do stuff on my own and have it supported by management.

I was doing a few tracks with Jake Fior at the time. It was supposed to be *For Lovers* the album. We were making it with Wolfman. Jake had ten songs he had a vision of me singing. We did get a number of tracks recorded, and those recordings are still knocking about somewhere, but Jake would get a bit infuriated by the number of people coming down the studio. I think the General got up his nose quite a bit, and the Wolfman had a tendency not to turn up. Actually, one of AmyJo's ex-boyfriends from years before, a jobbing musician and DJ, turned up in the band Jake put together for the recordings, a guy called Alex. That was quite curious for me, because I wasn't really in touch with AmyJo then – we'd fallen out about something, probably something to do with Mum and Dad. There were years when we weren't so close. She came back into my life with a vengeance when her musical career started to blossom and bloom in Spain, and we are almost as close now as we were when we were kids. We pieced the relationship back together. My dad had given up on me again at this time too. I think he said, I do not have a son at the moment.'

XXVI
Grace/Wastelands

2008–2009: Songwriting with an out-of-her-nut Amy
Winehouse. The day we met God – Lee Mavers. Black
magic with Peaches Geldof. Recording my debut solo
album, Grace/Wastelands. *Graham Coxon on guitar.*
Advice from Roger Daltrey. Thirtieth birthday party.

'I was trying to write music with Amy. I was so blown away and amazed by her, completely in love. I wanted to do something positive, but she was out of control a lot of the time. She was hard work the times she came to Sturmy when Blake was in prison.

She'd be out of her nut on medication and methadone. I'd have to carry her upstairs and put her in the spare room, and the next day she'd ask what had happened. Trying to do music with her was like a running battle between her excesses and her musical genius. I wanted to do something that would last, to show people, Look, we did some good music together, but it never came out that way. There are some recordings, bits on my laptop, of me and her jamming – some magical moments in the middle of the night – but the world never saw it or heard it.

I'm still a little bit heartbroken at the extent of how out of it she was a lot of the time. I don't know if there's a feeling I led Amy astray, but that definitely wasn't the case. I was definitely under manners to try and look after her. The people around her were wary of the relationship but didn't understand it. Her outfit was a lot more professional and commercial than mine – her band was a lot more organised. I was definitely seen as a danger from her camp, but I think that's an inaccurate interpretation of what was going on between me and her. In those moments when she would come to me, she would be in absolute chaos – as if she almost had to put herself in an extreme mental state just to be in my company. It was almost like her being with me was a chance for her to be completely out of her nut. I'd be the opposite so I could make sure I could look out for her. I could see how fragile she was. She wasn't really capable of using drugs constructively. She wasn't really a normal street addict who knew what to do or how to use – it was full-on chaotic using.

It was always mayhem around Amy at Sturmy – making any meaningful connection with her was very difficult. She was asking me to inject her a lot – something I vehemently refused to do. I was always 100 per cent no way, not in a million years.

When Amy was around at Sturmy, it was a period where I was making a lot of home movies for YouTube on my laptop. I think Kate was worried that after we split up I might put some stuff of me and her online, but the only video we did was with her and Sadie Frost in the red army jackets in the barn at her place in the Cotswolds. Those two dancing round in their red jackets. My favourite video from that time was the one I did when Lee Mavers came to visit Sturmy. I called it 'Didn't We All Have a Lovely Day the Day We All Met God'. It's me and Astile with Lee Mavers, and we're just getting him to play tunes – it's mesmerising. Some of those La's songs are the best ever, the lyrics and the guitar playing, like 'Over' and 'Son of a Gun'. Lee Mavers became a bit of an obsession, almost superhuman in my mind. There's not actually a lot written really about his past, the early '80s in Liverpool, but some people I've met said, Yeah, I remember him sitting on the side of the docks, staring mystically into the sea, and I used to do that, when I was at my nan's in Liverpool – I would just wander down the docks, staring into the sea.

It was a rich time creatively for me, but I think these were some of the worst days for gig no-shows too – became a regular thing. I was writing songs for *Grace/Wastelands*, really trying to capture a sense of Sturmy, which I imagined as like a mashed-up, skaggy version of Gracelands. I wanted it to be a pop-culture headquarters of some kind, but invariably people would come to stay and leg it after a couple of days in confusion – little things like occasionally no running water or no heating would put people off. Alan devised a character called Country Al, shooting jacket and massive boots, and we'd go on these massive treks across land and forest to a country pub. Alan and I wrote 'Sweet By and By' for *Grace/Wastelands*. I really rated that song. It was important to me, a kind of lament for the early days of The Libertines in a way, thinking about when we first went off on tour.

There were lots of comings and goings. Lindi came to Sturmy a couple of times. I tried to do some songwriting with Rini, and I had a lot of little songwriting sessions at Sturmy with Peaches Geldof. She was amazing, such a cool girl. She had these mad pagan tattoos of half-men half-goats on her abdomen. She was incredible, into black magic and the gear. Real creative force. I was always impressed with her. Again, like Amy, I don't know if people think I led her astray, but that's just not true. Not at all. We helped each other score quite a lot, or she'd turn up and have her own works, her own needles and that. She was pretty fucking wild. She made me feel like an old man, which I was, really, compared to her. She was a real live wire, talking about the black arts and unimaginable sexual positions. She'd just come and go. She was not in thrall to me or under my command – much the opposite if anything. There was never any, y'know – she was just a beautiful girl who was a really creative free spirit.

'Palace of Bone' on *Grace/Wastelands* was very much a Sturmy composition, sort of inspired by Peaches. I had this strange altar that she helped me set up with candles, snakeskins wrapped around candelabras, stuffed ducks and blackbirds, and lots of skulls. 'Palace of Bone' came from that, really. All the waifs and strays that would come and stay – just trying to make a creative refuge where everyone could 'come and dance in the palace of bone'.

Stephen Street was really keen on getting a lot of those solo-written intimate songs down, and he wanted to keep Mick . . . well, let's put it this way: he was definitely keen to get me working with another guitarist. Adam and Drew play a lot on *Grace/Wastelands*, so it is kind of a Babyshambles album, but Stephen also brought in Graham Coxon to play on the album. I liked him. We had a mutual respect. Well, actually, I kind of worshipped him, adored him, from the days on the army barracks watching the video to 'Beetlebum' as a teenager and thinking he was one of the greats, really, so I was honoured to have him on the record. I remember the first day of recording, and we were going to be doing a version of 'I Am the Rain' that I'd written with John Robinson from The Bandits who had supported The Libertines in the early days and were an amazing band, brilliant. We'd stayed up all night watching some old Hitchcock films, the murder mystery called *Murder!* – 'Sir John, Sir John, What are you going to do, Sir John?' That stuck in my head, and I gave Stephen Street strict instructions to have this Hitchcock sound excerpt on the album, but I think it cost too much.

I had a new song, '1939 Returning', that I wanted to be a duet with Amy. I had some recordings of her singing it on a phone that went missing. I was really concerned about losing it, but Stephen wasn't bothered at all and just moved on, and the song took on another form. We also did some of my old songs on the album, like 'Arcady', 'Lady Don't Fall Backwards' and 'New Love Grows on Trees', which refers to Carl and his moments of wanton despair early on when he was always talking about killing himself. It was great to get all these songs out. After *Shotter's Nation*, and the more commercial stuff, I wanted to just show that different side to myself, the more folky, poetic side of myself, as a singer-songwriter, the real me almost.

'Salomè' was a firm favourite from that album, based on the biblical story. I wrote that at Kate's country pile in front of the big fire, doing loads of gear and playing my acoustic guitar. I think there's a little bit of Mick in there, one of the really beautiful chord changes – B flat to E flat major 7 and back. Mick was always playing those chords over and over again, and it was like, Hello. 'Sheepskin Tearaway' from the album is one of my favourite songs of all time, actually. I wrote it with Dot Allison, and it was about Wolfman and Gemma, who was this girl who'd turned up at a gig in Liverpool in the early days of The Libertines with a ripped vest saying Arcadian Wench on it. She used to come and visit me in London, and her and Wolfman got together and were an item for fifteen years. I love that song so much. 'A Little Death Around the Eyes' came from the title of a novel Carl's sister Lucie wrote. I always liked that title, thought it'd make a good song, and the line 'Your boyfriend's name was Dave, I was bold and brave', which is quite an important bit of the song, was Carl's so that's credited to Doherty/Barât, but we didn't work together on it.

We'd seen each other at this fashion-show gig I did at the Prince of Wales for Gio-Goi. It was ships that pass in the night, a very brief encounter, a chaotic couple of songs on a small pub stage and then away into the night. That was filmed as part of the MTV thing, *Pete Doherty in 24 Hours*, that was shown in early 2009. It was all organised by Anthony Donnelly, and it worked out all right in the end, quite a little adventure. I think his book* covers all that quite accurately. Maybe the press made a big deal about Carl and me being back on stage together, but there was no way The Libertines were going to re-form at that time, although you do get a sense that things are thawing out a little bit, and in these brief moments maybe there is a feeling there's something inevitable about us getting back together. It was around the time he was breaking up with Annalisa. I think that hit him really hard, but it kind of paved the way for me and him to be able to get close again. I don't think with her in the picture there was ever a chance of that.

'Last of the English Roses', the first single off the album, was another old song – everything about it was ancient. The lyrics about 'cheeky' and 'saucy' are a *Carry On* films touch. Even though the lyrics say 'my famous Aunty Arthur', he's not a cross-dresser at all, my mum's elder brother who followed Percy into driving black cabs. When we'd go to Liverpool to stay at my nan's, she had all his old clothes from the '80s in a wardrobe. But who is the 'Last of the English Roses'? I don't know. I don't know who I was singing about, if I'm honest. One of the writers who influenced me was a Portuguese writer called Fernando Pessoa, who used to have this thing where he invented all these characters, and in his collected letters it was really hard to work out who he had invented and who was real – he'd write all these letters back and forth to himself, and it confused all his biographers. It turned out that they were all invented, all these noms de plume and different poets that used to contribute to his magazines. I think there is the same sort of invention in some of my songs, such as 'Last of the English Roses', but that title is also quite inclusive, quite rousing – it appeals to that sense of Englishness that I like to think I tapped into.

* *Still Breathing – True Adventures of the Donnelly Brothers* (Black & White, 2012).

It was strange because neither 'Last of the English Roses' nor the album sold that well in the UK – although over the years the album has maintained steady sales, and there's not a single solo gig that goes by where I don't play 'Last of the English Roses'. When it came out, I did a load of songs off *Grace/Wastelands* on French TV, solo, just a guitar and an amp. There was nowhere you could do that in England, just turn up with your guitar and go out live on TV doing what you want – it was such a great opportunity. It was a different environment in France around how I was perceived. It was a little bit nerve-wracking at the time doing that show, but I looked at it years later and really enjoyed it – it stands out as a good performance. I don't know where the kids in the audience came from – it wasn't advertised anywhere. I think the TV show just brought in music lovers who listened to the music and politely clapped. 'Last of the English Roses' is kind of my big number in France, and they love the album – people still talk about it, say it's their favourite album all these years later. I was really excited by the success in France and equally disappointed by the low sales in the UK.

Mick had felt excluded by the *Grace/Wastelands* recording, so it was good to get Babyshambles back on the road, touring Europe in late 2008. We did a Teenage Cancer Trust benefit gig with Roger Daltrey in Bristol in early 2009, and I think we ran through a few Who songs with him. Roger Daltrey was so cool – he was great to me. I was bang on the pipe and the gear, and he got me up against the wall by the scruff of my neck and was like, I'll drink any of my friends out of addiction, I'll do that for them – he sounded a bit like John Lydon. Look, some of my friends were addicts, and I drunk them out of addiction, is that what it's going to take? He demanded a bottle of whisky, and I was so terrified at the thought of him pouring this whisky down my throat and getting my drugs wet. He was good stuff but vehemently and aggressively anti-drugs. We got on. I think he was quite surprised we were all able to function. He pointed over to Mick and said, Can he even fucking walk, for Christ sake?

They wanted me to become an ambassador for the Teenage Cancer Trust. I played a little show at the funeral of this young fan of ours who died from cancer, Daniel Squires. He was only sixteen. I'd done that for Bluebell too – she was only fourteen when she died. I played at her funeral in Wales. She was disabled, loved loads of the obscure session tracks I'd posted online. I'd pop in to see her when I could, play those songs she loved. I was always stopping off at kid's houses – their mums would always be there, I hasten to add. It was a nice surprise for different kids, just play a gig in their back garden and have dinner with the family.

The Babyshambles tour went on for a few months. Between gigs, when I could, I'd do solo shows in London, at the Hackney Empire or Shepherd's Bush Empire, and I started doing guerrilla gigs again. We'd just post it last minute online – do these gigs at midnight. Always good fun, with skinny Clara wandering about in her fishnets and a sheepskin coat and sitting in the back office with Alan with his boots on the desk. Clara was someone I met through Mark Hammerton back when we were writing 'Can't Stand Me Now' together, really beautiful girl. She became a firm friend.

I was actually touring pretty much non-stop for about five months at the start of 2009 because Stephen put a band together, and we did a long tour, in the UK and Europe, to support the release of *Grace/Wastelands*. That was a great tour. Drew and Adam were in the band, and Graham Coxon came on the tour. We also had Stephen Large on keyboards, who'd done a lot of stuff with Blur and Madness. There was definitely a cohesion to the band, a good team spirit. It wasn't like a Babyshambles tour, where me and Mick would build a fortress at the end of the bus where we could do what we wanted with crack and heroin. Stephen and Graham were really professional. Lord Large brought his missus along to some shows – it was all a bit more family-orientated. Lee Mavers came and played with us in Birmingham, which was a great night. We took three string players on that tour and these two French ballerinas – Celine and Octavie. They were classically trained ballerinas. It was the start of a long association and working relationship with them.

After being slightly under manners on tour, not wanting to smoke crack on the bus in front of everyone, I wanted a real blowout for my thirtieth birthday. The Paddingtons came and played in the front room at Sturmy for this big party – it was great, but their birthday present to me was a shitload of temazepam, so I took a load, collapsed and woke up two days after the birthday party had finished with the house completely ruined, just a few stragglers in a few cupboards.

The police raided Sturmy soon after. I got caught driving under the influence. I think they might have found heroin in the car too. I know the bail they set was £50,000, which seemed a bit excessive. Whilst I was locked up, they went in the house and found loads of stuff, all the bits I'd hidden. They completely ruined my cigarette-card collection. I had loads mounted in frames, and they took all these frames apart, cracked them open, searched all these collectors' items which were filled with foam and bits hidden for emergencies. They went to town on Sturmy.

I had another implant put in after that, but they put it in while I still had opiates in my system, so I was in a bad way when we came to do Glastonbury that summer, 2009. I didn't think I was going to make it, so Andy Boyd turned up in a helicopter, landed by the stables, dragged me – in my shit-caked tracksuit bottoms – onto it. Amy guested with Babyshambles that summer. She was in a bad way too. She sort of stumbled on stage with us at the V Festival in August. Afterwards, she came to our tour bus, and we started fooling around. We were getting it on when her security turned up and literally pulled her off me. Adrian Hunter and her security were flailing on the stairs of the tour bus as Amy was getting dragged off kicking and scream- ing. The next day I saw her and said, So, what happened? and she claimed not to have remembered, which was a bit disappointing for me obviously.'

XXVII
Robin

2009–2010: Briefly dying at Sturmy and seeing Morrissey. A Nazi singalong. The flooding and freezing. Andy Boyd is jailed for hit and run. Robin Whitehead dies. The Libertines re-form. Amy on the prowl. A film role and six months for possession of cocaine.

'My heart stopped briefly one night at Sturmy. It was horrible. I don't think that was a straight injection overdose, but I could feel I was dying as my heart went into slow time. I remember thinking, This is it. I'd injected ketamine and taken a load of those weird Valiums that were knocking about – big pots of a thousand Valium that you used to be able to order from Thailand online. Before I collapsed, I remember thinking I was a taxi and running head first into the walls. One of the ballerinas apparently phoned the ambulance after I collapsed when my heart stopped.

I came round with no shoes on, no shirt, no pants, just a pair of green Adidas tracksuit bottoms that belonged to Andy Boyd. I was in intensive care in the Great Western Hospital in Swindon, and I don't know if it was some waking vision I had or what it was, but I remember being convinced Morrissey was in the same intensive care unit or had been recently. I was sure that a nurse had told me that. Then this other nurse came on duty, and I was like, That other nurse told me Morrissey was in the intensive care unit. It was an Irish girl, and she said, Who's Morrissey? I was absolutely dumbfounded. I said, Look, have you had like a male, in his late thirties with a sort of quiff, maybe he's in for, I don't know, suspended melancholy or something. She said, I don't know, I'll check. I was a in a bit of state when I came round, felt like I'd been hit by a bus.

Robin Whitehead was also into those Valium in a big way. Robin was going to make this film *Road to Albion* using unseen footage from the early days of The Libertines – it was all a bit vague, but she had access to this film-editing place in Soho. She would beg me to sleep with her on acid, and she got swept up in the Peaches Geldof 'black magic sex rituals' thing. I found her trying to inject herself with a blunt needle one time. I didn't want to see her using. She had this completely romanticised view of heroin, way beyond how I viewed it. To her it became like a pure tool for goodness and creativity, and she started making this new film, *Opium and the Romantic Imagination*. It was supposedly a complete celebration of me, Alan and Wolfman, our circle.

I can't begin to tell you how bad this period was. It was an assimilation of really dark events, one thing after another. This is like the peak of the demonisation of me by the tabloids. It started when I did some more solo dates in December 2009, and at this festival in Munich I sang 'Deutschlandlied', the national anthem. I didn't know the first verse, '*Deutschland, Deutschland, über alles*' (Germany, Germany, above all) was either banned or really contentious due to its association with the Nazi era. It really tapped into a strange atmosphere in Germany, that's for sure, politically, socially – definitely a sensitive area. I did it with some members of other bands, jamming on stage. We weren't supposed to be on stage, so that was bad enough, and then the only song I could think of to go into was '*Deutschland,*

Deutschland, über alles'. It was one of the all-time shocking headlines I think I've seen of myself: 'Doherty Sings Nazi Hymn'. I remember it was very tense afterwards, running round that festival with some people trying to kill me and some people with their unveiled appreciation of the fact I sang it, people saying, Well done, we love this song. Later on that night, I was arrested for smashing a car windscreen.

While I was away, the waterpipe collapsed at Sturmy, and the whole place flooded – all my stuff was ruined, my books and records. I don't know if you've ever seen real mould in action, but it's horrendous. It was all up the walls. The place had flooded and then frozen over, defrosted and then froze over again – all this happened in a couple of days. It decimated the place. It was completely fucked – I lost so much stuff.

I also had to go to court in December to be sentenced for the arrest over the summer. I got banned from driving for eighteen months, but the thing that stands out is a load of heroin fell out of my pocket, thirteen wraps, while I was in court. I was charged with another count of drug possession for that. Oh my god! The story was, and the story the court believed was, I hadn't worn the suit for a long, long time and that it was in my pocket from the last time I wore it. I suppose the truth is it was not very well hidden in my pants and fell down my trouser leg. I got off with a fine on that one.

Then just before Christmas Andy Boyd got sent down for twelve months. In September, near Ipswich, he'd knocked over a guy and put him in a vegetative state.* Jesus. It was a real tragedy and a massive shock to everyone. Not only was Andy driving my Daimler,

---

* Chris Corder, forty-two, was delivering church newsletters at the time of the incident. He suffered severe brain injuries and multiple fractures. He died in 2020, after ten years as a quadriplegic.

but he went on to tell the police that I knew he wasn't insured. I was on a ban, so I wasn't insured on it. He told them I'd given him permission to drive it, which makes it my responsibility. It got really complicated and really confusing. I remember the day before the court hearing going down to meet the lawyers at the Inns of Court and Royal Courts of Justice in Holborn, and it just being a clusterfuck of legal paperwork. There was a lot of confusion from the victim's family as well. When Andy turned up at court in Ipswich, there were people shouting at him, You're supposed to be a famous musician, mate, you're supposed to be a role model. They thought Andy was me. He didn't even admit to me he'd run someone over until the police contacted me and said mine was the car they were looking for. In court, he admitted dangerous driving and failing to stop at an accident scene.

Next, in January, Robin overdosed and died in Wolfman's bed at the Pink Tower. She was only twenty-seven. Alan and I had seen her the day before she died. She was pissed off that I wouldn't give her any drugs. I think after we left, she and Wolfman stayed up all night and then crashed out. Wolfman found her dead the next day. The police said the death was non-suspicious. I spoke to the police about Robin's death – they'd found drugs at Gill's place. In the end, at the inquest, the coroner said it was death by misadventure: they found a small amount of heroin in her blood, enough to kill someone who didn't take it regularly.

I was sick to my heart with sadness. Her family didn't want me at the funeral. Her dad, Peter Whitehead, who was a filmmaker, did the '60s Rolling Stones film *Charlie Is My Darling*, put a curse on me and threatened to kill me and Astile. He said he knew where my kid went to school, and he told Alan to watch out for potholes in the road. He thought we'd murdered his daughter. Even before she died, he accused me of leading her on and wasting her time. He came to Sturmy one time to oversee this so-called missing interview that I wouldn't do with Robin, but I was always happy doing interviews with her.

An offer came in from a French film director called Sylvie Verheyde. She came to stay at Sturmy for a couple of days. She'd just had a big hit with a French film called *Stella*, a great film. These were the final days at Sturmy. There was no electricity, and I just had a generator. The roof had started to leak too. She slept on a mattress on the floor – was quite a good sport. We had a good laugh – at one point the police were after me for something, and we had to run through the forest to escape from them. She was doing a period piece based on a well-known French novel by Alfred de Musset, *Confession of a Child of the Century* – it's the sort of things they teach French kids at school, the equivalent of Dickens or Wilde, part of their canon. She wanted me for the part of the lead character called Octave. Sylvie had quite a big budget, $5 million, and the film company got me a flat in Paris, an amazing gaff, for the early readings and the screen shots. There was a lot of trawling around Berlin and London too, trying to find the right costumes . . . getting fitted up for all these outfits. It was all really exciting. I always had aspirations to be an actor from the first time I was in a school play. I'd much rather have been an actor, or even a pantomime dame, than a musician. I love it. There are a few things that have fallen through over the years that I was a bit disappointed about – opportunities that came up that I didn't take. I was going to get a part in *EastEnders* at one point.

It was around this time that The Libertines re-formed too. Maybe I was in some huge financial crisis – it might have been to do with the money from that Andy Boyd car accident.* I was never fully aware of

---

* Corder was awarded damages in the High Court reported as running into seven figures. The Motor Insurers' Bureau – which compensates victims of uninsured drivers – was pursuing Boyd and Peter for the money.

my financial situation, but there was definitely a sense of panic. Maybe all of us were in a bit of a spot financially. They all had kids. Carl was sort of between homes, and then after that reunion he managed to get what he described as a muscular house, in Stoke Newington. We were booked to do Reading and Leeds Festival. There was a sense of celebration of us getting back together, and there was a lot of money involved, over a million pounds, but there was no new music, no new songwriting, and we weren't really hanging out apart from at rehearsals. I was still in full-on using mode, and very happy as well, because I was now supposed to be getting some proper bunce. I was also thinking maybe I could get Carl to see how I could be tolerable as a crack and heroin user . . . it wasn't the way to go about things. There were a lot of missing rehearsals on my part.

As a warm-up to the festival shows, we did a couple of nights at the Kentish Town Forum. Amy Winehouse turned up at the Malmaison hotel in Farringdon, where me and Carl were staying. She was going off on one about her new breast implants – she'd just had her boob job done. After Carl left, she was chasing me around the hotel room, but her security were in the corridor, and the tabloids were downstairs in the car park, so it was just not going to happen. I said, There's no peace here, but she was running after me like a lioness.

It was exciting to be doing the old songs, and I think people really wanted to see us. There'd always been a lot of females in The Libertines crowd, but I remember looking out at Reading and there being a massive teenage girl presence, which was surprising. I was a bit older, but the fans seemed to stay younger. It was quite a buzz playing massive gigs together for the first time with The Libertines. I'd never really done festivals with the band – we'd done a few Brixtons, but they'd been very fraught, with me running off stage. There was definitely a sense of unfinished business.

In September, following an inquiry into Robin's death, I was charged with cocaine possession, and Wolfman was charged with suspicion of supply. No one could believe I was being charged on video footage alone. The police were charging us on the basis of the film Robin had shot. It was really dodgy . . . the injustice of it all. The whole thing was madness. It was a complete frame-up. Robin had filmed me having a pipe, but there's millions of pictures of me having a pipe – I've never been nicked for them. It doesn't make any sense.*

It dragged on for ages, for months and months. In the end, after pleading guilty to possession based on Robin's film footage, I got a six-month sentence in May 2011. Complete travesty. It was hard to accept. At the sentencing, Robin's five sisters were all there in the court. Wolfman was so out of his nut. He didn't know what was going on, even when they announced he'd got twelve months. I had to tell him, You've just got twelve months, as we got led down. That's when he started to get upset. It was one of those things where you weigh it off, because standing in the dock looking at her five sisters . . . I was thinking, Right this is just going to be my time out to mourn, despite the fact it's completely unjust. I felt like in some way I had to pay some sort of penance, not because it was my fault but because the whole thing was horrible, the sorrow of it. Wolfman felt the same. It was like going into a big black hole and finally being able to mourn. There's something to be said for just getting your head down and getting it done – use it as a time to just clean up for a bit, albeit against your will. That was my mourning period, really, for Robin, who I really loved and so did Wolfman.

---

* The footage was shot on the day before Whitehead's death. Wolfe was filmed smoking from the same pipe before passing it to Whitehead and helping her to light it. Peter could be heard refusing to give Whitehead the crack pipe himself.

When I arrived in Pentonville, a lot of people were confused as to why I was in there – what I'd done or if I'd been shipping big amounts around. I said I hadn't done anything. I haven't even been caught in possession – it was on video. People would always say, How can you get six months for that? It was complete bollocks, that sentence, but what are you going to do? You've just got to take it on the chin. The Libertines were due to play Glastonbury that summer, and that had to be cancelled, and it all went quiet. I think the management announced it was all over. It fucked things up financially, a right old mess.

Being back in prison was the same old same old bang-up. There was overcrowding, and there was some trouble down in the block, different incidents, and they shipped me out to HMP Wayland in Norfolk, a Category C prison. It was supposed to be the most drug-free prison in England – just my luck. There were a few unpleasant incidents there with people wanting protection money, but I didn't have money to throw around. There were people coming into my cell, and I ended up having to defend myself, throwing the telly around, throwing chairs around, and not getting any help from the screws.

But there was a creative-writing course during that sentence, which was the first time I had anything like that available to me in prison. One guy on the course took me aside and threatened me, but all he really wanted was for me to write a poem to his girl-friend. I did that, and I was all right with him afterwards; apparently, she really liked the poem. They also asked me to put together a prison band. That was awful, terrible, trying to organise this one-armed keyboard player and this other guy who insisted he was going to do lead vocals – they were all a right bunch of cunts. There were punch-ups and people swinging at me all the time, and everyone outside in the yard pressed up against the window watching us rehearse. I got out on tag at the beginning of July, just before we were supposed to do a concert for the officers' annual dance or something. I did two months, and the conditions of the tag meant I had to be at home between 7 p.m. and 7 a.m. for the rest of the sentence.'

XXVIII
Sequel to the Prequel

2011–2013: Back in Camden. Amy dies. The imaginary
voices. Wolfman, Suzy, Elspeth and Adem – demos
and down at heel. Travelling Tinkers, touring with
Alan. Another huge drug debt. Meeting Carla Bruni.
A flop in Cannes. A third Babyshambles album.

'I'd only been out of prison a couple of weeks when Amy died in the small hours. I heard about her death the next morning. I hadn't seen her, even though she was just down the road – me on tag in this horrible basement below a key shop on Camden High Street, just a mattress on the floor and loads of foil and needles. I was using super heavily and not much use to anyone – just basically getting the tag out of the way and then see what was going to happen next in my life. Amy was someone I was deliberately keeping away from. She left a voice message on my phone not that long before she died. It just said, I'd like to see you. I kept it for ages.

In my memory, that summer there was the London riots, this rowing couple, and the ghost of Amy leaving her body and rising up over London. I recorded the rowing couple on my phone and used the recording on a song called 'Oily Boker' on the *Hamburg Demonstrations* album. It was a Scottish geezer and a cockney girl – really vicious argument. I'd gone to the door in my Camden hovel, and down this long dark corridor I could hear this god-awful screaming – he's accusing her of sleeping with his mates, and she's saying she's going to get her brothers to cut his dick off and stick it down his throat, You fucking cunt . . . At the time, I thought they were plotting to kill me. I was in such a paranoid state, in the depths of my addiction.

In fact, I'd sometimes hear threatening voices up until quite recently. For many years it would be a female Yorkshire accent, sometimes two females, and it was always very clear but completely imaginary. No one else could ever hear it. These two Yorkshire voices were there for a long time. I can't explain other than to say they were beyond being critical of me and my character and my life – it was completely poisonous rhetoric. One would say to the other, That fucking spineless cunt, who does he think he is? Look at him, he's disgusting, oh he's disgusting, I wouldn't touch him with a fucking barge pole, and I'm no princess. And the other one would go, You don't have to tell me . . . it would go on and on. It'd always be just outside the window, just out of view, so by the time I got to the window and looked out, sure that I'd finally be able to catch them, they'd shuffled off somewhere to a darker place. I never managed to get my hands on them. I imagined them as kind of like a Yorkshire version of the Fat Slags from *Viz*, but I can't confirm their appearance, because I never actually saw them.

A lot of this period I look at from a distance, because as long as I had a bag of gear – that was my orbit. There was definitely a lot of making or playing music to buy drugs. It seemed like it was going to be impossible for people to differentiate between me as a musician and me as a tabloid personality, and I couldn't really stomach that. I felt a lot happier and safer in my little drug bubble. All my money went on drugs for a long, long time. There wasn't really any creative satisfaction – it was a very dark time of just using and scrabbling together money from any little gig I could do, which I'd done for a long time, but maybe things were just a little bit darker and more desperate.

I was hanging out with Wolfman and a girl called Elspeth. She'd lived really close to Kate's country house but on a council estate in Oxfordshire. I met her because she worked in the local pub. She was quite young, twenty or twenty-one. Manchester Mike, who was also from Oxfordshire and in a band called Law Abiding Citizens, was also knocking about. He was mates with Bez, who took some huge manic canvases I'd been doing to auction off for one of his charities. Hopefully some good came of that. It was a weird situation, because that flat I was in was so small and bits of gear kept going missing and I didn't know who was taking it.

When I was living in Camden, I also got together with Suzy Martin, who ended up singing on a song on *Hamburg Demonstrations*. She was going out with Wolfman, and we had a stall together, Doherty and Martin, at Camden Market, quite good fun, selling all bits of stuff I'd collected over the years. She was a bit of an entrepreneur – she was flogging cigarettes that she said had Amy Winehouse's lipstick on. She used to run the Torriano pub in Kentish Town that Andy Boyd used to frequent. I did a lot of gigs down there. Alan and I used to put on folk-music nights and blues nights. It was where I met Miki Beavis, a violinist. We started jamming at the Torriano, and then we started doing music together. We did shows together – me and Miki and Celine and Octavie, just the four of us.

I also started recording with a guy called Adem Hilmi, a skinny London Italian kid, really small, really arsey attitude, rude to people but couldn't back it up, kept getting battered – quite cool but so annoying. Adem rented space in a studio over by Wormwood Scrubs and helped me put together 'Down for the Outing', and that song ended up on *Hamburg Demonstrations* too. Wolfman helped me write it, and there were some strange lyrics in that, plus these really emotional lines

I wrote – 'Sorry Dad for the good times that I had, they made me look so bad, sorry Mum for the good things I've done, gave you hope when there was none'. I used to have trouble singing those lines for a long time. The demos I did with Adem have a very distinct sound from the *Hamburg Demonstrations*, though – they're better texturally, they feel more interesting . . . strange sound effects, backward accordions. 'Nothing Comes to Nothing', which we did for the Babyshambles album *Sequel to the Prequel*, was demoed with Adem, a really good demo. I put it on online immediately. That was about Elspeth – 'An Amwellian do, a tongue soaked in booze, says he's filthy and much older than you'. The lyrics were about the stand-up comedy night we went to at Filthy's on Amwell Street. I was really happy to take her there and explain to her the history of the place and my relationship with it. The stand-ups were just taking the piss out of us, Yeah, what you wanna do – and then pronouncing her name wrong, they spent the whole night taking the piss out of her name – is get yourself an old junkie, that's always good advice. There was a lot of back and forth and throwing drinks at the stage.

I asked Adem to come on tour, a European solo tour that Adrian had sorted. I wanted him to play keyboards – he used to do weird sound effects with a Moog – but he got to the bus before me, and Adrian told him to fuck off, said he didn't know anything about it. As we were pulling off, I said, That's weird, I invited someone to come and play, and Adrian went, Oh, never mind, we'll be at Dover soon. Then I got a phone call from Adem saying what had happened and it all blew up. In the end, Adem did come on tour: him and Elspeth, and Wolfman, the ballerinas, this weird clique. It was a disaster.

After that, I started trying to do things on my own for a bit. I fell out with Andy and Adrian. It was an impasse at that point. I didn't really have any track of the money or any understanding of the money situation. Babyshambles was pretty much over. Alan and I would just go round Europe in any people carrier we could get hold of, any dodgy taxi driver we could find to do the driving, and we'd say we were doing a city-to-city tour. They were really chaotic gigs, just different low-grade promoters giving us ad-hoc gigs. Alan wanted to start a band called the Travelling Tinkers – that was always our dream.

It was safer for me being out of London. I'd built up another really bad drug debt with the dealer who used to come out to Sturmy – he'd been giving me a lot of tick, thousands and thousands. At the very end of filming *Confession*, there had been a lot of people flying out to bring me gear. Then this dealer turned up in a panic saying his uncle needed the money, twenty-three grand. Andy Boyd was living round the corner in Camden, and he helped me raise the money. I was really skint. He organised this exhibition at Cob Gallery in Kentish Town, *On Blood: A Portrait of the Artist*, and among the paintings he auctioned off all the things I'd brought away from my final evacuation from Kate's country house and from Sturmy, like this beautiful Louis XIV writing desk that had 'cunt' scrawled into it. Andy auctioned it all off, loads of my guitars and flags. James McCartney played a little concert with me at the gallery launch. We sold a blood painting of Amy Winehouse for £35,000 as part of the Cob Gallery international auction, and that was part of the debt clearance. Andy Boyd pulled it out of the bag. We did two solo gigs and sold the painting and got the whole lot in cash and paid off this drug debt. This dealer's uncle followed us round the whole time, parked outside wherever we were, reminding us every hour how long we had left to pay.

When my tag ended, I moved to Paris. I was working with Celine and Octavie on all my live stuff, and they were both doing really well for themselves in the dance world, with the French ballet, and they got a flat in Paris in their name, and I moved in with them. That was rue de

Copenhague, and that was where I lived for my longest spell in Paris. The *Confession* film was coming out at the end of the summer, and the idea was I was going to be a film star.

I also got involved with these three brothers who ran a high-end fashion label called The Kooples, a big name in France. We talked in depth about collaborating on a clothing range. It was great fun. I wanted to do skinhead, casual stuff, mod stuff, parkas, braces, hats, cool jeans, boots – prison shirts was a vibe. Rini, who was in Paris, did some of the modelling, and I did some of the modelling. I got my old friend Alize Meurrisse involved, and she designed the one item in the range that did really well, sold out immediately. I was going to swanky hotels, the Love Hotel in Paris was one, and doing interviews with fashion magazines and showing them the designs, really excited. There were loads of posters up in Paris, and I was quite proud of that fashion range.

I got invited to meet Carla Bruni the model and singer-songwriter who was married to Nikolas Sarkozy, the president of France. I went to her house, and we were working on a song. There were armed guards everywhere with automatic weapons. She gets quite a bad deal in France, but I thought she was cool. I really enjoyed that day with her. When the presidential car came to rue de Copenhague, Celine and Octavie were disgusted. Why are you going to her? She is not good, she is not cool. I was like, I'm going, I'm going to meet the president's missus.

Paris was where I first got to know Katia deVidas. We were married in September 2021. We were just friends for a long time. She was working freelance in cinema, mainly as an editor and camerawoman with the Stanley Kubrick Foundation in London. Jan Harlan, Kubrick's producer, was her boss. He was the brother of Kubrick's widow, Christiane. Sometimes the French magazine *Les Inrockuptibles* would hire her to film gigs. That's how she ended up on the road with Babyshambles and became part of the gang. She was somehow untouchable – I fell in love with her over the years. She started making a film about me, and later she'd join the Puta Madres on keyboards – more of both later!

I was still using heavily, and I've got a sense there was really a black hole in my life at the time. I was really struggling physically, getting a lot of abscesses and veins were just collapsing. Celine, Octavie and Katia were saying, You're dying, you've got to go to rehab. Adrian was trying to get me to go to Thailand, and I kept missing the flights. The girls were saying, Just fucking go, it's going to be great, you're going to have a great time in Thailand.

It was an amazing place, Chiang Mai. It was luxury. I had my own comfortable space, a wooden log cabin in what was a very expensive rehab surrounded by lots of rich European addicts looking for recovery or temporary respite from their chaotic lives. It was great. I did get clean there, but the second I got clean I thought, Shit, I've got to use. I had a bit of an argument with the director of the place, and it ended quite badly. One good thing that did come out of it was I met the assistant director there, a guy called Simon Mott. He wasn't my personal therapist – he was just a floppy-haired, barefoot ex-public schoolboy who had dreams of saving people from addiction. In the end, he set up his own rehab place in Si Racha called Hope, which is the place where I'd completely stick it out a couple of years later.

Confession of a Child of the Century was screened at Cannes. My mum came over for that. While I was still on tag in Camden, I'd been to Emily's wedding – she married a paratrooper – and I think people, my mum and dad, were surprised at how compos mentis I was despite all the tabloid stories.

Yes, the idea was I was going to be a film star, and this film was all set up. I had the lead role, it was made by a celebrated director who'd won loads of prizes, but it just didn't happen. The casting director, Phillipe

Elkoubi, gay guy, absolutely incredible, friend of Rini's, said Sylvie had an amazing cast, but the film didn't turn out so great. When she came to Sturmy, we had a little one-night fling. That's not a good situation to be in with a director.

They measure the success of films at Cannes by how long people applaud for after the film has finished – you have instances of people applauding for five, six, seven, nine minutes. I think we got to twelve seconds before people started filing out – the film's now available on DVD for two euros. Lily Cole pops up in it and all these quite well-known French actors – it was a bit of a star-studded film from the French point of view, but it just didn't hit with the public. I'm still hopeful the future might hold bounties in the film world. I actually started filming another French movie, *Le Fèvre**, with a really weird avant-garde French film director, Phillipe Grandrieux, but I pulled out when I went to Thailand for rehab at Hope.

Drew was responsible for getting Babyshambles back together and doing another album. He was really motivated. He'd had a nasty accident, got knocked off his bike by a bus or a truck. I'd gone to see him in Whitechapel General, and he was told he would never walk again. It was kind of a miracle he'd recovered. He came over to rue de Copenhague and said, What ideas have you got? He stayed over at the flat, set all his recording stuff up and we recorded basic ideas for *Sequel to the Prequel*. We demo'd things I'd written, like 'Penguins', which was a song for Katia, things he'd written, like 'New Pair', things I wrote with him, like 'Seven Shades', and things I'd written with Mick, like 'Farmer's Daughter', which was a belter. John Robinson was now sharing a flat with Drew, so there were some of his songs in the mix, like 'Fall from Grace'. Mick had some of his own ideas, like 'Dr. No', a really ska-heavy song.

---

* *The film was released in 2015 under the title,* Malgré La Nuit.

We were actually contracted to make one more album for Parlophone, and we all needed the money. 'Minefield', which was something to do with Amy, was written during a fun session we had when everybody came to Celine's dad's place in Perpignan, right out in the countryside. Her dad was an Italian sculptor. We holed up there and wrote 'Minefield' as a band, me, Mick, Drew and Adam – a different Adam.

Adam Ficek wasn't part of this album. He was just sick of all the drugs – that was how Babyshambles had been left, really. Mick and I were trying to get this working commune idea of a band going, where we all lived together, wrote together and had a real crack at it, and Adam had just had kids, was trying to pay for his home, and he was just sick of the chaos. Drew and Mick had some sessions in London with the drummer from Stereophonics, but in the end we used Adam Falkner on drums – he'd been playing with Amy McDonald, the big Scottish singer-songwriter.

It was a very fraught process recording the album. We did it at Question de Son, a small commercial studio in the very centre of Paris. It was all quite regimented – they were all staying in a hotel, a nice one. We were in and out of the studio every day. There was no trunk-load of artefacts being left round the studio, definitely no ketamine in there. Stephen Street was producing again, and he lost his rag a few times. At one point he said, I've come out here to make an album, and you're playing like a cunt, Pete. We were doing 'Stranger in My Own Skin', a song I'd written with Wolfman, and I couldn't get the intro right, and I started laughing. I wasn't fucked, it was just a tricky part, and he came out with this mad outburst. I said, Well, why don't you fuck off back to London then. I'd never heard him talk like that before. 'Stranger in My Own Skin' was a great song – there's a really good demo of it that I did with Adem Hilmi. I really liked 'Picture Me in a Hospital' on that album, and, again, I did a demo of that with Adem – very Morrissey-esque.

In the end, Stephen was really happy with my singing on that album, though – he said it a lot. He was really proud, he said. Katia did the video for 'Nothing Comes to Nothing', which was a single from the album, using footage from Place de la République, a gig Babyshambles did in the centre of Paris, but other than that I can't really picture any of that Babyshambles tour we did around the UK and Europe in late 2013 and early 2014 after the album came out. 'Maybelline', another song I wrote with Mick on the album, was a real banger live. We used to love playing it, especially at French festivals – it always used to work. It was quite a silly song, really, with lyrics nabbed from the Stone Roses, Iggy Pop and Chuck Berry, and the riff is Small Faces – an exercise in rock-'n'-roll history. 'Fireman' was a really punky one on the album that was fun live too. I was definitely injecting ketamine on that tour, because I remember at one point I actually did believe I was at a fire convention. I had the idea that I'd been transported down a telephone line to Buenos Aires to a firefighters' convention – they had to talk me down from that one. I was like, I've got to give this speech on fire regulations. No, you don't, we've got to get through customs. Danny Goffey joined the band live for some of the concerts – he was definitely part of the band for a while. Damien Hirst did the art for the album cover as a favour to Drew, who was teaching his son guitar, but *Sequel to the Prequel* almost doesn't feel like a Babyshambles album, even though there were a lot of good songs on it. It wasn't an album like *Shotter's Nation*, which had to be done, had a momentum all of its own – like a wild beast, it grew in strength. This one felt more like a job, but not a bad job, a good job.'

XXIX
Anthems for Doomed Youth

*2014–2015: A new life in Paris. Katia and the camper
van years. Barcelona with Rafa. Hamburg with Johann.
Recording Hamburg Demonstrations. The Libertines reunite
for Hyde Park. Hope in Thailand. Recording the comeback
Libertines album. The death of Alan. Another breakdown.*

'I moved out of rue de Copenhague and was living above a café, a tabac, in rue Pierre-Fontaine. I also ended up renting a shop space which I wanted to turn into a gallery. I holed up in there and did a shitload of canvases. It was a very productive time. I was making a new life for myself in Paris. Just down the road was the Bus Palladium, a well-known venue/restaurant/bar which opened very late, had a lot of live music. Cyril Bodin ran it, and I wanted him to manage me. I let him organise some gigs in France. Adrian came to see one, and Cyril wouldn't let him in.

This is also where Geraldine Beigbeder came in. She organised an art exhibition for me, *Flags from the Old Regime*, at a really flash place in Paris. Then she took that show to Geneva, Barcelona and Moscow. There was some big money involved in that. Geraldine had done some really high-profile collections, and she knew a hell of a lot of the right people – she's got a cousin called Frédéric who is a very well-known writer in France. At the opening night in Paris, she organised for television cameras and press, but I got there late, at midnight, and they'd all gone. We still had a good night – she was a right laugh, Geraldine. In Geneva, she sorted a private gig, with the paintings propped up in the background, in the front room of someone high up in the JP Morgan banking family. One of the wives of someone there bought some of my pieces as a collector. Geraldine also organised another exhibition of my paintings at the Rimbaud Museum in France. She's not involved with my art any more, although she might have some of my work still in storage. I've not been on good terms with her since she started adding her own ideas to the painting while she was curating. I started looking at some of the programmes for the events, and she'd changed the names of the bloody paintings. I always pride myself on having good titles, and that was sometimes just as important as the quality of the painting itself – in fact, it can make or break a painting with my collectors. Katia's mum did the last exhibition I had, in Etretat in 2021, and Katia and I organised the one in Paris just prior to that.

Things had moved beyond a working relationship with Katia. We bought a camper van together, a Peugeot Challenger 1986, the Bouboumobile. We got her uncle to renovate it, and we were travelling around a lot. We'd just find spots in forests or deserted beaches, especially in the south of France and east coast of Spain. It was great, especially in the summer, to set off with a guitar and a typewriter and let everything else go to hell. We used to weave about all over the place. We spent time in Perpignan, a very peaceful place to plot up, and got some local gigs, and travelled to Barcelona, a long trip from Paris, where I also did some gigs that I organised myself.

It was when we were in the camper van in Barcelona that I met Rafa Rueda, who is now one of my best friends. I was after getting some gear, and these kids said, Ah, we'll take you to the druid who runs a puppet shop. He didn't run a puppet shop – he just met them outside a puppet shop. I scored from Rafa a few times. He'd make me wait at a nice café while he went and got things from the Barrio de la Mina, a massive '70s social housing project, where they basically put a 30,000-strong gitanos (Romani) community. He'd say gringos can't go there. I did eventually – ended up queuing on a stairway with everyone from old ladies to kids. You went into the kitchen, and there's some woman with a gun in the back of her bikini and a big pile of heroin and a big pile of coke – ten euros of each or fifty euros of each.

Rafa was very involved in the squat scene in Barcelona. Once, on a separate visit to Barcelona, when I had nowhere to park the camper van, he invited me to go and stay with him. He lived in a place called La Floresta and had a drum kit in this cave underneath the house he was squatting. La Floresta is a forest area but in central Barcelona – the last haven for dilapidated networks of jugglers, musicians and anarchists. There's a strong creative vibe, people making pots and clothes. Whenever I stayed there with Rafa, I'd do a couple of shows at the weekend in the village square with all the other people, and in exchange the café feeds you and gives you drink. It's only ten minutes from central Barcelona on the train, so a lot of people, tourists or kids, come to see the punks, and there's wild boar running everywhere. They are a protected animal, and that's the symbol of the band I made with Rafa, the Puta Madres. Everyone has that sticker on their car bumper. I love it there.

I also took the camper van to Hamburg and did lots of little gigs in amazing bars there. I met a German fashion designer called Bent Angelo Jensen, who had a label called Herr Von Eden, amazing fella, and he took me to a party at a studio complex called Clouds Hill. I started doing the odd gig there for Johann Scheerer, who owned the place. The studio was part of this old compound of warehouses, and it had this amazing modern apartment downstairs, with a table tennis table and a telescope looking out onto the River Elbe. Johann and I came to this really simple arrangement that he was going to help me record a solo album, and we would put it out on his label, also called Clouds Hill, and I'd be able to stay in the apartment. That was the start of the *Hamburg Demonstrations* album.

Really, the main reason I was in Hamburg was the extraordinarily rich drug culture that exists there – you can get things easy. There was this place we used to call 'monsters from the deep', which is a methadone clinic but outside the clinic is this shanty town where people just sit and use in the street. I told Johann that Mick was going to be working on this album with me, but when Johann met him he acted really weird. Then when we went to start recording, he only set up one chair and one mic and one guitar, and he said Mick's not allowed in the studio. I said, What you talking about? He's gonna be working on the album with me. He said, No, he's not allowed in the studio. Maybe Mick was looking a bit rough round the edges. It was a really difficult situation, and I said, Right, we're getting in the Bouboumobile and we're off. Mick said, No, no, you need to do this, I'll just sit this one out. Which was really noble of him. We're still pals. He got clean before I did and is still clean. I've recently been offered a Babyshambles reunion – stranger things have happened.

Suzy Martin came to Hamburg as well – she was a right handful, dancing on the tables. She sang on a new song called 'Birdcage'. I also did a few older songs. The chorus of 'Spy in the House of Love', a title taken from the Anaïs Nin book, goes way back. I also did 'The Whole World Is Our Playground' for the album with Johann, another song which goes way back – it was on the *Babyshambles Sessions* demos, which makes it Libertines era, one of my old songs that never made it through. We also did 'She Is Far', one of the first things I ever wrote.

The recording of that album ended up being really problematic. It went on for well over a year, on and off. The plan initially was just to do a load of demos, and finally instead of whacking them online put them out properly, but that changed completely while I was in rehab at Hope. Johann got a load of musicians in who didn't even know how to play all the parts – that really pissed me off. I had a problem with him taking it and running with it, as opposed to just whacking out the demos, which would have been more the point – a collection of really rough-around-the-edge demos. It ended up being a long, long process of him fine-tuning everything. It's a collection of really good songs, but the production got away from me.

I did manage to get down some of the best new songs I'd written in years, like 'Kolly Kibber' and 'Oily Boker', which was a name Mick and I had for a crack pipe that was rich with oil and residue, the crust. 'I Don't Love Anyone (but You're Not Just Anyone)' was another great new song, about Katia.

When it did eventually come out, it was recognised as my second solo album, but it was all in someone else's hands, a very strange album. I did put a hell of a lot into the cover – really proud of that. It was the final bit of control I wrested after losing all control of the music.

There was a lot of legal wrangling over *Hamburg Demonstrations* – it went on for a long time. The recording overlapped with The Libertines getting back together to do a big-money show in Hyde Park, which led to us doing a new album. As soon as *Hamburg Demonstrations* started looking like a commercial prospect everything shifted, and Johann became a dirty word for Adrian. I don't know how that all turned so problematic, because our initial arrangement was so simple, and Clouds Hill was perfect for rehearsing. The Libertines rehearsed there for the Hyde Park show.

The Hyde Park gig went surprisingly well. It was quite ambitious. I think there was genuine excitement about it selling out, 62,000 tickets, especially for me and Carl. We used to go down and do Spaniel and Spaniel at Speaker's Corner with a broken guitar in 1997 and 1998, and now we'd sold out the park. They also put us up in a snazzy hotel, the Park Lane Hilton, and Carl and I had rooms 258 and 360, which were the numbers on Delaney Mansions, the Albion Rooms on Camden Road, which was sheer serendipity. All the families were there. It was a pretty special day. I remember waking up and looking out the window and seeing a lad in a three-piece suit in the colours of the Union Jack with a massive fedora bowling down Park Lane, and it got the juices going. It'd been a while since I'd felt that Libertines buzz, and it all came together – it was great, a cool day. The Pogues, with Shane MacGowan, were on the bill, and that was pretty magic, and Alan got to play as well. There were lots of surreal moments, like the naked bloke climbing the scaffolding while we played and Marc Almond knocking about back-stage with two massive minders.

After the show, I was really in a kind of spell, and there was just me and this little black woman in the trailer, and I couldn't work out who she was – I knew I'd seen her somewhere before. We got chatting about religion, and then she told me she was Mrs Powell, Gary's mum, and it was a really special moment. It's a genuine thing for me. I enjoy going to church, singing to God, just trying to get some idea of the relevance of the Bible. It's something that always fills my heart with I don't know what – the glory of God, really, feeling like I could be doing something as a servant of the Lord, rather than trying to set myself up as someone to be worshipped. I've always thought I could have gone to the church – I think I'd have been happy doing that. I'm a great believer in commu-nity and in faith – it's something that really attracts me. I think about it quite a lot – giving your life to service. It never really worked out, but it's something I'd like to pursue – even now I feel like I could do it.

I felt The Libertines were reconnecting on a different level this time around. We did more shows that summer. Carl and I were coming together slowly but surely, circling each other. It did take a while. It was little things, like before we did the three nights at Alexandra Palace, I went to his house for a visit – he was living right there by the venue. That's the sort of thing that wouldn't have happened in 2010 – those more personal avenues opening up, a sort of trust being regained and a friendship re-emerging. We did the Benicàssim festival in Spain, and that stands out as an amazing show, just striding on stage really confident and a massive crowd having it up. There was definitely more at play this time than the money – although there was a lot of that too!

After those big gigs, I went to Hope rehab in Thailand and started working with Simon Mott. It was a good three months getting clean. There was definitely a powerful moment in Thailand when Carl turned up at the rehab, and Gary and John as well – that was amazing, a real boost to the general sense of positivity. Lindi came to Thailand as well, with my daughter Aisling, and we spent what you might call quality time together. I'd met Aisling when she was a babe in arms. Lindi came to Paris with her, but it was all very tense. Aisling was two or three when I saw her in Thailand, a right little live wire. I never really understood Lindi – she'd changed so dramatically since we'd first met. I saw her as almost hippy-ish, into crystals and healthy eating and positive energies, but after she had the baby it all changed – her lawyer pushing for fortunes in child maintenance. It created a block.

When I left the treatment centre, I think it was Christmas Day or New Year's Day, Katia went online and said, Oh, look there's a little studio called Karma we can go and crash at and do some demos, and that turned into the next Libertines album. Initially, it was just me and Katia deciding to stay in Thailand for a bit and record some songs, Katia with the melodica and me with the guitar. We went in and demoed a new song 'Hell to Pay at the Gates of Heaven', and then someone, probably Adrian, who had been in Thailand with me too, had the idea of asking if the band wanted to come out and work on a new record. Carl came over, and it turned into an electric record, another full-on Libertines record. Before that, I sort of had the idea it was going to be a dusty folk album. I was prepared for a little dusty acoustic record, and I tried to swing it as much as I could that way with no success.

They were all so energised, Gary, John and Carl, and a lot of the album is quite in your face and fast, stuff like 'Fury of Chonburi'. Everyone was completely charged up to do a rock-'n'-roll record, especially the producer Jake Gosling, who'd done hip-hop records and was determined to make a noisy guitar record. For me to get back into that state of mind I needed stimulants, and I got back on the gear quite quickly. But it was a different vibe. I wasn't a complete mess because I'd been clean for so long, and also the stuff was so clean. I had this little connection, this little Thai guy. We were drinking whisky with a snake in the bottom of the bottle, everyone was having it right up, but I wasn't really into just getting drunk, so I was ticking along, kind of restrained for me. I was sleeping a lot and concentrating very hard on the writing sessions I'd have with Carl. We'd get a boat over to a little island, and the two of us would sit with guitars long into the night working on stuff like 'Anthem for Doomed Youth', the song, just really working hard on the lyrics – it was really important to both of us.

'Fame and Fortune' was another one we worked hard on. The tune dated back to the first night that Sandra danced out of the egg – that became the breakdown, and we fleshed the rest out by the pool. Lyrically it was a lovely rounding-off of fifteen years of space – we told the story of our beginnings, quite a funny little narrative, really Kinks-y, a Small Faces-type of song. 'Belly of the Beast' was another song I was really happy with. It had been one of the songs I'd wanted to record as a dusty folk thing, but it turned into a rockabilly song. It's a shame we don't do it live, but it's so tricky to play. 'Heart of the Matter' was a big song on the album – the lyrics are quite honest and intense, about our weaknesses, but the song really bounces along. The album had quite a bit of that back and forth between me and Carl, airing of the dirty linen, but more playful than poisonous – a lot of the poisonous gases from the swamp were evaporating. 'Milkman's Horse' has the line 'It must be lonely being you being me'. That was me to Carl, or him to me, or saying it to each other – as usual, there was a lot of wrangling over who would sing which line, because some of them were such belters.

Yeah, it turned out well, actually, that album – don't know how we pulled that one off, really. Thailand itself probably made it possible, just being in that space. It was a residential studio, so we were all living on top of each other, and we put a lot of pressure on ourselves to be the best we could be. It was quite an emotional time, especially when I sang 'You're My Waterloo' – not being able to choke back the tears, all the years falling away but in a really magical place. It was a kind of miraculous turn of events that record.

All the time I was in Hope and at the studio recording the Libertines album I was in communication with Alan. He was just so positive at that time, sending me messages of hope and positivity. His new slogan was 'a pint of beer and a spliff'. That's the way forward, a beer and a spliff, we're going to get clean, Pete. He was really positive about me getting clean and really proud I was doing the Libs record and it was going well. There were constant messages from him about staying strong and we'd see each other soon and he was doing really well. He said, This new injury has opened my eyes. The mezzanine at his flat had fallen on him, crushed his arm, split his main artery open. He was losing so much blood, and the lad who was there put a tourniquet on it to stop the flow and saved his life. He changed the band name to Alan Wass & The Tourniquet, and that was the name of the album he'd just finished recording. It was ready to be released, and he was unbelievably excited about that. He said he'd had this new lease of life, was glad to be alive, and then we heard he was in a coma after overdosing on heroin, and then I got this message from his wife Eliza saying that his Cadillac had been called up to heaven and they'd turned off the life-support machine. I was devastated. I'd wanted to fly back to London – it was the last day of recording. We were doing the vocals on 'You're My Waterloo'. It felt really wrong not going to see him in hospital, but it was impossible. Someone had injected him with heroin – he only had one working arm at the time.* I didn't know any of the lads who were with him. Their names appeared in the paper, but I couldn't work out who they were. No one knew who they were, just some lads he'd met . . . it was really awful.

That summer Dave Grohl out of the Foo Fighters had to pull out of Glastonbury at the last minute – he broke his leg – and they didn't have a band for the main stage, so we did it as a 'surprise'. That was another big moment for The Libertines, especially getting flown in by helicopter. We did quite a few festivals that summer. To have new music to play was a joy. I tried to do all the dates in the camper van, travelling behind the tour bus. I was determined to buck the system. I wanted us all to be in the camper van, really, but obviously with a crew and a professional money-making outfit it was not going to happen. After the shows, I used to see how many kids I could squeeze into the camper van, drive around, have a little party. I still liked a little pipe.

Simon Mason, a guy I met through treatment – he'd written a book, *Too High, Too Far, Too Soon* – was supposed to keep me on the straight and narrow. He was employed by the band. He mainly drove the camper van. We got nicked at the border going to a festival gig in

---

* Wass was thirty-three when he died, after eleven days in a coma, in April 2015. One person was arrested under suspicion of manslaughter, but no charges were brought, and the coroner recorded a verdict of unlawful killing.

Switzerland and instead of taking the drugs off me, he convinced the border guards he was my drugs worker, and said I was just going to have to score in the next town so they might as well give the drugs back. The Swiss border police gave him back three and half grammes out of seven grammes of heroin and just let us through. It was amazing – what a progressive policy. I'm sure there was inevitable disappointment from Carl that I was still using, but it was a lot more under control, or he'd come to accept it a bit more. Also, I think, in a moment like that, where we'd been nicked on the border and the gig was in an hour and a half, and we ended up making it on stage but an hour late, he was just happy, when push came to shove, that I'd made it to the gig.

I did end up missing one quite high-profile gig. We were supposed to be doing this album launch show at the Electric Ballroom in Camden, and I left them standing. I was in a motorway service station in the camper van on my own. I was really in bad way. I think I was heading for the Shetland Islands, planning to rough it out for six months. I'd got a supply of gear and a tin of baked beans. The drugs ran out before I got to Watford Junction, so I had to shuttle back and forward between London and the service station a few times – the Bouboumobile didn't do more than sixty. I was in a right state. I hadn't slept for days. It was a drug-induced psychosis of some sort. It's tricky looking back on it, because I haven't been in that state for so long. Now I look forward to the gigs, and even if there are nerves, there's no way I'm going to pull a gig. It's hard to put myself in that space where my own psychosis overrides everything, but it was not unusual in those years. Now the psychosis just bubbles under and it's manageable. But in the condition I was in back then, the last thing on my mind was whether or not I was going to do a gig. There is no sense of responsibility to anybody waiting – you don't even know what's going on. I probably didn't even know what day it was.

I pulled myself together, and we did quite a bit of promotion for the *Anthems for Doomed Youth* album. We did the Jools Holland show and

Soccer AM. Carl's very competitive by nature: any sport we take each other on at, whether it be table tennis or darts, he wants to win. Football was the thing I could always beat him at, until we went onto *Soccer AM* and did the 'Top Bins' challenge. He got the ball through the hole completely by chance, a toe punt, and I couldn't do it. Still a bit of a bone of contention that.'

XXX

Puta Madres

*2016–present: Libertines in South America. The start
of a new band, the Puta Madres. Investing in Margate,
the hotel – the Albion Rooms deluxe. Down and out in
Margate. Recording in Normandy. The breakfast challenge.
A final arrest in Paris. A new approach to life.*

'When I wasn't on tour or doing festivals with The Libertines, I was plotted up in Melun, a sleepy little town on the River Seine to the southeast of Paris, with a couple of camper vans in the front yard. I have really fond memories of that time. I was looking to get other things going musically. 'Flags of the Old Regime' had come out as a solo single while I was in Thailand, with all proceeds going to the Amy Winehouse Foundation. It was my hymn to Amy. I'd recorded it with Stephen Street during the time of *Prequel to the Sequel*. Katia did the video while we were in Thailand, and it proved to be quite a popular song. Adrian had sorted its release, but I wasn't getting on too well with him. One of the final nails in the coffin of our relationship – alongside the financial disputes – was the ongoing issues with the *Hamburg Demonstrations* album. I'd recorded 'Flags of the Old Regime' for *Hamburg Demonstrations* too, with Johann, and when I got back from Thailand I also recorded a version of 'Hell to Pay at the Gates of Heaven' with him. I wrote that song while I was in Thailand, and I couldn't work out why Carl didn't get on board with it, because it could have been wicked for The Libertines. It was written at the time of the Paris attacks and all the Islamic attacks on Europe. I was really proud of that song. We recorded it in Barcelona, and Rafa came to play drums on it.

This was when I asked my old school pal Jai Stanley to take care of my business affairs. I didn't know what was going on with my finances and money. Adrian had said, But you don't understand . . . and I said, OK, but this is all stopping. I got Jai to look at everything, and he became my manager. One of the first things he did was wrestle with the legal problems of *Hamburg Demonstrations*. He got it released finally. I think it probably sold a few copies for the Clouds Hill label. I did a couple of shows with those musicians Johann had hired at the studio complex in Hamburg, and then we did quite a big solo tour with a band I put together, the *Eudaimonia* tour. It was Drew, Miki, Katia, Rafa and an accordion player, Stephany Kaberian. It was great. Jai and I used to sit down and talk about why I wasn't really enjoying these colossal Libertines events. It was just that the band would only get together for intense rehearsals and then the gigs, and that wasn't how I wanted to be in a band. I wanted it to be a lot more organic, and that's how the idea for Puta Madres was born – as a way to try and get a band together that we controlled, that wasn't out of our hands, that wasn't all these diverse factions. I was not rubbing along well with Carl's management set-up at the time.

The Libertines did end up doing quite a big British and European tour for *Anthems for Doomed Youth*, with Sleaford Mods supporting us. We had a 'packaway' pub that we set up at every venue, a travelling pool table, darts board, bar stools, and everywhere we went it was someone's job on the crew to hire or find different burlesque dancers to wear the red army jackets and come on and dance for 'The Boys in the Band'. In London at the O2 Arena, the Docklands arena, Clara Mills was in charge of organising the dancers, and that was the best. She turned up with a right little motley crew of five or six girls and a boy. That was a good night. Clara took the dancers on stage for Sleaford Mods too, and they went crazy to all the mad beats – it was quite a good sight, that.

The Puta Madres came together in Argentina, ironically when The Libertines were doing a load of big venues in South America. The dream had always been to make a band with Carl and to become famous and acclaimed songwriters, but we had this other dream in the beginning: that we were going to go to South America and call ourselves Carlos and Los Libertines. I always had a feeling there was an audience for The Libertines in South America. When we were recording *Up the Bracket*, I received some picture of an all-girl Brazilian Libertines covers band, and there were some South American kids who popped up in Europe at gigs. So, those Libertines gigs in South America were a sort of fruition of those dreams, but we had this massive music industry machinery around us. We were staying in flash hotels, and it was all shuttle runs in expensive cars to big arenas and festivals. I felt a huge distance between us and the people, and we didn't really get to see anything. The Libertines at that time was just like a bullet going through. There was no kicking back with the lads. We were there on a mission to do these gigs, so we did it from that point of view, and there were moments when it felt good, but there were also occasions when I'd try and get a load of kids back to the hotel, and our own security would stop them coming in, and it would all kick off. Towards the end I had a massive row with The Libertines' tour manager, who was one of Carl's management's people, about all the trinkets I'd been buying, all my typewriters and stuff – he refused to include them as part of The Libertines' luggage. Ridiculous.

I wanted to get a real taste of South America, so after The Libertines played in Argentina, I just thought, I've got to stay here and investigate a little bit. That's when the Puta Madres were born. It all came together nicely when The Libertines flew off. I had my last night at the luxury hotel, and then I decamped to more of a flea-ridden place and settled in for the long haul. I got clean. I did cold turkey in this cheap hotel, and they all came out to join me: Drew, Rafa, Katia and Miki.

Jack Jones also came out to play guitar. I first became aware of Jack one night when I was wading through YouTube looking at some of Carl's stuff. Jack's band Trampolene had supported Carl at the Scala, and someone had said something about him doing poetry, so I immediately pricked up my ears and investigated. Two nights after I'd seen him on YouTube, I bumped into him by chance outside the Dublin Castle in Camden. I told him I'd seen him do one of his poems, 'Health & Wellbeing (At Wood Green Job Centre)', and it reminded me a little bit of my early bohemian performance poetry stuff, narratives about a young lad wandering round London skint. Jack was also an expert van driver. The Bouboumobile was an interesting challenge for him, so we had some adventures with him driving me around. I kind of gave him what I thought was an internship, taking him under my wing for a little bit. I could see he was really energetic and full of creative ambition. I'd be getting out of my nut, and he'd be looking after me.

The Puta Madres did it, what I really wanted to do: we just played loads of shitty little venues around Argentina, some really good gigs, and explored the country. We then came back and did some gigs in France, including two nights at the reopening of the Bataclan in Paris, after the massacre there. We came on stage and asked to have a minute's silence for the dead. I got Rini to say it in French, but after eleven seconds she just burst into shouting some mad poem. Afterwards, I said, Rini, you can't ask for a minute's silence and then after ten seconds start shouting, it's really offensive. She was like, It felt like a minute, and she did it the second night as well! I got someone to translate a review of that gig from a French newspaper, and they actually really liked Rini, they said it was very punk rock, but I thought it was diabolical. The whole band did. It was like, What the fuck is she doing? I was often on the fringes of certain things with Rini. Fat White Family was one of them. At the time, she was involved with getting them over to New York with Sean Lennon and doing that record 'Songs for Our Mothers' with all of John Lennon's old equipment. I was like, Hello! Fucking hell, Rini, what about your old mate?

The Puta Madres was sort of my dream band – ragged, a bit of rock-abilly, loose rock 'n' roll, bit folky, bit garage-y. With The Libertines, we'd be playing to a hard-core set of fans who expected certain things, but with the Puta Madres it wasn't really like that – we could do what we wanted. We could do mad long instrumentals and enjoy it, not worry about what anybody thought. It was all good as long as it was good music. I was completely in control with the sound – it had an organic vibe that reflected all our lives in general. Everyone's hopefully doing what they'd be doing anyway, not just turning up to rehearse, sort of living with each other. Also, it was understood that it was my band, so I could just sit back with the guitar and build songs around how I saw them. It was always an adventure. We went back to Argentina and toured South America. Uruguay was the most incredible trip. We played all across Europe. We were in and out of Barcelona all the time rehearsing and doing shows. My dad came on stage with the band for my birthday and sang 'What a Waster'. My mum and AmyJo were there too that night. We spent time rehearsing in Clouds Hill and recorded our first track as Peter Doherty & the Puta Madres with Johann, 'The Weed Smoker's Dream', a really old jazz number from the 1930s.

After we'd toured France and Germany, Drew moved on. He wanted a bit more security. I needed people who were just up for renegade stuff. Drew went off and joined Liam Gallagher's band, and Miggles,

Michael Bontemps, answered the call to play bass. I'd met him when he was a young lad outside a hotel in Paris in the early days of The Libertines. Back then he was in a band called The Parisians who wore brogues and jeans and Palestinian scarves, leather jackets – a bit like a younger version of me and Carl. I always tried to have their band supporting at various times to help them out.

I continued to tour with The Libertines. We had Jeremy Corbyn support us when we played a big gig at Tranmere football ground in 2017. That was such an honour. It was perfect, really. You just couldn't argue with the momentum he had behind him at that time. He talked a lot of sense, just basic old-school, left-wing principles. It seemed to me it was going to be the last opportunity someone like that would be given half a chance, definitely for a generation, and to see the young people singing 'Oh, Jeremy Corbyn!', I just felt something was in the air that was right. I really rated him. It was a shame he lost the election. People were poisoned against him. It's the old tabloid story – they do it to anyone they can't control or they don't really understand.

Jai made me see sense about The Libertines, and all the band really came to respect him. He would say, Look, do these gigs with The Libertines, get some money together to invest in other things, and let's just start making it so it works more for you, so you don't feel like you're just doing it for the money, so that you're enjoying it. It had basically been Carl's management and the people they hired and then separate to that my band of loyal crew. When Jai came on board, over time, my crew, Andy Newlove, Paul 'Brucie' Bruce, Iain Slater – my soundman since the Babyshambles days – took over the key roles on the roadcrew. Slowly but surely Carl and everyone saw these were real people, they got to know them and trust them, as opposed to just seeing them as Pete's people. So now when we play it's not strangers doing the guitars and sound. It's friends. We did an

Australian tour in 2018 that felt good: I managed to start enjoying those luxury hotels in Australia! There was quite a lot of camaraderie on that tour. The band really started to come together nicely – we did some belters, really good shows.

We used some of the money we'd made on the road to invest in The Libertines hotel in Margate, the Albion Rooms, which is now a viable venture, but it was so bad when I first saw it. Jai was involved, but Carl was really the driving force behind that idea. On the fateful day when Carl was going to show us this B&B we'd bought for the first time, I'd just finished another Puta Madres series of dates, and I went from Melun with Manu, a local taxi driver – he still drives me sometimes – to Margate. Basically, everyone went up the steps and went inside and, yeah, it was pretty fucking awful. Carl saw our faces, and he was like, Look, you've got to use your imaginations, you've got to think how great it can be, but it was all rotten green carpets and green doors with paint peeling off.

Jai also had this idea that seeing as we'd put a band and a crew together ourselves with the Puta Madres, we might as well put the records out ourselves, so the Puta Madres album and our own record label, Strap Originals, were born out of the same idea – just to be a bit more in control. I took the camper van to Margate, and the Puta Madres moved in to the old hotel while it was being renovated. It was a complete disaster, especially with Carl – the two worlds didn't welcome one another. Well, one didn't welcome the other, really. I think it was Carl's nightmare that the Puta Madres were in Margate, and that I was living in the hotel while it was supposed to be being developed. It was such a long-term project that I think initially the thinking was, Pete's there, but he'll be all right for a bit. But then as the development took shape and studio/rehearsal rooms were semi-usable, he began the long process of trying to extricate me out of Margate.

For me the hotel was heaven, because we suddenly had this

bricks-and-mortar place which was suitably dilapidated and in a kind of murky underworld area. They'll try like hell, but I don't think they'll ever be able to gentrify Margate – it's an incredible place to slip through the cracks. Or a terrible place to slip through the cracks, a tragic place in a lot of ways. But the hotel was a good place to squat – kind of like squatting in your own house. I was sort of shuttling back and forth between Melun and Margate. Unfortunately for Jai, most of the money I was making was going on drugs. He has managed, with a lot of perseverance, to turn that around, but there have been moments. I think it was the start of another Puta Madres tour when I went AWOL with his van and his credit card and went a little bit off the rails.

There were some desperate times in Margate actually, especially when I got the dogs, my two huskies – it was a right mess in the hotel. I was a mess. Jai arranged for me to go to rehab again – he found this place in Mauritius where they did an ibogaine treatment. It was sort of the last-chance saloon. Ibogaine is banned for use as a treatment in most countries, but some addicts who have tried everything else say it works for them. It was another wonderful paradise location with a privileged clientele in a flash rehab, full of crazy characters. I used to walk round singing until my supplies ran out. I took a massive box of cigarette cards with me where I had all my drugs hidden.

The ibogaine trip was so bad, a living nightmare. Ibogaine is basically a natural hallucinogenic harvested from the root of a plant – you get the effects of ketamine and acid. It was such a clinical environment, doctors coming in and monitoring you the whole time – it was really hard to have a positive experience. I had these weird flashbacks where I was back in my childhood with AmyJo playing on our street in Northern Ireland. That wasn't so unpleasant in itself, fine for a while, but six hours later and I was still stuck in my six-year-old self and my mouth was sewn up – in the vision my mouth was sewn up, so I couldn't speak. It's very hard to speak on ibogaine anyway, so I couldn't get any words out and explain what pain I was in.

I was determined at that point to return to England and get back on drugs as quickly as I possibly could. It was awful. I phoned Jai and said, I'll never forgive you for making me do this. Then the usual stuff unfolded. I managed to get one of the security guys to take me into town, and I met this taxi driver, and he took me to score in what was probably the most impoverished place I've ever seen – goats tied to tentpoles, naked children, people squatting in the dirt. To use heroin or to sell it over there is punishable by death, so it's really, really expensive. Looking back, I fucked up there, really. It could have been, but it wasn't, the end of my heroin use.

Then when I arrived back in Margate all my stuff was being taken out of the hotel. There was a line of blokes taking my typewriters out. I ran in, freaking out. I'd hidden things in certain desks, certain trinket boxes and they'd all gone into the back of this loading van. Everything was being shipped out of the hotel for the final makeover. Carl had had enough. I set up camp in this storage yard in Ramsgate, next to a breaker's yard. There was a fella selling fairground surplus, stuff like giant plastic models of the old woman who lived in the shoe and broken carousel horses, and I ended up living in a storage container I rented from him. This fella was taking payment in art until Jai realised he had shitloads of really good canvases. I was smoking a lot of crack again, and I was getting nicked as well. Same old – pulled mainly for driving offences, and then they'd find a bit of gear on me, but I never got any drugs charges. I was fined and banned from driving, though.

There were some good moments too with The Libertines coming down to visit. One time in the middle of the night we all made a fire on the beach with crates and petrol. Carl and I would have these mostly unsuccessful writing sessions at the hotel, we were trying to write some scripts together, and I was doing lots of little gigs around Margate, mixing with musicians and underground theatre people – there was an exodus of creative energy from London, people who couldn't afford to live there. I was bowling around Margate at five or six in the morning with the dogs, and I got to know all the other people walking their dogs at the same time, on those long, long beaches on the Kent coast. I'd be belting around on my electric scooter with the dogs in tow. I was working through a driving ban until very recently because of confusion over the law with that scooter – I didn't realise electric scooters are illegal to use on UK roads and pavements. I was out and about a lot in Margate, with Storm, a pal of mine, on scooters.

In the end, we recorded the Puta Madres album in Etretat, Normandy, in a house that belonged to Katia's parents. We did it really quickly. We had all this mad equipment in the front room, shitloads of proper equipment. It was a now-or-never moment. Jai produced it, although that wasn't really his preference, and he had a few people in mind for the job originally. At the start, I had the idea I'd be in control, but during the recording of the album I realised it's just not in my nature to be a music producer – all those years sat with Garageband was as far as it went. When it actually came to producing the album, I was just doing the recordings and wiping my hands of all responsibility. I put it completely on Jai and the engineer. Even when it was my own album in Katia's front room, I was still really not involved in the nuts and bolts.

Miki came to France for a couple of days. I'd played with her longer than I'd played with anyone else in the band. She was a constant over the years. Whenever I needed her, she was there, and the acoustic guitar and violin was always a beautiful combination.

The song 'Shoreleave' on that album was a perfect moment for me, the sort of moment I'd been trying to make over the years. Sometimes it happens with The Libertines – sometimes when we do 'Death on the Stairs', I feel it's the perfect combination of sounds and energy, but sometimes it spins a bit out of control and turns into slashy stuff. I tried not to let that happen with the Puta Madres, although it's quite easy to get caught up in the moment. 'All at Sea' was another song I was so happy with, a joyful moment. It had been a long time coming, trying to get that song right. If you hear The Libertines version we did in our very early days, it's too fast and doesn't work. I also tried to get it going with Babyshambles, and it never worked. It found its place with the Puta Madres. 'Paradise Is Under Your Nose' was a song Jack wrote, and Katia co-wrote 'Who's Been Having You Over' with me. I also gave Mark Hammerton a little credit on that song. Mark had some small part in its genesis – it was supposed to be about this mad theory he had about how Courtney Love had killed Kurt Cobain, and there's some lines in it pertaining to the DA and blood on the sofa. Katia also helped me write 'Travelling Tinker', which was a song about Alan.

The Puta Madres, the band, the album and the tours we did, wouldn't have happened without Jai. His idea to start our own record label with Strap Originals also got me fired me up. Knowing you've got the potential to put stuff out makes you get stuff done and finish ideas. Jack's band Trampolene is coming out on Strap Originals, and recently there's Vona Vella, a new young band we've been working with, a Burt Bacharach-flavoured couple from Lincolnshire. Yeah, it's looking really good for the label, all really encouraging. I'm really excited by all the young songwriting energy out there.

The same summer we recorded the Puta Madres album, 2018, I did the breakfast challenge at this café in Margate. If you ate their massive 'mega breakfast', you got it for free, and they put your name on their wall of fame. I didn't mind the chef taking a picture of me doing the challenge, but the picture was awful – he just took it on his phone. That was a terrible photo, but I did that café some favours, the Dalby Café. I had no idea what people were saying about that. In that Margate drug world I was inhabiting, I wasn't really aware of social media or what was being reported by the BBC or whoever. I was mainly writing songs and scavenging for drugs – of which there are a lot in Margate – so it didn't really affect me. I was really entrenched in the drugs. I used to read the local paper, but otherwise I was well out of touch. Now I follow the news quite closely, but for all those years I wasn't really paying attention. Obviously, Jai used to let me know. He'd say, It's blown up, this thing about the breakfast. I just thought that was hilarious, because I'd been building up to it – it was a like a personal thing to me, going in the café and watching people have a crack at the breakfast challenge. There were only three people's name up on the board at that time, and one was called Tiny, this huge fella, eighteen stone, a builder, and he had the record time.

It's funny because in The Libertines I have the nickname Pigman, which dates back to Daniel De'Ath in GCSE history. There was a fella called Otto Von Bismarck who led an early German push for imperialism in the 1860s, and he had this expression, It's time for the pig-sticking to begin, which we thought was hilarious. No one could say Bismarck in class or Dan and I would say, in an Irish Protestant accent, That's your da, so it is, you're a fucking bastard, you are . . . We'd shout it at any one, any teacher or anything – it caused quite a sensation. Carl and I did that routine in one of our first TV interviews on MTV. So Pigman developed from that, really – don't make me get the pig stick out. But I was more called Pigboy at Nico, or Yip Yip the Dog-faced Boy was another one. With Carl it became more Pigman, and then Piggles as well, because he used to have these paperback copies of *Biggles Flies East*, so Biggles was kind of his nickname, and I became Piggles!

But the meaning of Pigman changed over time. In those early days of The Libertines, I had this enormous capacity for eating, particularly fried breakfasts, as it happens. It was Carl's favourite thing, actually – if he couldn't finish his dinner, he'd push the plate over to me, and my party trick was to finish whatever anyone else hadn't. My nan used to say I had hollow legs. Over the years, that thing with Carl became quite a strain, because my appetite is not what it was, and I'm trying to watch my weight if anything these days. When The Libs got together for a socially distanced Newcastle racecourse gig in 2020, we had a pub lunch with everyone, and Carl was looking at me with puppy-dog eyes as he pushed his unfinished plate to me, as if to say, Go on, you used to be able to finish my plate. I was like, All right, give it here, c'mon. He was, Yeah, good old Pigman.

I was also unaware the hedgehog injury was made into a thing in the press at that time. During the tour we did with the Puta Madres when the album came out in 2019, I was holed up in a Manchester hospital for a while when my finger got infected by a hedgehog. I think I had to cancel a radio interview, and Jai said there were all sorts of rumours swirling about, but it was simply the dogs having it with this hedgehog, and I've gone in to try and save it, and that's what caused the cut – whether the hedgehog caused the infection is another thing. I don't know if people thought it was a drug-related incident. I haven't got great veins in my hands, so it wasn't from injecting – if I was going anywhere at the time, it would have been my feet or legs. The Puta Madres had just played Liverpool and Manchester, and I had a proper good connection in Liverpool, and he came by train and brought me ten of each, so I was lovely in that room with my fucked finger, smoking the brown and white in the hospital.

I was in the middle of a European tour with The Libertines in late 2019 when I was arrested twice in forty-eight hours in Paris. I was still travelling in the camper van, with the dogs. I wasn't on the tour bus because I still wanted a little rock after the gig. The problem was I'd started this buprenorphine injection thing, this blocker Buvidal, so heroin had no effect. I had nothing to take the edge off the crack. I was in a strange place. I got jumped by the police when I was scoring, and they proper battered me, and then within twenty-four hours of getting released for that small amount of possession, I got involved in a . . . I don't know what. Apparently, I was just laying into a bloke on his scooter. I think the scooter was going towards one of the dogs. It was outside a bar at two in the morning, and I just started punching this guy in the helmet. He's still trying to sue me, but it hurt me more than it hurt him, that's for sure – fucked my hand right up. When I got to the police station, I pulled my pants down and pissed all over the counter, was shouting stuff about the war, so I lost my tracksuit bottoms and my phone and my shoes. When they came to interview me, I was just in my QPR shirt and my pants and a piss-soaked blanket they'd given me in the cell. They kept me in for three days. There were fifteen of us in this one cell, and they were all moving away from me because I stank of piss where I'd pissed all over the police station and myself. It was just an absolutely disgraceful situation. I was very lucky not to go to prison again. They gave me a three-month suspended prison sentence for cocaine possession and affray, and I was put on probation for two years. Since then I've carried on doing Buvidal, the blocker. And it's worked – I've not taken heroin for two years now. It's a path I'm following – it gets easier, but for a long time it was just holding on for dear life.

Things settled down after that incident, and I did the rest of that tour clean. Alcohol and drugs were banned from the backstage area – not even the roadies were allowed to drink. Carl and I were in flat caps and braces – I think because the *Peaky Blinders* director came to one of the shows, in Manchester, and Carl was like, Look, we've got to look the part, he might give us some roles in the next series, but this director fella just ended up talking about how he couldn't get good-quality toilet paper in rural Ireland. By the end of that tour, at Brixton Academy, things came together really well – you've never seen a mosh pit like it. The word pandemonium springs to mind, back to throwing guitars into the crowd, but Andy Newlove, The Libertines' guitar man, makes them for me now, and he goes straight in, him and Brucie, and gets them back.

After that tour, I crashed in Normandy. I had half a mind of staying in Margate for ever, but the hotel was opening up, so I couldn't stay there. I've been in Normandy since then, plotted up in Etretat with Katia, and it's been great. When the pandemic first hit in March 2020, we needed a permit to leave the house, and the bars and public dining spaces closed down again in November, early December, and we were put on a 6 p.m. curfew. I was really lucky to be in Etretat, surrounded by beautiful, really inspiring, scenery. I'd go swimming in the mornings, walk the dogs along the cliffs. I still walk a lot. Katia and I even passed our boat licences – I learned to captain a boat.

I also recorded a new album with a French musician called Frédéric Lo that I think is my best yet, as good as anything I've written. Frédéric came to Etretat during the lockdown in the summer of 2020 with all these chords and said can you put any lyrics to these songs. It's usually not enough for me just to be happy with something – I usually look at it in terms of how people react to the music rather than how I feel about it – but I really feel it's a good piece of work. When I first heard the melodies and chords Frédéric presented to me, it reminded me of the early days with Carl: the guitar parts and orchestration were just too big not to at least try and write some lyrics for them. At the time when we were writing the album, *The Fantasy Life of Poetry & Crime*, I really got lost in a big melodic world, listening to songs like Black's 'Wonderful Life' and Tears for Fears' 'Everybody Wants to Rule the World' and 'The Boxer' by Simon & Garfunkel. For me, the album is a little bit like *Grace/Wastelands*.

I'm alive and well and sleeping every night now. I never used to believe in the private ownership of property, but I'm looking to get my own little farmhouse in Normandy. I do miss England, though. I saw Astile recently: he came to my mum and dad's house with me on a visit.

I've probably seen him more in the last couple of years than I have in all the years before. He's grown up into such a lovely lad. Relief is perhaps the wrong word to use, but it's hard to tell you how relieved I am he's so lovely. He's obsessed with Morecambe and Wise as well, which is curious. I do not put them in the same class as Hancock. Even though I'm obsessed with aspects of vintage comedy, I don't rate Morecambe and Wise at all. The relationship with my mum and dad is healing too, which I'm really happy about.

I feel part of a community in Etretat. I always enjoy strolling down to the village, having a large rum and coffee, and reading some periodicals. I subscribe to the *London Review of Books*, the *New York Review of Books* and the *TLS*. The *New York Times* is the only English-speaking paper in the village. A dream of mine is to open a bookshop in Etretat. I've been discussing it with a local fella, Christian Fevret, who started the magazine *Les Inrockuptibles*. The idea is we'd have a printing press out the back to run off pamphlets. I'd maybe do some art there too. Etretat has a strong literary and artistic heritage. Maurice Leblanc, who created Arsène Lupin, is an Etretat boy. Katia's mum says her aunty and Maurice Leblanc played together as kids in the streets, and he used to call her the girl with the purple eyes. They've got amazing eyes in Katia's family. Katia's mum and all her sisters and brothers, they've all got these incredible blue eyes. Katia has the most beautiful eyes. I don't know if I can say how I feel about Katia in just a few words. She saved my life – the most incredible woman. And her film about me is finished and that's incredible too. It's called *Stranger in My Own Skin*, and there's interest in showing it from various film festivals around the world.

It's all changed so much, all slowed right down, especially over the six months we were doing this book: I feel really detached now from drugs. I'm not really even drinking very much. I'm longing for Libertines gigs more than anything. I love doing those songs with Carl. And that's why

I never did those songs without him with Babyshambles. I can do some sort of Libertines greatest hits with the Puta Madres or when I do solo shows, and Carl will do stuff if he's doing a solo show, but doing them with The Libertines is different.

We played a one-off gig for Terry Hall in Coventry in August 2021 when the Covid restrictions lifted in the UK, and we were really together – all the lads spent the day together at Terry's festival watching the bands play. Carl was really mindful that I wasn't going to be doing anything before going on stage, so we all went on in the same state, so to speak, and it really worked. We had three days' rehearsal before the show, and Carl was playing around with some new ideas, and I knew it was going to be the start of a great new song. I got the same old feeling that I'd had back when we first started, sat in the library at Queen Mary, thinking, This is something bigger than us as individuals that we are tapping into. That's a really beautiful, powerful feeling.'

Acknowledgements

The authors wish to thank Janine Stanley, Jai Stanley, Kevin Pocklington, Katia deVidas Doherty, Jackie Doherty and Carl Barât for feedback during the draft stages of this book. Their corrections and suggestions were greatly appreciated.

Simon also thanks Shirley and the late, great Kieron Flynn, aka 'Big Ronnie Fabulous', or, as Peter knew him, 'Ronnie Richardson'.

Peter sends all his love to Jai and his family, to Katia and the deVidas family, and to his mum and dad and sisters.

In loving memory of Alan Wass, Amy Winehouse, Robin Whitehead, Robert Chevalley and Lee Brown.